GIBRALTAR

Sir Joshua Reynolds' magnificent portrait of General George Eliott who commanded the Gibraltar Garrison throughout the Great Siege (1779–83), the most important event in Gibraltar's turbulent history. (National Gallery)

GIBRALTAR

MAURICE HARVEY

Foreword by
Field Marshal Sir John Chapple
Governor and Commander-in-Chief
Gibraltar 1993–95

SPELLMOUNT
Staplehurst

British Library Cataloguing in Publication Data:
A catalogue record for this book is available
from the British Library
Copyright © Maurice Harvey 1996, 2000

ISBN 1-86227-103-8

First published by Spellmount Limited in the UK in 1996

This paperback edition published in the UK in 2000 by
Spellmount Limited
The Old Rectory
Staplehurst
Kent TN12 0AZ

Tel: 01580 893730
Fax: 01580 893731
E-mail: enquiries@spellmount.com
Website: www.spellmount.com

3 5 7 9 8 6 4 2

Printed in China

CONTENTS

FOREWORD

by Field Marshal Sir John Chapple
Governor and Commander-in-Chief
Gibraltar 1993–95

MAURICE HARVEY has undertaken to cover the whole known history of Gibraltar to give the reader an understanding of its turbulent and troubled history; and also a flavour of what influences have affected the character of the people who live there.

He has done this in an admirably clear and concise manner, bringing alive the colourful episodes in its history and emphasising how the importance of Gibraltar has varied over the years; and how its fortunes have waxed and waned – not always directly connected to its importance.

Gibraltar is the most densely fortified corner of the world and up to the eighteenth century was probably the most fought over. The fortress mentality is still apparent, although it has not been directly attacked for two hundred years. The feeling of threat however remains, and the evolution of this feeling is well set out in this book.

Gibraltar is a small place, with an inclination towards intense feelings. It is still a very integral community, with a very high proportion of the population living near their place of birth (a rare phenomenon in the Western world today). People know each other well; close relations live nearby. The feeling of community is strong. The tolerance between people of different views and beliefs is remarkable. But the world does, to those who live in Gibraltar, centre on Gibraltar: any news story anywhere else in the world always comes second to the local story.

It is this that makes Gibraltar such a fascinating, as well as friendly place. They seek what most people seek – to find a secure, stable and sustainable future. They realise that some part of these legitimate aspirations are dependent on someone else who can either deliver or prevent these being delivered.

This book tells the story of Gibraltar's past and sets the scene for the dilemmas which Gibraltar and the Gibraltarians face today.

Acknowledgements

ALTHOUGH I had visited Gibraltar on a number of occasions during my career in the Royal Air Force, I had not studied its fascinating history in any detail until I started to write this book. I must, therefore, first acknowledge two books on Gibraltar which gave me a thorough insight into the long and varied history of this formidable fortress. First was George Hills' *Rock of Contention* (Robert Hale, London, 1974) and secondly Sir William Jackson's *The Rock of the Gibraltarians* (Gibraltar Books, 1987). These two introduced me to the wide range of primary and secondary sources which have charted the development of the Rock over nearly twelve centuries.

In Gibraltar I would particularly like to pay tribute to the help received from the Governor (1993–95) Field Marshal Sir John Chapple GCB GCVO KBE DSO, who not only read and commented on the whole book, but also allowed me to see and use those sources retained in the Convent. He has also kindly contributed a Foreword. It was Sir John who also introduced me to another valuable contact, Lieutenant Colonel Eddie Guerrero OBE, Chairman of the Gibraltar Heritage Trust, which is doing some splendid work in preserving and restoring the historic buildings of Gibraltar. Tito Vallejo, a member of the Trust, took me in hand and showed me virtually all sites of historic interest in Gibraltar as well as reading and commenting on several of the chapters, providing a fascinating panorama of the nooks and crannies of local history – as well as some of its more controversial aspects. Christopher Terry who was restoring Parson's Lodge Battery to its former imposing grandeur was a valuable source of information and also took time to show me some of the more interesting areas such as the Naval Victualling Yard and the King's Bastion which are not yet open to visitors.

I would also like to thank Dr Clive Finlayson, Director of the Gibraltar Museum, for reading the first three chapters and his brother Tommy Finlayson for commenting on my chapter on the nineteenth century. John Searle gave me access to the Garrison Library and Sam Benady pointed me towards a recent discovery that Gibraltar was sold to the Conversos of Cordoba in 1474. Dr Sheelagh Ellwood, the Assistant to the Deputy Governor, was particularly helpful on the last chapter. Finally in Gibraltar, I would like to thank the manager and the ever-friendly staff of the Rock Hotel for making my several visits to Gibraltar so comfortable.

In England I owe a particular debt to Reggie Norton who made available to me the unpublished manuscript of the late Sir Gerald Pawle who had intended to publish a history of Gibraltar in the 1970s. The above-mentioned General Sir William Jackson GBE KBE MC (Governor 1978–82) kindly read and commented on the last chapter on the modern history of Gibraltar.

As illustrations I have mostly used my own photographs as I was particularly keen to show many of the historic buildings and artefacts as they may be seen by the visitor today. But I am also grateful to the following for permission to use their illustrations: National Gallery (London), National Portrait Gallery (London), National Maritime Museum (Greenwich), Imperial War Museum (London), Royal Engineer's Museum (Chatham), Budapest National Gallery, Gibraltar Museum, Garrison Library (Gibraltar) and the Gibraltar Heritage Trust. Individual attribution is given with the appropriate illustration.

Finally I should like to thank my publisher, Jamie Wilson, and my editor, David Grant, for their unfailing help and advice.

11

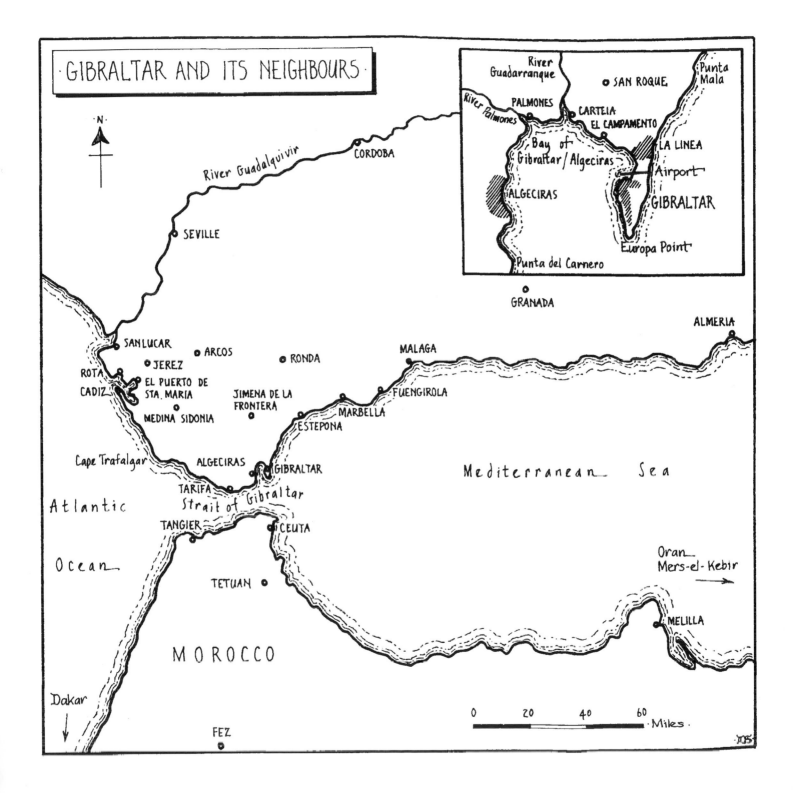

1 THE END OF THE KNOWN WORLD BC – AD711

THERE IS USUALLY a best way to approach any city for the first time, to see at a glance its predominant features and even a glimpse of its character. For many cities shrouded today in dreary suburban monotony, the most satisfactory approach is by sea – Venice and New York immediately spring to mind, or from a dominating river – London, Paris and Budapest. Few perhaps are best first seen from the air when individual features are subsumed in a miasma of sprawl and smoke, and often on an approach to an airport several miles from the city. Gibraltar, however, falls indisputably into that latter category. Not only does an approach by air banish the dismal journey past the sprawling petro-chemical works of Guadarranque, the unappealing tower blocks of La Linea and the drab formalities of the frontier controls, it enables the traveller to take in the Rock in all its splendid isolation, the little community nestling in its shadow to the west, and to discern at a glance the reason why this tiny entity insecurely attached to the southern tip of Spain has assumed such importance over a thousand years or more.

The vast sweep of the lonely Atlantic on one side and the equally expansive but more intimate glimpse of the Mediterranean on the other are segregated by what appears from the air like a narrow strip of water probing between two massive peaks – gateposts in a silver sea. Indeed it is as gateposts – guardians of the strait – that the two rocks have generally been seen. The reality is not as simple as that; for much of their history the rocks could more accurately be envisaged as stepping stones – inviting passage, in both directions, between the two great continents of Europe and Africa. East-west, north-south, whichever the predominant direction at any one time, the flow of humanity has been almost continuous from early pre-historic times to the present day. Sometimes the north-south flow has been relatively unimportant or impeded, but it has usually been replaced by an east-west flow – of peoples, culture and trade, and more often than not, of warfare.

At some stage in the very far past it is almost certain that Europe was joined to Africa and that the Mediterranean was no more than a string of lakes. At that time there would have been at least a land bridge between what is now Spain and Morocco. But about 5 million years ago, the whole Mediterranean area, indeed extending as far as the Indian sub-continent, was racked by folding and fracturing which allowed the Atlantic to flood into a gap created in the mountain range that runs along the southeast coast of Spain before turning back eastwards again into the Atlas mountains of north Africa. It is not surprising therefore that the landscape around Gibraltar appears to bear a closer resemblance to north Africa than it does to the more familiar green and lush country of western Europe. W. H Auden called Andalusia 'that arid square, that fragment snipped off from hot Africa'.

From the air the Mediterranean Sea generally exudes a calm composure compared with the mobile, darker, menacing expanse of the Atlantic Ocean to the west, and for early travellers the passage of the Strait marked the transition from the comforting certainty of the known world to the dark terrors of the unknown. The Rock of Gibraltar, with its twin across the water, formed the boundary between security and stability, and apprehension and mystery. But two popular misconceptions should perhaps be laid to rest at once: Gibraltar is not the southernmost tip of

Europe; that distinction falls to Tarifa some 20 miles to the west. Furthermore, the narrowest point of the Strait, at 12½ miles, is not abeam Gibraltar; that too lies just to the east of Tarifa. Seen from Europa Point, the southernmost tip of Gibraltar, is the Spanish enclave of Ceuta, about 16 miles distant, although it looks far less in the brilliant, shimmering light of a clear day.

Once on the ground, the Rock simply dominates the airport in a way which cannot be matched anywhere else, even by Beacon Hill and Lion Rock looming over the airport in Hong Kong. In the bright summer sunshine, as it is usually seen by the casual visitor, the Rock can appear benign and protective; but wreathed in cloud or encircled by lightning, it assumes an altogether more brooding, threatening presence. George Borrow, who visited Gibraltar in 1842 called it 'a terrible couchant lion whose stupendous head menaces Spain'. Not surprisingly, the Rock can cause problems for the pilot, particularly when a strong wind is blowing from the south-west causing eddies and wind sheer close to the point of touchdown on the short, if reassuringly wide, runway. The towering, awe-inspiring north face of the Rock as seen from the terminal building can also generate a feeling of being trapped, hemmed-in by an overwhelming force. This impression could be particularly acute for the British Servicemen working at the airport when the border immediately behind them was solidly barred and patrolled by the Spanish military. Now at least the open border provides a psychological escape route from the brooding presence forever filling their vision.

Before the days of steam, or even radar, the passage of the Strait, particularly from east to west, was rarely easy. Powerful currents, frequent fog, rocks and sandbanks regularly took their toll of sailing ships. North-south passage on the other hand was relatively simple, encouraging the interchange of people and goods between Europe and Africa from the very earliest times. From the rise of Islam in the seventh century, the Strait became a Saracen sea as successive waves of African Muslim mercenaries rescued Muslim Spain from the excesses of its rulers and then shipped its riches back to Africa. It was not until Dom Joao of

Portugal captured Ceuta in 1415 that this stranglehold was broken, and in the process condemned Granada, the final Muslim outpost of Spain, to inevitable extinction. The vacuum was filled, however, not by Spain but by the piratical Corsairs of the Barbary Coast. It was not until the beginning of the sixteenth century that 'northern' ships began to open up the passage into the Mediterranean and Spain at last took an interest in controlling the Strait. Indeed, from the time of Charles V, the western Mediterranean became a Spanish sea, in almost constant opposition to the eastern sea controlled by the Turks. Two centuries later it was England, with the assistance of that other great maritime nation, the Netherlands, which took control of this increasingly important area. Control is, however, perhaps too strong a word, for until very recent times, it was quite easy for ships, or even whole fleets to slip through the Strait unseen under the cover of fog or darkness. Furthermore, until the advent of long range artillery in the twentieth century, there was often little that could be done to prevent passage even when it was observed.

Most people today would regard the strategic significance of the Strait of Gibraltar as essentially a gateway to the Mediterranean, the focal point of an east-west axis of fundamental importance to the control of this vast inland sea embraced by two continents. The Romans regarded the Mediterranean as their sea – *Mare Nostrum* – a concept which the Spaniards were not slow to adopt in later years. But for long periods it has been, as we have already seen, the north-south axis which has been of greater consequence. It has been as a bridge between Africa and Europe, rather than as a tideway between the Mediterranean and the Atlantic, that the Strait and Gibraltar have enjoyed such prominence over the years. Even in periods when the east-west axis has been more important, Gibraltar has sometimes been more of a staging post than a guard post. At other times it has not been particularly important either way. This ever changing emphasis is a constant theme, and it is the strategic importance of Gibraltar which has dominated its history, and which will concern us most in this narrative.

Gibraltar is, however, best known as a fortress, and it has been in this capacity that

it has witnessed its most dramatic moments, particularly in the Great Siege of 1779-83 when Spain made her most determined attempt to recover her lost possession. The best place from which to gain an overall appreciation of the defensive attributes of the Rock is the sea front esplanade in La Linea. Here one can see confirmed what was already evident from the air: that whatever advantages Gibraltar may have as a military location, it has few, if any, as an area for peaceful domestic settlement. This would have been even more obvious in the eighteenth century when the sea lapped either side of the narrow causeway connecting the Rock to the mainland and right up to the walls protecting the town from the sea. The whole foreshore, now occupied by high rise flats and office blocks as well as the extensive port complex, is a development of our present century, most of it on land reclaimed from the sea. It is, therefore, to its role as a fortress that Gibraltar owes its existence and, given its prime location at the entrance to the Mediterranean Sea, it is not surprising that it has been fought over some fourteen times within the last six hundred years.

It is possible also from our viewpoint in La Linea to reach some basic conclusions regarding Gibraltar's military strengths and weaknesses. The north face of the Rock is a sheer façade some 1300 feet high, and although not visible from our present position, the east face is scarcely less steep. The land access to the town, which shelters at the foot of the more gentle western face, can only be approached across the causeway dominated by the north face and funnelled into a narrow entrance at the Land Port Gate. It is readily apparent that there is little mileage in an offensive action from this direction even though it was often attempted. Furthermore, a blockade could never be effective unless the defenders could be cut off from re-supply by sea. Looking towards the south, the aspect becomes slightly less daunting: the ground slopes less steeply towards the south and south-west, and a force securely lodged ashore here could contemplate the town walls with rather greater expectations of at least a siege conducted on more equal terms. Closer inspection will also reveal a tiny inlet, Rosia Bay, as a possible landing site, and in the

The western face of Gibraltar from La Linea.

eighteenth century a strip of sandy beach would have been visible to its north. However, an approach from this direction would be hazardous, if not impossible, unless the attackers could be reinforced, supplied, and if necessary evacuated by sea. The key to Gibraltar is therefore immediately self-evident; the defending force must have command of the sea, without which it can neither withstand a sustained blockade nor perhaps successfully fend off a land attack from the south-west through the Red Sands or Rosia Bay. Furthermore, as will be seen in 1704 (although not in 1782), a naval force with total command of the sea could batter the town into submission.

Another factor may also be discerned from our vantage point in La Linea. Although obscured now by the moles and quays of the port, it is clear that Gibraltar has no natural harbour and is wide open to the south westerly onshore winds from the Atlantic. Algeciras,

on the other hand, lies on the western side of the bay and is protected by an off-shore island as well as, to a lesser extent, the Rock itself from the easterly Levantine wind which blows for much of the year. Furthermore, Algeciras has better communications with the hinterland of Spain, but is overlooked by surrounding hills which provide an advantage to an attacking force. The conclusion to be drawn is that Algeciras is the better settlement location in times of peace or where the occupying power has the military ascendancy; but in less stable periods, the security advantages of Gibraltar come into their own. And so it has proved throughout history; for hundreds of years Algeciras, Tarifa and Carteia flourished before Gibraltar was more than an isolated and uninhabited rock. It was only when the Moorish dynasty began to fragment and become dissociated from its north African base that Gibraltar began to develop as a fortress.

*   *   *

The eastern face of the Rock falls almost sheer to the Mediterranean Sea and the highest point to the north (1398 feet) towers over La Linea across the border.

The Rock of Gibraltar is a massive limestone outcrop, mirrored by the Djebel Musa across the Strait, surrounded by newer sandstone rocks such as those which now form the low-lying lands northwards to the Sierra de Montecoche. The Rock at the highest point towards its northern end stands 1398 feet above the sea, its most precipitous faces looking towards the north and east. Water percolates readily through the rock eventually forming caves, of which more than 140 have been discovered, and for which man has found a use from earliest times right up to the present. Some of the larger caves may have been formed by the separation of the limestone bedding plates as a result of earth tremors. Although the glacial sheets which periodically covered Europe from 1.8 million years ago never reached Gibraltar, they still had a major effect on the eco-climate as the sea alternately fell and then rose again with the advance and retreat of the ice. The highest sea caves are now about 1000 feet above the current sea level. At times the sea also flooded the isthmus leaving Gibraltar an island more than a mile off the coast. Wild animals such as lions and leopards roamed the plains, and remains of their presence have been discovered on Gibraltar, as have those of the great auk, found in Gorham's Caves, a bird which became extinct in the nineteenth century.

In earlier days the western slope of the Rock was well wooded, but the removal of the trees, started by the Moors and the Spaniards, was completed by the British during the Great Siege when every scrap of available wood was required for fuel. The presence of goats which roamed the Rock then ensured that the natural vegetation did not regenerate and it was not until the Upper Rock was fenced off for military reasons that a dense scrub (*maquis*) appeared, called *Garigne* in Gibraltar, which is the natural characteristic of the Rock today. Stone pines were later replanted alongside the roads leading to the Upper Rock to provide shade for the military, and these provide a welcome variation to the ubiquitous scrub. Today the western face of the Rock looks quite green with wild olives, many self set seeded by the passage of migrant birds, and the imported eucalyptus. Other exotic species, native and imported, now grace the

public and private gardens, which with the abundance of wild flowers make an attractive show in spring and summer. The diversity of plant life for such a small area is impressive – around 600 species have been identified, a few of which like the Gibraltar Candytuft are unique in Europe and the Green Sea Lavender possibly unique in the world. The strongly alkaline soil compared with the acidic soil of the hinterland makes Gibraltar distinctively different from the surrounding areas of Andalusia.

Although not rich in animal life, there is one mammal which is, of course, internationally renowned – the famous Rock Ape. Correctly described as Barbary Macaques, they are not native to Gibraltar and are thought to have been introduced as pets in the 18th-century by the British. They now live in a semi-wild state on the Upper Rock where they perform for the tourist with

The Rock Ape was introduced from north Africa in the 18th-century.

The severe shortage of building space, and consequently one of the problems for heritage conservationists, is well illustrated in this picture which shows the Moorish Castle hemmed in by post-war building.

Old guns mushroom on almost every corner in Gibraltar. This 32-lb muzzle loading cannon dating from the 1870s has recently been installed in front of the new Queensway Apartments.

unfailing arrogance. Like the Ravens of the Tower of London, they carry the heavy if legendary responsibility of ensuring by their procreation that Gibraltar remains British. Spain may have missed a trick in not mounting a surreptitious raid on the Ape's Den! In fact, during the Second World War, the ape population dwindled to four and Winston Churchill is said to have ordered that some be imported from Morocco lest Hitler took it as a good omen.

Whatever it lacks in mammals, Gibraltar has an international reputation for its bird life. The Barbary Partridge, another British introduction, is found nowhere else in Europe, and a unique variation of the Blackcap as well as large numbers of Blue Rock Thrush and Sardinian Warbler are among the resident population. But it is in the spring and autumn migrations that the

Rock comes alive as vast numbers congregate before setting out across the sea and the Sahara, or rest and feed after their arduous northbound passage. Many migrants pass their winter on the Rock before returning north to their breeding territories. Even so, many past residents such as Bonelli's Eagle, Egyptian Vultures, Ospreys and even Ravens have succumbed to the pressures of modern development, and strenuous efforts are now being made to preserve and improve the remaining habitat.

*　　　*　　　*

Two aspects of Gibraltar immediately strike the first-time visitor. Space for man's ever-increasing needs is at an absolute premium – if the ground is reasonably level, or can be made so, it is occupied by buildings of one sort or another, commercial, military or domestic. Much land for building has been reclaimed from the sea and the process continues. Secondly, even today, the city exudes a military atmosphere: military aircraft often dot the airport and naval ships nestle busily at the quaysides. As you walk around the city you are never far away from a military fortification – line wall, bastion or battery. Ancient cannon are apparently almost casually abandoned in squares, at street corners, or sitting imperiously rusting on the ramparts. Even the street names are evocative of the military presence – Line Wall Road, Flat Bastion Road

Attractive features of the old town are the splendid wrought iron balconies which adorn many houses.

and Victualling Officer's Lane – and what would be called a hill in any other town is known here as a Ramp, a sure indication that it previously led to a gun battery. Nevertheless, the scene is slowly changing as the armed forces which provided the raison d'être of the town for more than six hundred years are substantially withdrawn and other more commercial ventures seek to replace the economic powerbase of a military fortress.

Many visitors to Gibraltar have remarked on its resemblance to a rather old fashioned

The 19th-century Anglican Cathedral of the Holy Trinity displays its Moorish antecedents.

English seaside town. Laurie Lee in *As I Walked Out One Midsummer Morning* wrote: 'To travellers from England, Gibraltar is an Oriental bazaar, but coming in from Spain I found it more like Torquay – the same helmeted police, tall angular women and a cosy smell of provincial groceries.' Well, the policemen are still there and the rash of duty-free shops may suggest a bazaar, but in most respects the comparison with an English town is only superficial. As you walk along Main Street, lift your eyes above shop level and note the tiled house façades, the ornamental wrought-iron balconies, and above all the ubiquitous wooden shutters: you could hardly mistake this for Torquay. The atmosphere, if anything, is more Italian, perhaps Genoa or Naples, certainly not Spain just across the way. It is true that some of the larger, older buildings in a solid Georgian style have a genuine English appearance, hardly surprising in view of their military squirearchical provenance. The 15th-century Franciscan Convent, now the Governor's residence, would not be out of place in a quiet English cathedral city, but the military guardroom immediately opposite is pure Aldershot. The 19th-century Anglican Cathedral is anything but Victorian

in appearance, its façade enlivened by colourful Moorish horseshoe arches. Immediate post-war building, slab-sided office blocks and garish high-rise tenement flats studded with television aerials, are as depressing here as anywhere else in Europe. Later developments in that ubiquitous post-modernist 'European Classical' style are better, but are beginning to have a monotonous regularity which may wear equally badly.

As you pass out of Main Street, through the South Port Gate and up the hill, you enter into another Gibraltar. The exotic subtropical Alameda Gardens are perfectly complemented above by the colonial haven of the Rock Hotel, home in its time to personalities as varied as Winston Churchill and the Spanish musician Segovia. Above you, as everywhere in Gibraltar, towers the Rock itself, less formidable on its gentler western and southern slopes, but still an all-embracing presence. It seems impossible to believe that less than a mile to the east, on the other side of the Rock, lies the little fishing village and holiday resort of Catalan Bay. And so south to Europa Point with its red and white Trinity House lighthouse, looking across the Strait to the equally towering mass of Djebel Musa on the distant shore. From the airport on the Spanish border you have traversed less than three miles, and the peninsula is only three quarters of a mile wide: in all it totals 2¼ square miles. Into that tiny area, in addition to the Rock itself, are packed some 30,000 people of British, Spanish, Italian, Maltese and Portuguese descent, not to mention the sizeable numbers of resident aliens of Indian and Moroccan origin. But although all this is a comparatively recent development, the presence of man on Gibraltar and the neighbouring hinterland has a very long history.

*　　*　　*

The remains of the first recognisable man – '*Homo erectus*' – up to two million years old, have been discovered in Asia and scattered sites in Africa and Europe. Some of them almost certainly crossed the Strait of Gibraltar, which already existed at this time although probably narrower than today, into Iberia and France, and their primitive stone tools have been discovered in southern Spain although not yet in Gibraltar itself.

A more secure dating stems from a skull found in the Neander Valley near Dusseldorf in Germany in 1856. It was then recognised that a skull found in Forbes' Quarry in 1848 and now in the Gibraltar Museum dated from the same period. In 1926 another Neanderthal skull, that of a child of about five years old, was unearthed in Devil's Tower Cave. What sort of people were these early inhabitants of the Rock, the first '*Homo sapiens*', who lived between 100,000 and 35,000 years ago? Short, squat and powerful in build, they were generally cave dwellers but occasionally built camps in the open air. They used fire and a variety of stone implements and hunted small and medium-sized animals with wooden spears. There is also possibly some evidence of cannibalism and primitive forms of religion. Some of their artefacts, found in Gorham's Caves, are displayed in the Gibraltar Museum along with imaginative displays of modern archaeological processes.

About 10,000 years ago, the Ice Ages

The Alameda Gardens, laid out at the beginning of the 19th century, are a haven of peace in a bustling city.

departed for the fourth and last time and there is ample evidence that Bronze Age peoples flourished in Andalusia which is as rich in archaeological remains as anywhere in Europe, although as yet not so well documented or displayed. Near Jimena de la Frontera, only 20 miles from Gibraltar, are the excellently preserved cave paintings of late Neolithic age (about 4000 years ago) which contain some of the first known paintings of boats, a clear reminder of how people arrived from across the Strait. By now humans had been living in cane huts for a thousand years or more and using caves only for sanctuary and ceremonial and burial purposes. If the Rock was inhabited in Palaeolithic times it is probable, as man progressed from hunting to farming, that he now moved to the mainland hilly areas where food would be more abundant. Primitive man did not tend to linger in the low-lying areas surrounding the bay which were lands of stagnant waters infested with malaria.

As we progress into more recent and better documented times we must move briefly from anthropology to mythology to consider the legend of the Pillars of Hercules of which Gibraltar forms the northern tier, with the Djebel Musa its mirror on the southern side of the Strait. The Pillars are said to have been created by the Greek god Heracles (Hercules) who, driven mad by Hera, killed his wife and children and fled to Tiryns to expiate his crime. Of the twelve 'labours' imposed by the king of Tiryns, the tenth was to capture the oxen held by the three-headed monster Geryon living in the distant west. On the successful completion of his quest, Hercules commemorated the event by setting up the two mountains; or in another version, clove the mountain in two thereby allowing the sea to pour through the gap and create the Mediterranean Sea. In Greek times, shrines to Heracles were possibly erected on the Rock, but visitors would not have lingered long in what was universally regarded as a hostile environment.

Throughout the first millennium BC and up to the eighth century AD, five distinct ethnic groups can be distinguished in the vicinity of Gibraltar. The indigenous race, the Tartessians (and their neighbours the Turdetanians), were the descendants of the Bronze Age peoples, but they were eventually joined by Phoenicians and Greeks and all became collectively known as Iberians. The Romans and Goths were later arrivals. This rapid turnover is itself an indication of a developing and turbulent world, but most of these groups made only a small contribution to the history of Gibraltar and rate only brief mention. Nevertheless, although the Italian poet Petrarch is supposed to have been the first man to climb a mountain simply for the view (in 1327), it is difficult to believe that some of these early colonisers would not have scaled the most prominent height for miles to survey their new domain, to wonder at the mysterious mountain landscape across the water, or to search the horizon for signs of ships bringing news from their ancestral homeland. It was not, of course, known as Gibraltar in those days – the Phoenicians called it Alube and the Strait Melkartes, and the Romans later gave it the more familiar name of Mons Calpe and its sister peak Mons Abila.

The Tartessians were a mysterious race whose main city, still not precisely located, is believed to have been at the estuary of the Guadalquivir river in southern Spain. However, its famed wealth in gold and silver was sufficient to attract the next wave of settlers, the Phoenicians (from modern Lebanon) and the Greeks, who created settlements along the coastal plains either side of the Gibraltar peninsula. The Phoenicians' main settlement was at Gades (modern Cadiz), but they established small fishing settlements in Guadarranque and Guadiaro. Their successors, the Carthaginians who were also of Phoenician origin, founded a settlement in 940BC on the banks of the Guadarranque river upstream of the later Roman Carteia.

Recent explorations in Gorham's Caves on the east side of Gibraltar have disclosed many Phoenician and Carthaginian artefacts which it is believed people left there as offerings to the gods before embarking on a long journey. Most prominent are Egyptian scarabs (tiny personal amulets worn in necklaces and rings which had mystical significance) of the 6/7th centuries BC. Many of these depict the god Bes and it is thought that they may represent a cult directly associated with the Strait. Scarabs were precious possessions which were usually left in tombs on death, and the fact that they were deposited in Gibraltar suggests that considerable importance was attached to the rituals performed by these ancient peoples in these inhospitable caves. Other remains discovered include pottery bowls and plates of between the 4th and 2nd centuries BC which may have been made in Iberian workshops.

The ruthless exploitation of the Carthaginians led inevitably to conflict with that other major power in the Mediterranean, the Romans, resulting in the three Punic Wars. The Romans were not such intrepid sea travellers as the Phoenicians, who had wandered as far as Cornwall in search of tin, and it was they who coined the phrase '*non* (or *ne*) *plus ultra*' which has been variously interpreted as 'nothing beyond' or more loosely 'go beyond at your own peril'. Whichever is preferred, the early Romans clearly regarded Mons Calpe as effectively the end of the known or at least the secure world. Following the First Punic War (264-241BC) the Carthaginians, who had already lost Sicily, Sardinia and Corsica, concentrated their forces in south-eastern Spain. The Second Punic War (218-206BC) led to their defeat in Spain and occupation by the Romans. The latter soon made it clear that they intended to remain and in about 190BC they established their main settlement in the Gibraltar area called Carteia. It lay only two miles from the Rock at the mouth of the Guadarranque and according to Livy was founded as a concession by the Roman Senate for the 4000 sons of Roman soldiers and Spanish women between whom there was no legal right of marriage. The town prospered under the Romans with its own mint, amphitheatre and temples. Sadly the site today is largely occupied by a petro-chemical refinery: a few ruins remain but most of the stones of Carteia have long since gone to build San Roque and neighbouring villages. In its time it was a flourishing port for the fertile hinterland and was also colonised by the Greeks. The Romans also built settlements at Portus Albus (modern Algeciras) and at Tarifa, and set up colonies at Tingis (Tangier) and Saepta Julia (Ceuta), once again introducing a north-south flow across the Strait.

The Romans' talent for organisation soon manifested itself in Spain and Calpe fell within the newly created province of Baetica which produced both the emperors Trajan and Hadrian, as well as the philosophers Lucan and Seneca. Roman remains have been discovered in Gorham's and the nearby Bennett's Caves and lead anchors recovered off Europa Point where ships waited for a favourable wind. Carteia may have declined in importance after the battle of Munda to the north of Ronda in 45BC between Pompey and Julius Caesar.

As Roman power waned, Carteia was sacked by the Vandals at the beginning of the fifth century AD as various tribes of Asian origin swept down from the north, displacing the Germanic tribes in the valleys of the Rhine and Danube. Although Carteia may have continued to exist as a small village under the Visigoths, the Vandals' successors, its days of wealth and splendour had disappeared for ever. In all this time Calpe was ignored as an infertile and inhospitable eminence, unvisited except perhaps for the occasional religious rite, and useful only as a barrier to protect the harbours from the prevailing easterly wind.

The Visigoths were not quite the uncultured barbarians popularly depicted by history. They were Christians, although of the Arian rather than the Roman Catholic creed of their Hispano-Roman predecessors, and they assimilated many of the administrative organisations bequeathed by the Romans. But religious and racial differences militated against a stable society and they suffered, furthermore, from that bane of medieval civilisation – weak kings and overmighty nobles, exacerbated by an elective rather than a hereditary system for selecting the ruler. St Boniface, writing in the eighth century, was quite clear regarding their weakness; he attributed 'their decline to the Goths' moral degeneracy and their homosexual practices'. It was the usurpation of the throne by a noble, Roderic, in 709 which led directly to their downfall, for the dispossessed Aquila appealed to Count Julian, the Vandal governor of Saepta (Ceuta), for military aid to recover his throne. It was not, however, Julian who was to be instrumental in ridding Spain of the Visigoths, for a far more powerful and explosive movement was taking place in north Africa at the end of the seventh century – the invasion of Islam.

Islam means 'submission to the will of God', whose message has been expressed through a series of prophets culminating in Mohammed. Muslims believe that God has spoken through Mohammed and that his Word is contained in the Koran. Mohammed had been born in Mecca as recently as about AD570, banished to Medina in 622 and only acclaimed in Mecca in triumph in 630. Inspired by religious zeal, the forces of Islam had already entered Egypt and occupied Alexandria by 643. Cyrenaica soon followed, but the indigenous inhabitants of north Africa, the nomadic Berber tribesmen, offered stronger resistance. The difficult country of the Maghreb was eventually subdued and in 681 the Arab forces arrived at the gates of Count Julian's fief at Saepta. It is the speed of the spread of Islam at this time which is so remarkable. In addition to their spiritual fervour, one of the great strengths of Islam at this stage of its development was that it did not have the missionary zeal of conversion that was later to overtake it: subject races were not forced or even encouraged to become Muslims. However, a special tax was levied on infidels and this encouraged many to take the new faith for economic reasons. This is one of the reasons why so many Jews in Gibraltar over the years have had names of Arabic origin.

Although the Arabic tribes retained for themselves full spiritual and political power, the absence of coercion meant that both Christians and Jews could live at least in some harmony with their rulers. This was to have important consequences for the subsequent history of both Spain and Gibraltar.

Power in the heartland of Islam had by now settled in the Umayyad Caliphate of Damascus (661-750) and the initial religious zeal was already being corrupted by the more prosaic ideals of power and dynasty. The first Islamic approach to Saepta had been little more than a reconnaissance in force, but nearly 30 years later in about 707 a much larger army under Musa ibn Nusayr took effective control of the whole north African littoral – at about the same time as Julian was being asked to intervene in Spain. Not surprisingly, Julian, who was obviously keen to move the Arabs onto other pastures, suggested that they might care to undertake the invasion instead. Although Musa was initially less than enthusiastic, he nevertheless in 710 authorised a reconnaissance of the Spanish coast in the vicinity of Gibraltar, and set in motion a conquering force which was not to turn back until it was defeated by Charles Martel at Poitiers in the heart of France in 732-3, and to remain in southern Spain for another seven hundred years.

2 COMPETING KINGDOMS 711–1309

THE INVASION OF SPAIN by Islam was an event of profound significance in the development of western Europe and it had a relevance which spread far beyond the Iberian peninsula. It brought to the barbaric northern countries the superior cultural, scientific and philosophical achievements of the Greek and Persian civilisations which had in turn been inherited by the Arabs of Damascus and Babylon. The debt is still manifest today in language, architecture, and the arts and crafts. Nor was its influence restricted to Europe, for much of South America, colonised by Portugal and Spain around the time of the Christian reconquest still bears the imprint of an Islamic inheritance. On the other hand, the Moslem advance was partly instrumental in converting western Europe from an outward looking, albeit backward, trading society into a structure of landlocked agrarian and feudal realms. From whichever viewpoint one looks, the Islamic invasion of Iberia was to have a resounding influence on the development of Europe throughout the Middle Ages which still lingers today.

Except for two brief periods, Gibraltar was to play no significant role, or indeed any role at all, in the first six hundred years of the Moorish kingdom or the Christian king's efforts to regain their patrimony. Nevertheless, this period cannot be glossed over too quickly as the struggle often raged in nearby Algeciras or Tarifa. These two towns were the 'baseports' for the north African Arab and Berber control of their possessions and interests in Spain. Furthermore, as it became recognised, somewhat belatedly, that one of the keys to power in Spain lay in control of the seas and of the Strait in particular, it was inevitable that sooner or later the strategic advantages of this great natural feature could no longer be ignored.

The Arab occupation of Spain is usually described as the Moorish period, although the Moors were strictly the Berber races of north Africa. In fact, the majority of the settlers in all periods were Berber, but the inspiration and power behind the armies, at least in the early stages, were almost entirely

The Apostle St James of Santiago was the patron saint of the 'reconquista', according to legend appearing in person at the Battle of Clavijo in 844. *St James the Greater Conquers the Moors* was painted by Giovanni Tiepolo in 1759. (Budapest Museum of Fine Arts)

Arabic. The Moors also took their stimulus in culture and learning from the east at least until the tenth century. Apart from the Tower of Homage the Moors have left only a handful of visible imprints on the Gibraltar of today, but one does not have to proceed far beyond the isthmus to find the evidence, and in Granada, Cordoba and Seville the remains of Moorish Spain are powerful and eloquent.

Although the primary focus of the Crusades was always the recovery of the Holy City, the Christian nations could hardly ignore the infidel resident within their own backyard. Nevertheless, the task of dislodging the intruder – the 'reconquista' – fell largely to the remnants of the Christian races in the northern provinces of Spain itself, the descendants of the Iberian, Roman and Gothic races in Castile, Aragon, Galicia, Navarre and Leon. The mythology of the 'reconquista' survives powerfully into modern times; in Richard Fletcher's words: 'It was a sacred patriotic struggle to wrest power from alien hands and restore Christian dominion.' But it was something more than that; it was born also of an unrelenting quest for secular power, wealth, status and land, and thus beset with the intrigue, treachery and greed which has always dogged and often undone the idealistic crusading spirit. This struggle was to endure, somewhat fitfully, for over seven hundred years.

Despite the habitual intensity of their leaders' squabbles and the diversity of their racial background, there is no doubt that a commonality of spirit existed among the Christian community: an inhabitant of Spain saw himself as a Spaniard as much as one of England considered himself an Englishman. The word 'Hispania' was used throughout the Middle Ages to describe the geographical area of the Iberian peninsula, and a few even kept alive a vision of reviving the 'Hispania Citerior' and 'Ulterior', which had been united under the rule of Rome. This humanist ideal, however, was in practice usually submerged beneath the pervasive influence of the politics of power. The real driving force of the 'reconquista' was as much an expression of aristocratic domination as it was a question of the Faith. With the passage of time the great nobles of Castile became sated with the establishment of their great estates, the 'latifundios', and tended to forget the original divine purpose of their intervention. The 'reconquista' was also frequently diverted by the Crown of Aragon's interest in imperial expansion elsewhere, particularly in southern Italy. That the 'reconquista' took so long to complete was a consequence of the diverse and quarrelsome nature of the residual Christian rulers; and that it was eventually successful was due as much to the steady disintegration of the Moorish dynasties as to the brief period of unity forged by the marriage of Ferdinand and Isabella in 1469.

*   *   *

We have already noted that Musa was somewhat reluctant to undertake an invasion of Spain even though he was regaled by Count Julian with accounts of the riches to be found there. Furthermore, it must have been evident to Musa, and his Caliph in Damascus, that the invasion would provide a useful outlet for the repressed tensions of their new Berber subjects. With their victory in north Africa behind them it could hardly be that the Muslims lacked the confidence to continue their conquest. Nor was it likely to have been the sea barrier which gave them pause: for though not numbered among the great maritime nations, the Arabs at this time controlled the whole of the western Mediterranean. Perhaps the rapid expansion of the Islamic Empire had outrun its administrative tail and needed to gather breath before taking on the numerous Gothic hordes to the north. Whatever the reasons, Musa soon overcame his doubts and launched the Islamic invasion of Europe.

There is much conjecture attaching to the early history of Gibraltar and archaeological evidence is almost non-existent. Furthermore, the sources for the early years of the Islamic invasion are scarce and confused by the Gothic penchant for legend and mythology. Although small Arab expeditions may have crossed the sea in the early years of the eighth century, it is clear that in the summer of 710 a raiding party, perhaps about five hundred strong, under a Berber, Tarif ibn Malik, crossed from Tangier to Mellaria. Subsequently named Tarifa, it is said to have been the origin of the modern word 'tariff' on account of customs duties levied by the Moors at the port. The reconnaissance was outstandingly successful and Tarif soon returned with ample evidence of the booty foretold by Julian.

It was the reassurance engendered by this initial sortie which evidently led to Musa sending a far more formidable force across the Strait the following year. This was led by Tarik ibn Zeyad, variously described as a 'freedman' of Musa, probably an Algerian, but certainly a Berber. Tarik had about 7000 mainly Berber troops of which 500 were cavalry and the rest infantry; auxiliaries may have brought the total force up to about 12,000. He did not use the Tarifa route which the Visigoths might have anticipated and there is evidence that he went to some lengths to conceal his intentions. Legend maintains that he landed on Mons Calpe which he named Djebel Tarik (Gibraltar) on 27th April 711, but there is no clear evidence of where he actually disembarked. Later sources suggest that he made an initial landing which was repulsed and went to another part of the coast. It is known that he had only four merchant ships and had to ferry his troops across in relays which could have taken up to fourteen days. It may be assumed therefore that his point of entry was sufficiently far from Portus Albus (Algeciras), where the Visigoths had a garrison, to avoid an early confrontation, and ideally out of sight of observers from the port. This would seem to preclude anywhere within the Bay of Gibraltar although the initial landing referred to, which may have been a feint, could have been near Carteia. The most likely conclusion is that Tarik sailed round the Rock to the east and landed somewhere north of the isthmus. The beaches in this area were suitable and there was pasture for the horses and fuel for cooking fires; but most telling of all, the landing would have been screened from the Visigoth garrison.

So what was the role of Gibraltar in the invasion? The answer is probably very little directly, but it is conceivable, even probable, that Tarik put an observation party onto the Rock to keep him informed of the enemy's movements across the bay. There are reports that he built a fort on the Rock although no signs of this remain, or indeed of any walls or other fortifications from this period. It is possible that he made some provision for a defensive fallback position on the Rock, but it is unlikely that it was maintained for long after the capture of Algeciras and Tarifa. But even so Tarik apparently saw fit to give the Rock his own name rather than, for example, the major settlement in the bay at Portus Albus. Thus the bestowal of his name on the Rock must be largely symbolic – it was undeniably the most impressive natural feature in the area. There is, however, another possibility that the name could have a spiritual derivation more in keeping with the times. The Arab word *tariek* means path, in which case Djebel Tariq could be defined as the 'The Mountain of the Path (of Islam)'. Whatever its derivation, the reconquest of the Rock in both Moorish and British times came to represent a symbolic value out of all proportion to its contemporary strategic importance. It was certainly regarded as a potent image by the time of Queen Isabella when it was specifically mentioned in her will, and the Spanish claim today lies deep within their souls.

Wherever he landed, Tarik appears to have maintained an element of surprise and it is certain that he quickly captured all the settlements around the bay. Although properly we should continue to refer to the Rock as Djebel Tarik, from here, for ease of reference, I shall call it by its modern derivation – Gibraltar. Likewise the names Algeciras and Tarifa also stem from this period and modern Andalusia acquired its Moorish name of Al Andalus.

After this brief claim to fame, Gibraltar almost disappears again from history for over three hundred years. Whilst the Moors remained unopposed in southern Spain they had no use for the potential defensive qualities of the Rock and were quite content to develop the more convenient ports of Tarifa and Algeciras which became the main gateways for trade and, when necessary, reinforcements from north Africa.

We need consider only briefly the events of these years until a new threat arises in the eleventh century. Tarik made rapid headway after his initial successes, defeating Roderic in July near the town of Medina Sidonia in an unusually prolonged battle for the period of seven days. From there he made rapid progress northwards, capturing the Visigothic capital Toledo through the treachery of its Jewish inhabitants later in the same summer. For what was intended only as a reconnaissance in strength, Tarik had been remarkably ambitious, so much so that it attracted the attention of Musa who brought another 18,000 troops, mainly Arabs, across to Spain in 712. Tarik and Musa quarrelled, and summoned to Damascus, both ended their years in disgrace.

The Umayyad dynasty in Damascus was toppled by the Abbasids in 750 and the focus of the by now vast Arab empire moved to Baghdad. But one of the surviving Umayyad sons, Abd al-Rahman, escaped to Spain where he set up an independent Emirate at Cordoba. This dynasty ruled Moorish Spain for nearly three hundred years in some splendour as may be seen today in the mosque at Cordoba and the nearby now largely destroyed palace at Madinat al-Zahra. But it was basically an unstable regime, and although generally tolerant of its indigenous Jews and Christians (Mozarabs), they for their part were ever ready to support any rebellious factions among the Arabs and the Berbers. The organisation of the country was still basically tribal despite the centralising efforts of the emirs. And at the same time the displaced Christian kings were nibbling away at the periphery.

The most glorious period of the Muslim dynasty was the tenth century. Cordoba was one of the main cities of the western world, perhaps as large as Constantinople and half the size of Baghdad. Although briefly threatened by the Fatimid dynasty in north Africa, which eventually settled in Egypt, Al Andalus was able to reverse the situation of the early years and maintain a hegemony over the mainland Berber tribes, reinforcing their hold by capturing Melilla in 927 and Ceuta in 931. Relations with the Christian states fluctuated, but in general Cordoba had the better of their military encounters, noticeably so at the end of the century under the regent Almanzor. At other times relations were more harmonious: in 964, as a gesture of good will, the Emir sent his personal physician to treat King Sancho the Fat of Leon for obesity. But in the eleventh century the country degenerated into chaos, Cordoba was destroyed and Al Andalus disintegrated into what is known as the 'Age of the Petty Kings'. Except for brief periods when it passed into the hands of the Berbers of Malaga or to rebellious petty rulers, Gibraltar became part of the Arab kingdom of Seville, the most powerful of the petty kingdoms.

*   *   *

Throughout these three hundred years there is no evidence as yet of any significant settle-

This is a section of the earliest Moorish wall in Gibraltar. It is of rubble construction and may date from the 11th-century.

ment in the vicinity of the Rock. Around 860 two Norse pirates from the Loire, by the name of Bjorn and Hastein, ravaged the coast of Spain including burning the mosque in Algeciras on their way into the Mediterranean. They did not apparently land on Gibraltar. The Algecirans gained their revenge after a later raid when they made doors for their mosque out of the planks of captured Viking ships. However, in the middle of the eleventh century a new threat was emerging in Africa. From the Senegal basin in the western Sahara, a nomadic Berber tribe, the Lamtuna, embarked on a wave of conquest in the name of religious renewal, leading eventually to the Almoravid dynasty of Yusuf ibn Tashufin. Their religious zeal and enthusiasm for expansion and war naturally worried the more worldly Arabs in Seville and in 1068 Al-Mutadid ordered the Governor of Algeciras to build a fort on Gibraltar. This was perhaps more correctly an observation tower both to watch across the Strait and to monitor shipping to the east of the Rock – remembering Tarik's landing in 711, Al-Mutadid would have known that he would need the maximum warning to assemble his garrison troops to oppose a landing. However, it is not known whether Al-Mutadid's orders were carried out, for he died the following year and his successor was a much less able military strategist.

As a further complication, an old threat, the 'reconquista', was again on the march. Ferdinand I of Castile and Leon had already exerted sufficient pressure to extract tribute money from many of the petty kingdoms, at times even including distant Seville; and in 1082 his son, Alfonso VI, raided deep into Moorish territory, briefly reaching Tarifa. It

was also the time of the legendary El Cid, Rodrigo Diaz, extolled as a kind of Spanish Robin Hood, but in reality little more than a mercenary brigand. In 1085, Alfonso captured Toledo and the Moors had no alternative but to plead for assistance from the Almoravids, an option which cannot have been entirely agreeable to them. Yusuf, the leader of the Almoravids in Morocco responded, and with the Moors reasonably united for once, inflicted a crushing defeat on Alfonso at the battle of Sagrajas near Badajoz on 23rd October 1086. To the Moors' relief Yusuf returned to Africa, but retained control of the Bay of Gibraltar and its hinterland, clearly suggesting that he may not yet have finished with Spain. Indeed he had not, for he returned in 1090 with a large army and took control of the whole of southern Spain as far north as Badajoz and Granada. As Richard Fletcher has aptly commented: 'The world of the party (petty) kings was suddenly and brutally swept away when the cats came face to face with real lions.' If it was ever built, Al-Mutadid's fort on Gibraltar would have had a short active life.

The Almoravids did not enjoy power for long, for although they brought a new reli-

Jimena de la Frontera, about 20 miles from Gibraltar, is a good example of one of the castles of the 'petty kingdoms' of Moorish Spain.

gious intensity to bear on the rival Arab and Berber tribes, the power structure quickly languished into decadence on the luxuries of Al Andalus and dissolved into another system of petty quarrelsome emirates. In Morocco the Almoravids were soon upstaged by an even stricter and more extreme grouping, the Almohads. They were descended from the sedentary Masmuda Berbers of the High Atlas and by the middle years of the twelfth century had gained control of most of Morocco and Tunisia. Their regime in its religious zeal bears a close resemblance to fundamentalist Islamic doctrine today. Power in the Almohads passed, by 1133, to a very able general and administrator, Abd al-Mumin, and in 1146 he invaded Spain through Tarifa with 12,000 cavalry and 20,000 infantry.

These developments in north Africa were mirrored to a certain extent in a revival of Christian zeal within Spain with Alfonso VII of Castile occupying Cordoba, albeit briefly, and ravaging the kingdoms of Seville and Granada. But of more significance to Gibraltar was the use of Catalan/Genoese naval forces to capture Almeria in 1147, only some 180 miles along the coast to the east. It was the first time the kings of Spain had used naval power and it opened up a new approach to the strategically important Bay of Gibraltar.

It took many years for Abd al-Mumin to restore the Moorish position in southern Spain, for not only did he have to contend with the Berber petty kingdoms, but also to repel the revitalised forces of Christendom. He was generally successful in pushing back the boundaries and his son and grandson extended his work. However, Moorish Spain was no longer an independent entity; it was now firmly ruled from Berber north Africa and Gibraltar itself, as opposed to its bay, was at last beginning to play a strategic role.

It is known from the Arab Chronicles that Abd al-Mumin decreed in 1160 that a fortified town should be built on the Rock to be called Medinat-al-Fath (City of Victory). He inspected the site himself and ordered that the town should be enclosed by a wall with a single gate, the Bab-al-Fath (Gate of Victory), and contain a mosque, palaces for himself and his sons, and reservoirs connected by aqueducts to the domestic build-

ings. A small stone air vent still to be seen on Rosia Road (of Spanish reconstruction) originally formed part of this Moorish water distribution system. Windmills were to be erected on the Rock for grinding corn. The extent of the town is not known exactly although its main fortification was probably a smaller building on the present site of the Tower of Homage. A stretch of wall on the Upper Rock above the later Charles Vth wall may date from this period. Nor is the precise purpose of the town at all clear, but given Abd al-Mumin's reputation as a general it is tempting to suggest that its function was mainly military, to monitor and if possible forestall any Christian naval movement round the Rock towards the important ports of Algeciras and Tarifa. But even after the loss of Almeria in 1147, which in any case had been recaptured ten years later, it had taken a long time to recognise this potential threat. Furthermore, the presence of several palaces and the employment of one of the leading architects of the day, Ahman ibn Basu, suggests that the intention was perhaps rather more ceremonial and administrative than defensive. The imposing position on the Rock would have given the town an exclusivity and status which could not have been so easily achieved at low-lying Algeciras.

It is not known how much of the town was actually built, for Abd al-Mumin died in 1163 and his son preferred the softer ambience of Seville. It may be assumed that the majority of the building work stopped, although with the war against the Christians still being waged strongly, it would be surprising if its defensive and observation aspects were totally neglected. Today we have to go to Tarifa, where the walls and gateways, although of a slightly earlier period, are still standing to get some indication of what Medinat-al-Fath may have looked like.

The next one hundred and fifty years present a confusingly complex picture as the three competing elements, the Berbers in Spain, the Berbers in Africa and the Christians competed and cooperated with each other in a web of conflict, alliances, treachery and intrigue. Portugal had emerged as a sovereign state in 1147 under Afonso, son of the illegitimate daughter of

One of the builders of Medinat-al-Fath, Ahman ibn Basu, was also responsible for the Giralda and the Patio de los Naranjos in Seville. This print is by Gustave Doré.

Not much remains of Medinat-al-Fath in Gibraltar, but a typical Moorish walled town may be seen at nearby Tarifa.

Alfonso VI, and for many years compounded the problems of Castile. Gibraltar played no known part in this matrix, but war frequently raged in the vicinity. It also brought to the forefront the factor that was thereafter to play an increasingly important part in Gibraltar's history – the rise of sea power.

The Almohads' power in both Africa and Spain steadily waned over the first fifty years of the thirteenth century which, particularly during the reign of Ferdinand III (1217-52), was by far the most successful 'reconquista' to date. Cordoba fell in 1236, Valencia in 1238, and Seville succumbed to a Christian siege in 1248. By 1252 most of Al Andalus had been lost and only Murcia and Granada remained as Moorish strongholds in Spain. These were independent of each other and also of control from north Africa at this time. Granada was the more important and its territory extended from Almeria, which had been recaptured from the Christians in

1157, round the coast to Cadiz, including the Bay of Gibraltar. In line with the increasing acknowledgment of naval power, Alfonso X, who became King of Castile in 1252, recognised the importance of control of the Strait in future operations against Granada, for any military success on land could be quickly nullified by Berber reinforcement from Africa. Although he maintained a naval force in Seville to harass Berber shipping, it was too far away from its home base to be really effective in the Strait. Furthermore, Alfonso was distracted by wider concerns – he became Holy Roman Emperor in 1268 – and did not pursue his advantage as strenuously as was desirable, for disruption was looming again in north Africa.

Yet another Berber tribe, the Marinids, led by Abu Yusuf Yakub, were steadily conquering the Almohad dynasty, finally gaining control of Morocco in 1269. The Marinids were not possessed of the same religious fervour as the Almohads, but were quite prepared to use the religious war, the jihad, to further their secular interests. Meanwhile in Spain, Muhammad I, founder of the Nasrid dynasty to which we owe today the glories of the Alhambra, had seized Granada in 1237. Yusuf conspired with his successor, Muhammad II, a cunning and treacherous rogue, to try to recapture Cordoba despite the truce that he had recently agreed with Alfonso. A desperate defence followed and thanks largely to Prince Sancho, Alfonso's brother, Cordoba was soon retaken, with Yusuf retiring once again to the relative safety of Algeciras. Alfonso decided at last to attempt what he should have done 20 years earlier after his father had captured Seville and make a determined effort to capture the Moors' 'baseports' in the Bay of Gibraltar. If he could control the passage between Africa and Spain, he could subjugate the Moorish sultanate at leisure. He fitted out a fleet of 80 galleys and supporting sailing ships and in October 1277 besieged Algeciras. The following year he advanced with an army and laid siege to the landward side of the town. Despite terrible privation the town held out and Alfonso's grip began to weaken in the face of sickness, desertion and that bane of all armies, and the Spanish in particular – not enough money to pay the troops. Yusuf eventually intervened although he only had 14 galleys of his own, and with the help of a providential gale destroyed the Spanish fleet: Alfonso had no option but to raise the siege and retire. Another truce was agreed.

The ensuing thirty years was a period of shifting alliances, internal conflicts and short-lived truces which, with one exception, left the situation the same as it had been in 1278. Simmering differences between Alfonso and Sancho erupted into open warfare in 1281 with Yusuf supporting his erstwhile enemy Alfonso and Muhammad of Granada supporting his opponent. However, when Alfonso died in 1284, Yusuf switched his support to Muhammad although prudently retaining control of Malaga as well as Algeciras. Yusuf displayed only an intermittent interest in Spain, but he well recognised the importance of the baseports on the northern shore of the Strait, as indeed did Sancho for Castile. Internal dis-

sension and foreign ambitions kept Sancho occupied for a few years, but in 1292 he made another sortie to the south and captured Tarifa fairly easily, installing as governor Alonso Perez de Guzman, whose family was subsequently to play an important role in the history of Gibraltar.

Yet another internal player, Sancho's younger brother Prince John, now entered the fray. He offered his services to Yusuf's successor, Yakub, to lead an attack on Tarifa. It was hardly an opportunity that Yakub could ignore and he provided ships and cavalry as well as the Algeciras garrison. John mounted a prolonged siege of Tarifa which was ultimately unsuccessful, but which produced one of the romantic legends so dear to Spaniards. As a result of one of the earlier shifting alliances, Alonso de Guzman had placed his son as a page with Prince John who now produced him under the walls of Tarifa threatening to kill him if Alonso did not surrender. Alonso threw his sword from the walls saying that he would provide the weapon to enable this, and that he would rather his son died, and five more sons if he had them, than to hand over the town which belonged to the King. Sad to relate, his son was killed before his eyes, but the town survived and ensured Alonso a revered place in history as 'El Bueno'.

The death of Sancho in 1295 led to further internal dissension in Castile as his successor was his nine-year-old son Ferdinand IV. The Regent, Ferdinand's uncle Henry, whose motives were suspect to say the least, wanted to sell Tarifa to Muhammad, but was thwarted by the Dowager Queen. At the same time, Yakub, tiring of his Spanish adventures which had not been over-rewarding, sold Algeciras to Granada. The advent of the new King led to a settling of differences between Castile and Aragon, and when Ferdinand came of a age another determined effort was made to revitalise the 'reconquista'.

The six hundred years which had passed since Tarik landed in the vicinity of Gibraltar had seen a slow but inexorable decline in the Moorish power in Spain. The essentially tribal nature of the Arab and Berber society had led to a fragmented authority with periods of strong and often cultivated rule giving way to petty warring

Commemorating a hero of the '*reconquista*', this modern statue of Alonso de Guzman – '*El Bueno*' – is in the public gardens in Tarifa.

kingdoms. Centralising influences, when they occurred, invariably came across from north Africa, but with each succeeding invasion, interest in Spain had become increasingly distant and intermittent. The '*reconquista*' might well have succeeded much earlier than it did if only the Christian kings had been able to engender a modicum of cooperation or to preserve internal loyalty. However, despite the internal dissensions, by the beginning of the fourteenth century the Moorish domain was restricted to the Sultanate of Granada which included Gibraltar and Algeciras, but no longer Tarifa, Seville and Cordoba. The '*reconquista*' had been largely accomplished by land battle, but thanks to Alfonso X it was now recognised that sea power had a prominent role to play; and with this realisation, Gibraltar began also to play a more significant part in the ongoing history of Spain.

3 FLUCTUATING FORTUNES 1309–1462

After the decline of Medinat-al-Fath in 1163, Gibraltar disappears almost completely from the documentary accounts for nearly one hundred and fifty years. The town may even have been temporarily deserted for, with Algeciras and Tarifa as secure 'baseports' for communications with north Africa, the barren rock had little to commend it as port, fortress, and certainly not as a home for domestic settlers. The only worthwhile tracts of land available for cultivation were across the isthmus and, with the war temporarily far distant, there was no incentive to colonise territory which had few domestic or commercial advantages.

Nevertheless, as the thirteenth century progressed, the 'reconquista' moved inexorably closer and it is difficult to believe that the Rock did not again figure in the military planning of the competing factions. We do know that when Gibraltar suddenly reappears in documented history, in 1309, a small fortified town existed on the northwest side of the Rock. There are several reasons to support the theory that this town owed its existence to the capture of Tarifa by the Christians in 1292. Although it did not happen, it was widely expected that Sancho would besiege Algeciras after Tarifa, for as always control of the two 'baseports' would sever the Moors' lifeline to north Africa. After the fall of Tarifa, the Moors in Algeciras would feel somewhat isolated with a hostile garrison to the west and a vacuum to the east. A stronghold on Gibraltar would provide some protection in their rear and provide a fallback position in the event of the expected attack on their town. Secondly, the increasing importance of seapower required them to keep watch on the enemy's movement by sea as well as overland, and Gibraltar provided a splendid lookout post

overseeing both the approaches from the west from the Christians' main naval base in Seville and down the east coast from Catalonia and Valencia. Finally, the refugees from Tarifa had to settle somewhere and it is likely that many of them, the memory of defeat in the forefront of their minds, were

A 14th-century Moorish lookout and signalling base high on the Rock.

The mosaic pavement which formed the courtyard of the mosque built by the Moors at Europa Point.

looking for a more defensible location on the coast whilst still keeping open their lifeline to north Africa. It was therefore in everybody's interest that the Rock should be occupied and defensible.

Nevertheless, it does not appear that the town on Gibraltar was either very large or strongly fortified. Its population was probably little more than a thousand and its walls were susceptible to a prolonged siege. It was situated in the area of what is now Casemates Square and would have been surrounded by a stone wall with small bastions and perhaps one more substantial tower in the curtain wall. As there was no natural protection for ships, there would almost certainly have been a harbour or a mole to allow maritime access. But this is only speculation as no archaeological evidence is available. There is, however, one interesting monument which is believed to date from this period. At some time around 1300 the Moors built a mosque at the southern tip of the peninsula at what is now Europa Point.

It is believed to have contained a tower with buildings, now destroyed, around the other three sides of a small cloister. The courtyard remains and contains a mosaic paving, unfortunately now a little overgrown, with a typically Moorish star-shaped design. The small mosque, converted by the Spanish to a chapel, has been extensively rebuilt over the years and during the British period used as an army storehouse. It is now surrounded by a military housing estate but has been restored as the Shrine of Our Lady of Europe and contains a small polychrome wooden statue of the Virgin and Child.

The long expected siege of Algeciras at last commenced under Ferdinand IV in July 1309 and within a few days he had sent Juan Nunez and Alonso Perez de Guzman, the hero of Tarifa, and a few hundred men to besiege Gibraltar. Two siege engines were employed and the walls, which could not have been either extensive or substantial, were breached within a month. The inhabitants thereupon quickly surrendered and

Ferdinand agreed that they could be exiled to north Africa. For the first time in six hundred years Gibraltar was in the hands, albeit only briefly, of the Christian rulers of Castile. It was the first of the fifteen sieges that were to be the fate of the Rock over the next six hundred and fifty years. The King visited the town himself and soon appreciated its strategic value, ordering that the walls should be repaired, a keep built, and a dockyard constructed for the protection of galleys. This may have been the origin of the Old Mole, now the location of the Devil's Tongue Battery outside the Water Port Gate. The tower is likely to have been on the site of the present Moorish castle, but again there is no direct evidence on the ground. Having captured a by now deserted site, Ferdinand had to establish a garrison and settlers from Castile to provide those many domestic services required to support it. Understandably this was not very easy with Algeciras and the coast to the north still in the enemy's hands and Ferdinand had to provide generous incentives to encourage the mere three hundred households that were considered necessary. Inhabitants were not required to pay taxes to the Crown and grants of land across the isthmus were freely available. The Town Council was granted the right to levy harbour dues except on warships and food. Even so, the King's Letter Patent of Incorporation of February 1310 still implicitly encouraged the settlement of thieves, murderers and evildoers of all kinds except for traitors to the King or their feudal lord, or anyone running away with his lord's wife! Alonso Guzman's son was named as military governor, Alonso himself having recently been killed in battle. He was required to maintain a garrison of 300 men at the King's expense.

Ferdinand found Algeciras a much harder nut to crack. Unable to storm the walls, he settled down to blockade the town by sea and land. But he had started the siege too late in the year and was unable to prevent the occasional blockade runner from north Africa breaking through the net. An exceptionally wet winter brought the usual problems of sickness, shortage of supplies resulting from the appalling state of the roads, and the inevitable desertions and low morale. Conditions on the blockading ships were equally foul. As so often happens with Gibraltar, witness the Spanish siege of 1704, the incarcerated were living in better conditions than the besiegers. That perennial Spanish scourge, the disaffection of over-mighty nobles began to cause problems, and in February 1310 Ferdinand was forced to call off the siege although he secured surprisingly favourable terms from the Moors. In fact the Moors too were experiencing their customary difficulties of intrigue and internal coups, and a stalemate ensued for the next few years, albeit with sporadic skirmishing which generally favoured the Christians.

The failure to capture Algeciras left Gibraltar in a precarious position. Whilst Algeciras could be partly neutralised by the possession of Tarifa and Gibraltar and the superior Spanish fleet, Gibraltar itself was surrounded by towns controlled by the Moors. Castellar, less than 15 miles from Gibraltar, Jimena de la Frontera, Ronda and Estepona were all Moorish fortified towns, and a further complication ensued in 1316 when Abu Ismael granted these forts to the King of Fez (Morocco), Yusuf ibn Yakub, in return for the declaration of a jihad. Castile was now ruled by the five-year-old Alfonso XI after the death of Ferdinand in 1312 and was under the regency of Prince Peter, the late King's brother. Ferdinand had instructed that the defences of Gibraltar should be strengthened and another bastion was built to protect the dockyard. This was the Giralda Tower, now superseded by the North Bastion. No attempt was made to improve the southern wall as it was believed that any threat must materialise from the landward approach across the isthmus. Given the strength of the Spanish fleet, this was perhaps an understandable but nevertheless unjustified error, and one which was to be repeated in the future.

A sea battle in the Strait in 1327 under the capable Admiral Jofre de Tenorio seemed to confirm the Spanish superiority, but protection from the sea in this area of strong currents and fickle weather could never be assured. Gibraltar's situation was further compromised by a corrupt governor, Vasco Perez de Meira, who misappropriated funds intended for the improvement of the defences and the provision of food supplies.

King Alfonso, now come of age, had the insight and talent to have been a great military commander, but at this early stage was more concerned with the pomp of state and the pleasures of the flesh. Furthermore, he always had to watch his back against the insidious intrigue of his relations and nobles. The time was ripe for a Moorish initiative and the new ruler of Fez, Abu'l Hassan, grasped the opportunity of another attempt to recover Gibraltar. He entrusted the siege to his one-eyed son, Abd'l Malik, a capable general, who managed to slip across to Algeciras with 7000 troops in February 1333 whilst Jofre was revictualling in Seville. This is usually regarded as the third siege of Gibraltar, but the second was in fact an insubstantial affair in 1315 which was quickly forestalled by the Regent, Prince Peter.

A rapid response by Alfonso may still have retrieved the situation. He quickly despatched Jofre to transport food and supplies to Gibraltar by sea, but his openly disloyal nobles were very reluctant to supply troops and Alfonso was equally reluctant to proceed south with his own army leaving rebellious subjects at his back. Muhammad IV of Granada inadvertently helped him by attacking the most powerful of the recalcitrant nobles, Juan Nunez, and stinging him into retaliation. The perennial problem of acquiring money to pay the troops was also delaying Alfonso and the siege had been in progress for four months before he was at last able to move south. Further difficulties ensued when he reached Seville where the Council of War tried to persuade him to abandon Gibraltar on the grounds that he was now taking on both Granada and Fez at the same time. Although Alfonso's personal peccadillos are often blamed for the tardy response, it has to be admitted that, for a very young and insecure ruler, he showed considerable resolution in very trying circumstances.

By this time Abd'l Malik had a strong grip on the town. He had recognised the vulnerability of the southern approaches and had captured the dockyard, and it is recorded that he had siege machines on the Rock above the castle. Looking at the ground today this seems improbable: medieval siege machines were large and unwieldy constructions and it is difficult to conceive how these could have been manoeuvred into a position above the castle. He may, however, have had some form of catapult on the Upper Rock. Jofre meanwhile was sitting impotently off shore with fifteen galleys and six sail, but had to withdraw when Malik turned his catapults on the ships. However, notwithstanding his pre-war peculation, Vasco was proving a remarkably determined defender of the walls and Malik was making only slow headway despite his vastly superior force. The precarious situation may yet have been saved if only Alfonso could have accelerated his departure from Seville. By mid-June the conditions inside the town were desperate, food was all but exhausted despite frantic attempts by Jofre to use catapults to hurl bags of flour over the walls. Even so, Alfonso was only a day or two away when news came from Jofre that the town appeared to have surrendered. Vasco had indeed given up the struggle on the 17th of June. That he believed he would be held responsible for his misrule is supported by his flight to north Africa, and Spanish history still regards him as a traitor. Alfonso has also been blamed for the loss, but perhaps the most significant reason was the greedy aspirations of the nobles who failed to support the young King in his hour of need.

Alfonso was still more determined than his feckless subordinates and immediately sought the agreement of his Council of War to attack Gibraltar before the victors could consolidate their success. It was a sensible move: Jofre still dominated the seaward approaches and resupply by land would be slow and difficult. With some reluctance they agreed and Alfonso's army set out from Jerez towards the end of June. They soon recognised that they were being shadowed by a force of about 6000 Moors, but they made no effort to interfere until Alfonso was encamped on the Sierra Carbonera above Gibraltar. The Moors' tactics were now apparent; they would fall upon the Christians as they descended the steep slopes towards the isthmus, or alternatively entrap them in the lowlands between the besieged town and the hills. Alfonso was alive to this danger and left his rearguard conspicuous on the ridge while he infiltrated a force of archers and cavalry through the woods on the Moors' flank. As soon as they were in position, he enticed the Moors onto the ridge by withdrawing his rearguard while at the same time the flanking force slipped in behind the enemy. Meanwhile the rearguard had halted as soon as they were out of sight below the crest and were now rejoined by the main force. The pincer movement worked exactly to plan and the Moors were driven in disarray towards Algeciras. It was one of several examples of Alfonso's skill as a tactical commander, faultless in planning, timing and execution.

As so often, however, Alfonso could not keep control of his subordinate commanders once battle was joined. Despite his orders to the contrary, they pursued the fleeing Moors almost to the gates of Algeciras, leaving themselves horribly exposed on the wrong side of a river. They were rescued only by the resourceful Jofre who had a force of 100 archers rowed up the Palmones river to cover their retreat. The day had been won, but not without distractions and indiscipline which was to plague Alfonso again as he set about the fourth siege of Gibraltar.

Alfonso's plan was sound, indeed it was the only viable option. The key to Gibraltar in medieval warfare was to gain the high ground above the walls, and the only way this could be achieved in strength was by landing troops on the Red Sands to the south of the walls. It is a mystery why this obvious landing area was not enclosed within the walls, particularly by a defender who could not guarantee control of the sea. The first force ashore of some 1500 men was transported by Jofre's galleys without difficulty and landed on the Sands. But instead of remaining in the vicinity of the beach to protect the second wave from the by now alerted Moors, they instead clambered onto the Upper Rock from where they could only watch helplessly as the second wave was cut to pieces by the Moorish archers as they disembarked on the beach. The numbers ashore, without heavy equipment and siege material, were totally inadequate successfully to breach the walls, and far from becoming a spearhead had become a liability. Indiscipline had once again thwarted Alfonso's carefully laid plan.

This setback, along with a shortage of supplies, was sufficient to persuade the Council of War that all was lost and Alfonso

was forced to order a withdrawal, leaving the 1500 men to their fate: it appeared an ignominious failure to a King who had vowed before they set out that he would not rest while one Christian flag still flew on the Rock. His evident distress this time, however, was sufficient to test the consciences of even the most irresolute of his knights and after another Council of War they retraced their steps to Castellar. Their new found courage had its reward, for as they reached the hills overlooking the bay they saw the welcoming sight of their reprovisioning fleet arriving from Cadiz.

Alfonso made another determined, and this time successful, attempt to land a sizeable force on the Red Sands. Every available boat was used to move the best troops, cavalry and crossbow men, in a concerted rush on the beach. Under a hail of fire the Moors fled behind the walls and the cavalry, already mounted, were able to ride ashore and join their relieved comrades on the Rock. The hard work was still to come for, although there was now an adequate number of troops ashore, the walls still had to be breached. It was a return to medieval siege warfare which, before the discovery of gunpowder, was a long and tiresome ritual. Siege machines were summoned from Seville, Cadiz and Jerez, and sufficient food laid in for a long investment. Gaining the high ground above the castle, siege catapults were hoisted up the east face of the Rock to batter the main fortress and the dockyard where the galleys were protected by a stout wooden roof. An assault on the latter from the sea was unsuccessful.

The merlons and parapets of the tower were destroyed and the walls damaged, but still not breached. Mining operations were tried, leading to some desperate hand to hand fighting right under the walls, and some of the siege towers were set on fire by burning pitch dispensed from portholes hastily cut in the walls. A long static siege, with no succour for the defenders from the sea, would undoubtedly have succeeded. But Alfonso too had his problems of resupply: Abd'l Malik and Muhammad were sitting patiently on the hills overlooking Gibraltar, too weak to attack with much hope of success, but blocking the communication routes overland. Food therefore had to be obtained via the sea, and in these times this was at best unreliable even in the summer. Alfonso dug a defensive trench across the isthmus, but in reality he was now as surely besieged as those inside the walls of Gibraltar itself. Furthermore, both besiegers and besieged had their internal problems. Alfonso's notoriously rebellious nobles, who had agreed to mount diversionary raids into Granada, were in fact threatening the King's own castles. On the other side Morocco was again under threat of revolt, and Muhammad was as usual more intent on feathering his own pocket at the expense of serious warfare.

It was in fact a classic stalemate: Gibraltar might fall at any time, but in practice had only to hang on until the winter. On the other hand Alfonso could certainly not delay matters so long, and news of the death of his infant heir quickly persuaded him to react favourably to a tentative offer of peace from Abd'l Malik and Muhammad. Alfonso withdrew his siege machines from Gibraltar, sending them to Tarifa, and marched his troops back to Seville. On the way he entertained Muhammad to a banquet where they exchanged rich gifts, but the unfortunate Muhammad was subsequently slain by some of his zealot followers for consorting with the Christians. There was a risk of renewed war, but a general four year truce was agreed in 1334 and Malik returned to Africa to help his father. Gibraltar, not without considerable alarm, had successfully withstood its fourth siege. Before leaving for Africa, Malik ordered the defences of Gibraltar to be strengthened. A massive keep, which still stands today, was built on the site of the former tower at the summit of the walls and these were extended to encompass the Red Sands beach, a long overdue improvement. It is from this period that we can first see on the ground substantial remains of the extensive concourse of fortifications that encircle Gibraltar today.

*   *   *

There is a problem in dealing with the fortifications of Gibraltar because they have evolved, albeit in some periods somewhat spasmodically, from the twelfth century through to very recent times. The work of no period has been totally obliterated, but as the weapons and tactics have changed over the years, so the defences have been modified and developed, often overlaying the work of a past generation. Furthermore, in the modern period when static defences have become outmoded and before the world became aware of the desirability of maintaining its historical heritage, commercial development has often encroached upon the fabric of the fortress. Although there is still much to see today, it is sometimes difficult to fathom from the remaining constituents the structure of the overall plan which was largely, but not entirely, complete by the end of the nineteenth century.

There is little documentary and no archaeological evidence to support the building of any fortifications on the Rock at the time of Tarik's invasion of 711. The first sure documentary evidence of fortifications comes in 1160 when Abd al-Mumin built a tower and an enclosing wall with a single gate. But, whilst the tower was probably on the site of the present Tower of Homage, there is no evidence on the ground, and nor is there any sign of a subsequent rebuilding of the tower in the time of the brief Spanish occupation of Ferdinand 1V in the early fourteenth century.

Apart from isolated stretches of wall, the

Shorn of its merlons, the castle as seen today is largely the work of Abu'l Hassan after 1333.

first evidence of the fortifications of Gibraltar which may be seen today is therefore the imposing tower, now called the Tower of Homage, but known to the Moors as '*Al Qasabah*' and to the Spanish as '*La Calahorra*', and the surrounding castle complex which was built after 1333 by Abu'l Hassan following the recapture of the town by the Moors. The castle occupies a commanding position facing north and west at the point at which the gentle west facing slope gives way to a steep escarpment about a third of the way up the Rock. The tower which is one of the largest in Moorish Spain is almost intact, shorn only of its merlon battlements. It is faced with *tapia*, a hard lime mortar with an unattractive concrete texture, and bears many traces of shell damage from later periods. The topmost floor contains chambers for the governor, one room with a ribbed dome was possibly a mosque

and is shown refurbished as such today, and another with star-shaped apertures which would have contained coloured glass served as an ablution.

Attached to the tower is the large redoubt, which is also 14th-century, although built in a 12th-century style, not an unusual characteristic of Moorish architecture. It has large blocked arches to the west flanked by lines of alternating large and small stones, typically 14th-century *Taza* work. Below the redoubt and zig-zagging down the rock is the best preserved stretch of Moorish wall. It was constructed in the 14th-century of rough masonry with bricks and mortar from the Red Sands; there are signs here of embedded masonry from an earlier wall. The wall of the Qasbah below the castle is also intact and contains both square and a bow-shaped tower built into the wall above the main gateway. The latter, although rebuilt

This view of the 'Tower of Homage' from the north shows the redoubt and the zig-zag wall running down towards the Land Port Gate.

The bow-shaped tower, complete with merlons, built into the south wall of the castle complex.

The gatehouse to the west of the castle was the main entrance to the Qasbah. Although on a Moorish foundation, the 14th-century building seen today was built during the Spanish occupation.

by Portuguese engineers in Spanish times, still has Moorish vaults similar to those in the tower above. It is an impressive structure with its elliptical domed roof and small cupola looking somewhat like an overturned bathtub: it originally had a right angled gateway, a typically Moorish feature which can still be seen in nearby Castellar. Today the Tower of Homage is approached from above and is well worth a visit, but the rest of the complex is difficult to see. The Qasbah has disappeared under modern tenement flats which press right up to the Moorish wall, and the redoubt and its environs is now a prison, best seen in all respects from outside. In fact the whole complex is probably now best viewed from below near the Land Port Gate. Hassan also strengthened the Casemates and extended the Line Wall as far as the Red Sands. It is believed that the southern mole was constructed at this time, later to be rebuilt in much the same location and called the New Mole.

The Moorish baths below the Gibraltar Museum.

Another splendid Moorish survival of this period is the *Hammam* or baths, situated under the Gibraltar Museum. Similar in concept to Roman baths, it contains four large rooms connected by open round arches. The entrance hall, now reduced from its original size, has star-shaped apertures in the roof and leads into the impressive Main Room which may be compared to the Roman *Apodyterium*, a changing and resting room. This has a domed ceiling with pillars of polished stone and Roman, Visigothic and Moorish capitals, the former probably recovered from Carteia, and would have been divided into cubicles by curtains. The Main Room leads in turn into the Cold Room, again with star-shaped apertures in the ceiling and a large shallow bath about 15 inches deep at each end. Beyond is the Hot Room containing a plunge bath complete with lead pipes for hot water. Built shortly after 1333, the baths were probably no longer used after 1462 and certainly not after 1567 when such baths were banned in Spain. The principal mosque was situated where the Cathedral of St Mary the Crowned now stands on Main Street. Although this was largely destroyed during the Great Siege, some remnants of the Moorish construction are still visible.

*   *   *

Alfonso used the truce to engage in a war with Portugal and to subdue his barons, an undertaking he might profitably have implemented earlier. In the meantime, Malik's father had successfully subdued the rebellions in Morocco and all was set for a resumption of hostilities in Spain. In this period the balance moved very favourably towards Alfonso and with a little more luck and resolution he might well have crushed the Moors altogether, nearly one hundred and fifty years before it was eventually achieved.

Malik, having again returned to Spain and substantially reinforced the garrison at Gibraltar, was comprehensively beaten and killed at a battle in the Sierra de Ronda in 1339. There was a new spirit of Christian zeal amongst Alfonso's troops and the Moors were well beaten again later in the year. There was a setback however when, in the Winter following, a large Moorish fleet of 60 galleys and 250 sail slipped across to Gibraltar and Algeciras while Jofre's back was turned. Stung by remorse and a suggestion, probably false, that Alfonso had doubted his integrity, Jofre mounted a suicidal attack on the Moorish ships in the bay. Unsupported by the majority of his captains, he mounted an heroic but extraordinarily rash assault on the Moorish ships. He died gloriously, but completely unnecessarily, and his fleet was routed as well, only six out of thirty three galleys returning to Cadiz.

Hassan, Malik's father, who had now come over to Spain to try to avenge his son, took the obvious first course of seeking to recapture Tarifa and thus regain his stranglehold on the sea approaches from Africa. Alfonso's response, a hastily contrived fleet of foreign ships, soon ended in disaster in the Bay of Gibraltar, and even as far away as on the rocks of Valencia after the sailing ships had been driven through the Strait in a storm. A land advance, however, was totally successful in the decisive battle of the Salado river near Tarifa in which Alfonso displayed the tactical mastery which had previously been glimpsed in the earlier battles. This was the first occasion on which Spain had been truly united in an attempt to expel the Moors and Alfonso also had the welcome help of the King of Portugal and 1000 knights. Pope Benedict XII, in exile in Avignon, gave his blessing and decreed that this would have the official designation of a Crusade to counter the jihad that Hassan had already declared. The Moors were routed and Hassan fled to Gibraltar, but he did not dally there long as the Aragonese fleet looked poised to attack and his son ready to rebel in Fez. Yusuf, Muhammad's successor, returned in haste to Granada.

What remained of Moorish Spain was now there for the taking – Yusuf's army was defeated and for once there was no likelihood of a favourable intervention from north Africa. In particular, Algeciras and Gibraltar without moral or material support must have quickly capitulated, and the prospect of further forays from north Africa probably permanently eliminated. But Alfonso, tactically so talented, did not possess the strategic insight or good luck which would have made him into a great commander. He led his army back to Seville for restocking, and the majority of the troops, sated on African gold, jewels, gems and fine silks, deserted in droves to cash in their new found wealth as far away as Paris and Barcelona.

*   *   *

The patriotic and spiritual fervour had vanished as quickly as it had arisen, but Alfonso still had his navy and he had found another admiral, Egidiol, as competent and resourceful as the unfortunate Jofre. Even the most efficient of admirals, however, was at the mercy of the weather, winds and tides and it was not too difficult for Hassan, if he picked his time carefully, to keep the garrisons of Algeciras and Gibraltar well stocked with food and troops. This he managed to do, but at great cost – in the three years to 1342 he lost nearly three quarters of his galleys, sunk, shipwrecked, or merely penned within the bay at Algeciras. Although he could with difficulty still maintain the supply run, he no longer had the capacity to ship a large army across to Spain, and without his cooperation Yusuf was too weak to bring the King to battle.

By the summer of 1342 Alfonso was at last ready to make another attempt to capture the troublesome 'baseports' of Algeciras and Gibraltar. The more important of the two was Algeciras: it was much larger and had a far stronger garrison, perhaps as many as 800 cavalry and 12,000 infantry. Without the backing of Algeciras, Gibraltar would become a last ditch defensive outpost, its limited port facilities virtually impotent. It was towards Algeciras, therefore, that Alfonso first turned his attention. At the outset his army was smaller than the garrison forces and certainly not capable of a frontal attack on the town's strong walls and forts, and his strategy therefore was to mount a blockade by land and sea whilst whittling away at the towns defences. Unfortunately, he had started the campaign in July, too late in the year to avoid committing himself to a winter siege, never an easy enterprise even in the climate of southern Spain.

The siege was notable for two aspects: it was one of the earliest encounters in which the cannon was employed as an offensive weapon, and marked the first appearance in this part of the Spanish peninsula of English troops. Gunpowder had been known to the Arabs for upwards of a hundred years and all of the main ingredients – saltpetre, charcoal and sulphur – were readily available in this area. The lethal results of 'the great iron bolts from the sky' caused considerable alarm in the Spanish camp, but it was not decisive and the Spaniards patiently developed their network of siege diggings and slowly moved their stone catapults up to the walls of the town. They also coped very competently with the occasional forays out of the town by the numerically superior Moorish troops. Gibraltar, meanwhile, was cordoned off by the occupation of the Tower of Cartagena to prevent its small garrison of 600 troops from interfering in the siege, and perhaps more importantly stopping the inhabitants harvesting their crops across the isthmus.

The English intervention has been portrayed, particularly by Chaucer, as a chivalric enterprise inspired by the spirit of the Cross against the infidel; indeed the Pope had declared another Crusade. Alas, its motives were more mundane and self-interested. The 100 Years War between England and France had now been running for some five years since the seizure of Aquitaine by Philip VI of France in May 1337. But by 1340 something of a stalemate had developed with an uneasy truce. Edward III, however, had noted the rise of the Castilian fleet and recognised that some form of dynastic alliance with Alfonso directed against France deserved serious attention. He therefore dispatched two of his most trusted and experienced soldiers to investigate the possibilities. Henry Lancaster, Earl of Derby, and William Montague, Earl of Salisbury, arrived with a company of knights in May 1343 and, despite the ulterior motive for their expedition, set to with a will to further the King of Spain's cause. They helped with the siege operations and fought vigorously in a major skirmish between the opposing forces in the open ground in front of the walls during which two English knights actually penetrated the town, for a time causing great alarm among the defenders. Derby also had the opportunity of observing the Spanish ships in action at first hand. By August their intelligence survey was complete and Derby departed for Rome on a diplomatic mission, but Salisbury, taken ill in Seville, expressed a wish to be carried back to Alfonso's camp to join in the long awaited great confrontation with Yusuf. He died in 1344. The English intervention was held in high regard in the Spanish chronicles of the time, unlike the contribution of the French knights who were castigated for disloyalty and cowardice. In the event, the alliance of England and Spain was not to be consummated until the Treaty of Medina del Campo in 1489.

The blockade of Algeciras had been maintained throughout the winter of 1342/43, but to no great effect. Yusuf meanwhile had been gathering his forces in the area, supplemented by those few reinforcements from Africa who had slipped through the net. By April it appeared he was ready to relieve the siege and he moved down to the area east of Algeciras, forcing Alfonso to relinquish the Tower of Cartagena from which he had been keeping watch over Gibraltar. But the stalemate persisted throughout the summer and it was not until October that the Moors at last managed to transport a sizeable force of cavalry to Spain when Egidiol's fleet was distracted by a storm: the long expected major confrontation appeared imminent. Surprisingly it did not materialise, for Yusuf, as unpredictable as ever, asked Alfonso instead to state his peace terms. The negotiations continued throughout a winter of heavy rain during which Yusuf made tentative moves, always repulsed, to move his army into a more favourable position.

Continually plagued by unrest at home, Hassan began to lose interest in Spain and without his help Yusuf was impotent. Even so the terms eventually agreed for peace were extraordinarily favourable to Alfonso given that his troops, after nearly two years of the debilitating conditions of a siege town, were in no better state to continue the war. The old town of Algeciras was surrendered to Alfonso on 26th March 1344 which he entered in state, symbolically holding a Mass in what had been the great mosque. The garrison was allowed to depart in peace and many of the inhabitants moved across to Gibraltar with all their chattels. A ten-year truce was agreed and Hassan was to pay an annual tribute to Alfonso of 12,000 doblas.

Algeciras had at last fallen to Castile, but Gibraltar remained a troublesome thorn, perhaps rather more in Alfonso's conscience than in his strategic thinking. By the terms of the truce, however, he could legally do nothing to ease it until 1354. Yet another coup in Morocco, in which Hassan was deposed by his son, gave Alfonso and Yusuf, who had recovered some of his courage, the opportunity to declare the truce broken. Yusuf made war on the towns in the Kingdom of Ronda, which was still under the nominal suzerainty of Morocco, and Alfonso announced in

December 1348 that he was to renew the siege of Gibraltar.

In August 1349 he was in position in the area of Carteia and constructed trenches across the isthmus, indicating once again that he was not strong enough to contemplate a frontal attack. It was, however, the first occasion on which cannon were used against the walls of Gibraltar, although presumably with no great effect. Alfonso built barracks for his troops in what is now La Linea and moved his mistress, Leonora de Guzman, and her children to the new town: he was clearly contemplating a long wait. But a greater plague than the Moors and the usual winter storms now descended on his troops. The Black Death which had laid a swathe across Europe reached the southern tip of Spain in the early months of 1350. Large numbers succumbed and the Council of War recommended retreat, but Alfonso, perhaps recognising that this was to be the last chance to gain the prize which had always eluded him, insisted that the siege be maintained. That peculiar sense of honour, at least to our eyes, which could not countenance a fear of death, constrained the reluctant army to persevere. The end, however, came with startling suddenness and finality: Alfonso was suddenly taken ill and died on Good Friday, 27th March 1350. According to the Moors' contemporary historian, 'Allah in his great wisdom favoured the Faithful in their extremity'.

*   *   *

With the death of Alfonso XI the first great period of the 'reconquista' as a spiritual and dynastic crusade comes to an end, not to be revived until the time of Ferdinand and Isabella nearly one hundred and fifty years later. It was a time of petty intrigue, jealousy, decadence and fluctuating alliances reminiscent of the earlier centuries after the Muslim invasion. Until 1350 the issues had been comparatively clearcut: on the one hand there was a relatively united Islamic cause, not, it is true, without differences between the Moors of north Africa and those of indigenous Spain, but generally they could depend on at least some degree of mutual support. The stronger and more determined the kings of Spain, particularly Castile, the greater the cooperation of the rulers of Fez and Granada. On the Christian side, the differences were rather more marked. Not only were there the contrasting aims of the kings of Castile and Aragon, but there was continual strife between the ruler and his overpowerful nobles, particularly his closest relations. As we have seen, the main opportunity of ridding the peninsula of its Moorish rulers during the reign of Alfonso was lost not so much through his own indeterminate strategy as the lack of support of his greatest nobles and commanders.

The Iberian peninsula in 1350 was, nevertheless, largely Christian. The King of Fez still maintained his own sovereignty over Gibraltar and the kingdom of Ronda, comprising a ring of forts and towns stretching in a crescent from Jimena through Ronda itself to Estepona and Malaga on the coast. The Emir of Granada ruled a smallish enclave to the north, rimmed and protected by mountains on its northern frontiers and by the Mediterranean to east and south. He was encircled from Algeciras through Cadiz, Seville and Cordoba by Christian fiefdoms in which the dukes and counts were becoming ever more powerful, and who were to play an increasingly prominent role in the future of Gibraltar. To the north the Crown of Aragon overlooked the shrinking emirate.

The next one hundred years is a confused and complicated saga, dominated by two conflicting and interacting forces. In the first place, the Moorish homogeneity disappears with increasingly open conflict between Spain and north Africa; never again were they to combine in united opposition to the Christian encroachments. On the Christian side it is a period when the kings became even more distant from the most powerful nobles who profited from the distractions at court and showed a much greater propensity to operate independently, both of the king and each other.

Alfonso was succeeded by his young son Peter, called 'the Cruel' – with some justification. He first murdered his father's mistress, Leonora de Guzman, thereby setting in train perpetual hostility from her son, Henry de Trastamara, leading eventually to Peter's own murder by Henry in 1369. In the meantime he had treacherously murdered with his own hand the Emir of Granada, the usurper Muhammad VI, after inviting him to dine in his sumptuous new Alcazar in Seville. This

splendid building and gardens, mostly in the Moorish style and inferior only to the Alhambra in Granada, was largely built by Peter and is as clear an indication as one can get of the extent to which the Moorish culture was absorbed by Spanish Christianity. France and England joined in the argument over the Spanish succession with the latter supporting Peter with the formidable military assistance in Galicia of the Black Prince, Edward III's eldest son.

The new King of Fez, Abu Inan Faris, strengthened and extended the walls and a contemporary description cites the splendour of Gibraltar with 'its walls, towers, gates, citadel, dockyard, mosques, munition stores and corn granaries'. But the uncertain rule of Gibraltar suffered another hiatus when a new governor, Isa ibn al-Hassan, appointed in 1356, declared himself King of Gibraltar in defiance of Fez. His reign was short, for he soon upset the Gibraltarians who sent him in chains to Ceuta where a grateful Abu Inan had him executed, only to

be murdered himself by his vizier a year later. The topsy-turvy politics of Spain at this time found the emirs of Granada alternately fighting or supporting the rival kings of Castile, but in 1369, Muhammad V, who was reinstated after the murder of his predecessor by Peter the Cruel, turned against the latter's successor, Henry de Trastamara, who had at last exacted his revenge against Peter. He made a lightning swoop on Algeciras and captured it in two days, undoing all the hard effort of Alfonso XI and in effect returning the territorial status of Spain to that existing in 1292 when Sancho initially captured Tarifa, now once again the only Christian outpost facing Morocco.

But there were differences in the new state of relations between Morocco and Granada. Gibraltar was now a potentially hostile base against Muhammad and consequently Algeciras inherited the mantle of the vulnerable outpost, menaced both by Gibraltar and the kingdom of Ronda which encircled it. Muhammad therefore razed Algeciras to

The Moors had a small harbour in the area of Casemates Square. The 19th-century Grand Casemates Gate is on the site of the old Water Gate.

the ground and made his peace with Henry II, a truce which lasted for forty years. In the meantime Muhammad, in somewhat obscure circumstances gained control of Gibraltar, probably as a reward for helping the King of Fez with his own internal problems. An inscription on the south gate of the castle, now erased, clearly indicated that at some unspecified date the castle was in Muhammad's control.

An outbreak of hostilities in 1407 led to a sea battle in the vicinity of Tarifa which the Christians won comprehensively and, after a brief reconciliation, the rulers of Morocco and Granada were once again at odds with each other. The upshot was that in 1410 Gibraltar rebelled against the rule of Granada and declared for Fez, and the new Sultan, Fayd, quickly sent his brother with 1000 cavalry and 2000 infantry to retake control of the town and the surrounding forts in the old kingdom of Ronda. Their success was not long lasting, for in the next year Yusuf III of Granada not only recaptured Marbella and Estepona, but laid siege to Gibraltar. Treachery from inside the town soon ended the sixth siege and Fayd asked Yusuf to execute his brother as a traitor. There was, however, yet another twist in the story, for Yusuf now allied himself with the defeated brother, Abu Said, to dethrone Fayd in Fez. The reader who is still with me after this narrative of intrigue and treachery will hardly quarrel with the conclusion that both the Christian and the Muslim rulers of north Africa and Spain had descended to a new low of decadence, disloyalty and self-interest by the early years of the fifteenth century.

The next attempt to capture Gibraltar was hardly a siege and quickly ended in tragedy. Henry, Count of Niebla and grandson of the hero of Tarifa, Alonso de Guzman, had established himself in a strong position north of Tarifa from which he had revived the old Roman tunny fisheries. By 1436 he was becoming increasingly angry at raids on his property by Berber pirates based on Gibraltar and, with the aid of neighbouring towns, gathered together a force of 3000 infantry and cavalry in 20 ships to attempt a landing on the Red Sands. In support was a force of 2000 cavalry and infantry which marched overland to Gibraltar under his son, Juan Alonso, and took up positions on the isthmus by the end of August. The Count began to disembark his troops on the Red Sands which were now isolated from the town by a sea wall, a development of which Henry seems to have been unaware. The defenders made no attempt to interfere for reasons which soon became obvious, for the incoming tide was trapping the Count's forces between the wall and the sea. Henry ordered a withdrawal, but seeing some stragglers on the beach ordered his own boat to return inshore to the rescue. Unfortunately, the numbers were too great for the boat which overturned, drowning Henry and forty of his knights. The rest, including Juan Alonso, departed in disarray and the siege was over almost before it was underway. The defenders, however, in their moment of triumph made a fatal mistake which ultimately cost them Gibraltar, for they hoisted Henry's dismembered body high on the walls, a pointed reminder to the departing Christians of their loss of honour. The gate in this position is still called 'La Barcina' – the wicker basket.

And so the matter rested for another twenty five years. It was again a time of incessant civil war in Christian Spain eventually leaving Henry IV on the throne of Castile. But the dishonour of the barbarous treatment of the Count of Niebla rankled in Andalusia: Talleyrand's later comment would have been particularly apt at this time – 'it was worse than a crime, it was a blunder'. It had to be avenged and in 1462 it was, for the Muslims lost Gibraltar for the last time.

4 SPANISH INTERLUDE 1462–1704

FOR NEARLY THIRTY YEARS after the abortive attempt to capture Gibraltar in 1436, Spain, Muslim and Christian alike, passed through one of the many low points in its troubled history. Castile was ravaged by civil strife and endured weak and degenerate kings and over-mighty and quarrelsome nobles. Henry IV had little intention of pursuing the 'reconquista', but feebleness in the court of Granada had enabled him to place on the throne his nominee, one Ali Abu'l Hassan, better known as Muley Hassan, which precipitated, albeit indirectly, the capture of Gibraltar by the neighbouring nobles. This event marked the end of Moorish control of the Rock, but the circumstances were enveloped in acrimony and farce exceptional even in the annals of military history.

It was set in train by a refugee from Gibraltar, Ali el Curro (Ali the Beau), who went to Tarifa in August 1462, ostensibly to become a Christian, but also to tell Alonso de Arcos, the military governor, that all the senior men of Gibraltar together with their retainers had gone to Granada to pay homage to the new ruler, leaving the Rock virtually defenceless. He must have been a persuasive young man, for a sceptical Alonso gathered together a small force of 80 cavalry and 180 infantry and marched overnight to take up positions right under the walls of the town. The following morning they apprehended three scouts who confirmed Ali's story that the garrison under Muhammad Khaba was very weak. Alonso hesitated; weakly defended though they might be, the walls from below still looked formidable enough, and instead of taking action he summoned assistance from the neighbouring frontier towns and the two main nobles in the area, the Duke of Medina Sidonia and the Count of Arcos.

The frontier towns responded with troops and a few ships and Alonso was persuaded to mount his assault. That his earlier fears were at least partly well founded was confirmed when the attack failed with many casualties. Many of the aggressors were now all for returning home, but the stouter hearts were encouraged by the arrival of 400 cavalry and additional infantry from Jerez. Ali the Beau, who could see his credibility fast disappearing, if nothing worse, pleaded vociferously for the assault to be renewed. The defenders were also having second thoughts, for the following morning a messenger presented himself to Alonso declaring that the Moors were willing to surrender provided that the inhabitants could leave within four days for Granada with their movable possessions and receive compensation for what they left behind. Alonso, who must have been one of the most indecisive of military commanders, replied that he would need to consult his superiors.

The first to arrive was the son of the Count of Arcos, the 19-year-old Rodrigo Ponce de Leon, who if not the sole villain of the piece, rapidly emerged as its main hothead. The Moors, by now anxiously looking for anybody to whom to surrender, were willing to submit to him, but Rodrigo said they would have to await the arrival of his father and the Duke of Medina Sidonia. In the meantime, the knights of Jerez entered into secret talks with Muhammad and suggested that the inhabitants would be safer under their protection than that of Rodrigo and that he should surrender unilaterally to them. Muhammad was eager to oblige and the knights entered the town, thereby provoking Rodrigo to rush in his own men along with those of Arcos. A physical confrontation between the Christian knights was only narrowly averted and the inhabitants of the town, seeing the way the wind was blowing, prudently retired into the castle.

Fortunately, the arrival of the two principals cooled an explosive situation to a certain extent, but did little to remove the petty quarrelling between the victors. The first to arrive was the Duke of Medina Sidonia who was willing initially to wait for the arrival of the Count of Arcos to enable the surrender of the castle to be accepted jointly, but then double-crossed Rodrigo by accepting an offer from the Moors in the castle to surrender to him alone. Rodrigo was furious and again threatened unilateral action, for his were the troops which now actually controlled the town. Eventually a compromise was reached by which Medina Sidonia and Rodrigo would jointly occupy the castle with 100 knights each. The arrangement did not last long for Rodrigo soon discovered that the Duke had insinuated another 200 men into the castle and seized the Tower of Homage. Rodrigo then evacuated his knights to await the arrival of the Count of Arcos. When at last Arcos did arrive with reinforcements, Rodrigo was all for taking a force to capture the Duke and kill him. Whilst it is possible to feel some sympathy for Rodrigo at this point, Arcos fortunately rejected so drastic a solution. However, after fruitless discussion with the Duke as to who would accept the formal surrender, which in practice had occurred some days previously, Arcos formally challenged the Duke to single combat to decide this point of honour. One can imagine the bemusement at these bizarre transactions of the long-suffering Moors, who only wanted to disappear quietly. The Duke wisely refused and waited patiently in his lodgings until the enraged Count of Arcos eventually departed with all his men.

Gibraltar at last nominally belonged to the King of Castile although he had done nothing to deserve it. The moral of this unruly event was not, however, lost on the two eventual rulers of Spain, Ferdinand and Isabella, who recognised that something would have to be done to curb the political power and factional behaviour of the great nobles if Spain was to drag itself from the morass into which successive kings had allowed it to sink.

*   *   *

Although the Duke of Medina Sidonia had been left in sole possession of Gibraltar, Henry IV soon claimed it as his own and added King of Gibraltar to his many other titles. Medina Sidonia departed surprisingly quietly after burying his father, who had embellished the walls in his wicker basket for twenty six years, in a room in the Tower of Homage which he converted into a chapel. He was not, however, yet quite finished with Gibraltar.

That Henry recognised the strategic importance of Gibraltar is confirmed by the charter he bestowed upon the town in December 1462 which specifically drew attention to its role in guarding the Strait and preventing the flow of reinforcements and supplies to the isolated kingdom of Granada. Its nominal area was extended substantially into the hinterland, taking over the lands of the ruined settlement of Algeciras; and like Ferdinand IV the King gave substantial encouragement to potential settlers and their families. In this he was relatively successful, for the threat from north Africa had largely subsided thanks to the efforts of the King of Portugal. However, despite its growing strategic significance, successive rulers of Spain, albeit with short bursts of enthusiasm for building fortifications, frequently neglected the defences of the town as events would soon prove.

The internal unrest which had dogged Spain for so long was at its height in the ensuing years. It is not necessary to follow the complicated quarrels which led to the accession of Queen Isabella in 1468, but one of the actions of Henry in 1463 eventually resulted in another siege of Gibraltar. The King had appointed as Governor his favourite Beltran de la Cueva who in turn had appointed Esteban de Villacreces as his lieutenant. This patronage, which owed nothing to the capture of the town, infuriated the Duke of Medina Sidonia, and on the deposition of Henry in 1465 he soon obtained a warrant to invest Gibraltar from the heir apparent, Prince Alfonso. In April 1466 he duly appeared at the gates of Gibraltar with a force sufficiently large to deter Villacreces from seeking battle and to persuade him to withdraw into the castle. Despite breaching the walls with mortars, however, it took fifteen months of blockade to force Villacreces into surrender. Medina Sidonia repaired the walls and encouraged further settlement, particularly with his own supporters; but both he and Prince Alfonso died in 1468 and his son quickly made his peace with the restored Henry IV. The lands of Gibraltar, now extended out to 40 miles from the peninsula, were formally restored to the Dukes of Medina Sidonia.

The next generation saw Gibraltar settle into a period of economic growth. The old dockyard was re-established and ship repair facilities developed on the estuaries of the Palmones and Guadarranque rivers. As a freeport, Gibraltar attracted merchant ships from north European ports exploiting the tunny fishing industry which had always been one of the planks of the Medina Sidonias' wealth. Vines were grown on the hinterland and cooperage and wickerwork provided employment for the new settlers in Gibraltar. The population at this time, however, is not thought to have been greater than about a thousand.

An interesting episode recently brought to light by Diego Lamelas was the sale of Gibraltar to the Conversos of Cordoba in 1474. The Conversos, about 100,000 in number and widely distributed in Spain, were Jews who had been baptised following persecution by the Christians. They had achieved preference at court and were prominent in tax collecting and banking, none of which endeared them to the rest of the population. This hostility was particularly pronounced in Cordoba and there were violent clashes in March 1473 which prompted their leader, Pedro de Herrera, to open negotiations with the Duke of Medina Sidonia to allow them to settle in Gibraltar. Both drove a hard bargain, and in the resulting agreement the existing inhabitants were to be evicted and Pedro was to become solely responsible for the military and administrative control of the town. In return the Conversos would become largely responsible in the first two years for the cost of maintaining the garrison, thus allowing the Duke to misappropriate the bulk of the 5000 doblas which he extorted from the citizens of Seville, ostensibly to defend Gibraltar. The agreement may justifiably be described as a sale, for the Conversos obtained their refuge at the expense of the original inhabitants and the taxpayers of Seville whilst handsomely lining the pocket of Medina Sidonia.

About 4000 Conversos from Cordoba and Seville settled in Gibraltar in August 1474 although many soon quarrelled with Pedro and returned home. The arrangement did not last long, for by 1476 Medina

The Jews have had a long connection with Gibraltar: they tended to concentrate in an area near the South Barracks known as 'Black Jerusalem'. There is a Jewish Cemetery off the road to the Upper Rock, opened after 1713, with good views across the southern end of the peninsula.

The Franciscan Church in the Convent which is now, as the King's Chapel, the garrison Anglican church.

Sidonia was regretting his greedy impulse and looking for an excuse to evict the Conversos. He not only feared that they were plotting to deliver the town to the Crown, but also recognised under the original agreement that after two years he would again become responsible for the costs of defending the town. His chance came on the pretext of attacking the Portuguese enclave at Ceuta just across the Strait, but instead he suddenly descended on Gibraltar with the bulk of the force and deposed the Governor. The Conversos were expelled and presumably some of the original inhabitants were restored as the episode did not seem to impact on the continuing prosperity of Gibraltar.

The first of the many religious orders to settle in Gibraltar, the Franciscans, established a house there in 1490. It was they who in 1528 built the Convent, that delightful red brick building in Main Street which has been the residence of the Governor since 1704. The Convent was partly rebuilt in 1864 but remains a large irregular building of mixed Moorish and Spanish monastic character with a fine garden containing a dragon tree probably over five hundred years old. Although the Convent is not normally open to the public, the King's Chapel, the church of the Franciscans next door should not be missed. A church was built in

the Villa Vieja, now Casemates Square, and a later Renaissance doorway from this church was re-erected in modern times at the top of Main Street near the South Port Gate. The defences were not entirely neglected and a permanent garrison of about 450 cavalry and infantry was established. But Gibraltar was by no means yet developed into an impenetrable fortress and few remaining works can be attributed specifically to this period. Occasional incursions were inevitable, but a raid by Muley Hassan from Granada in 1477 was soon seen off by the timely arrival of a Castilian fleet, albeit only after a short eruption of panic.

The accession of Queen Isabella to the throne of Castile in 1474 at last heralded a period of stability in the Spanish monarchies, although for five years she had to wage war against the King of Portugal and his adherents in Spain to secure the possession. The first modern historian of Spain (W. H. Prescott, 1838) claimed it was 'the most glorious epoch in the annals of Spain', and although more recent historians might not go quite so far, it was undoubtedly the mainspring to Spain's prominence in the European scene in the next two centuries. The key was her marriage to Ferdinand of Aragon, for the energy, shrewd intelligence and martial competence of Ferdinand was complemented by Isabella's determination, presence and diplomatic gifts. They realised that the warring tendencies of the aristocratic families must be curbed as a precondition of the completion of the 'reconquista' and in this they were generally successful. The long-standing feud between the Medina Sidonia family and that of the Count of Arcos, later the Marquessate of Cadiz, which had stemmed from the time of the capture of Gibraltar in 1462, was finally laid to rest.

The expulsion of the Moorish dynasty from Spain was at last achieved in 1492: what had taken the Moors seven years to conquer had required the Christian kings seven hundred to undo. Gibraltar played little part in the final rites of the expulsion of the Moors, for with Tangier and Ceuta in Portuguese hands there was no back door for the crumbling kingdom of Granada. Ferdinand's failure, however, to extend the conquest to north Africa was to prove a fatal mistake as the coast became a haven for the Barbary pirates of whom we shall hear more in the ensuing pages.

The year 1492 marked a turning point in Spanish fortunes. For not only were the Moors finally defeated, but Christopher Columbus discovered the New World, portending the 'Golden Age of Spain' in the sixteenth century when only the shadow of the war in the Netherlands seemed to cloud the burgeoning wealth emanating from Hispaniola (Haiti and the Dominican Republic). The time was now ripe for Isabella to assume full control of Gibraltar even though the Medina Sidonia family had been loyal adherents during the latter stages of the 'reconquista'. She made her move in 1501 by telling the duke that Gibraltar was of too great a strategic importance to remain in private hands. Somewhat surprisingly the Duke agreed despite all the effort his family had spent in acquiring the territory and developing its new found commercial prosperity, and in December 1501 Gibraltar was formally attached to the Crown of Castile. It was at this time that the town received its coat of arms – a key suspended by a chain from a three-towered castle – that may be seen so frequently as one walks around the

city today.* The original parchment, however, is now in the town hall in San Roque just across the isthmus. The formal handover to the new governor, Garcilasso de la Vega, revealed that the dukes in recent years had been less than diligent in maintaining the defences of the town. In November 1504 Isabella died and another period of uncertainty hove onto the horizon.

As always the succession was disputed. Isabella's daughter Joanna was of unsound mind and her will had stipulated that Ferdinand should be regent if her heir was mentally incapacitated. This codicil was ignored by Joanna's husband, Philip the Fair of Burgundy, who protested that he should be king, or at the very least regent. In 1506 the Duke of Medina Sidonia, still presumably smarting from his loss of Gibraltar to Isabella, took the side of Philip, asserted that the latter had revoked the Queen's assumption of control, and promptly laid siege to Gibraltar. But it was a half-hearted affair and when the inhabitants declared for the Crown, the Duke was soon persuaded to withdraw. He could perhaps see which way the wind was blowing – Philip was dying and Ferdinand was clearly gaining control over the confused Joanna. The citizens of Gibraltar were granted the appellation 'most loyal' and amply compensated for any damage caused in the last siege – already the tenth the settlement had sustained in its brief history. It was the last time that the Guzman family was to play a major role in the history of Gibraltar. The grandson of this duke was to achieve fame, or perhaps rather notoriety, as the leader of the Spanish Armada in 1588.

*   *   *

If Joanna was mad and her husband weak, their eldest son Charles of Ghent inherited none of their disabilities. Devoutly Christian, a dashing military commander, and indisputably the greatest of the Habsburgs, he was the third member of that contrasting trio, with Henry VIII of England and Francis I of France, who dominated and contested the leadership of Europe for the first half of the sixteenth century. Charles, as Holy Roman Emperor, saw in himself the reincar-

---

* Gibraltar was described in many documents of the time as a city rather than a town. But the distinction between the two is sometimes contentious (it is not, as tradition would have it, simply the existence of a cathedral which determines its status). Nevertheless, I have generally speaking called Gibraltar a town until the two cathedrals were established in the early 19th century.

nation of that first great crusading emperor Charlemagne: that he ultimately failed was less a reflection of his considerable ability than of the extravagance of his ambitions. In fact, the reign of Charles exactly coincided with the break-up of Christendom as the Reformation took hold throughout Europe except in Spain and Italy. As a consequence, England and Spain, who had largely ignored each other hitherto, became potential or actual enemies, depending mainly upon which side of the fence France was currently sitting.

Charles' assumption of power in Spain in 1516 as a gawky youth of 16 on the death of Ferdinand was far from straightforward, and he did not establish full control until about 1522. Pedro Lasso, the Governor of Gibraltar at the time, sided with the communes against Charles, but the citizens again showed their loyalty by failing to join the revolt. In the sixteenth century the main external threat to Spain, and indeed the Empire as a whole, came from Turkey and its surrogates, the Corsair pirates of the Barbary coast. And Charles, who also ruled over most of Italy, was in the forefront in confronting this new Muslim upsurge.

Charles V (actually the First of Spain, but generally known as the fifth, his Empiric title) had little direct impact on Gibraltar, but in 1535 he made the apparently extraordinary choice of an 8-year-old boy, Alvaro de Bazan, as Military Governor. It might have been a supernaturally inspired selection, for Alvaro quickly grew into a notable sailor who achieved his first success against the French at the age of 17 and achieved distinction in that epic sea battle against the Turks at Lepanto in 1571. The King's choice, however, appears slightly more comprehensible when it is recognised that the boy's father, Alvaro the Elder, was Captain General of the Fleet and was expected to be the real Governor until his son reached maturity.

The early sixteenth century saw the final abandonment of the old conventions of warfare in which the ancient and eccentric rules of chivalry were generally respected. War increasingly began to impact on the nation at large and great advances were made in military science and equipment. It was also incidentally the period in which the cost of warfare usually exceeded the means of the

princes to wage it. This is probably the reason why, despite their insistence on the strategic importance of Gibraltar, the Spanish kings were consistently lax in providing an effective defence. Garrison duty was unattractive and the royal finances were always in too parlous a state to provide strong fortifications and modern weapons. Such was the state of the defences in 1540 when the town suffered one of the most effective and humiliating attacks in its history. At the time Charles was heavily involved in his struggle against the Turks who had major outposts in Tunis and Algiers under their renowned sea captain Barbarossa. With an avowed and competent enemy so close, one would have expected the Gibraltarians to have been acutely aware of their safety. In fact they basked in supreme complacency, not even manning the watch towers adequately and allowing most of their menfolk to be absent in the fields or at sea fishing. One other factor should have given them pause for thought. Alvaro de Bazan had imported a number of Turkish slaves to Gibraltar to work in the shipyards despite the law which prohibited their presence on the coast, and alarm bells might have rung when a mass escape of about 100 slaves to Algiers occurred in July 1540.

Their leader Caramani reported to Barbarossa's lieutenant, Hassim Aga, that the defences of Gibraltar were dangerously deficient and undermanned and that the city lay open for the taking. Hassim was persuaded and mounted a 1000-strong raiding force under Caramani in 16 galleys rowed by 1000 Christian slaves and manned by 1000 infantry. Commanded by his own sea captain, Ali Hamat, the ships arrived off Europa Point after dark on the 8th of September. Realising that they had been spotted by Medina Sidonia's men at Melilla, Ali sent a reconnaissance ship round the Point to land on the isthmus and spy out the land. Quite incredibly they managed to enter the city through the Land Port Gate and report back that all was quiet.

As dawn approached Caramani landed his force near Europa Point. Although their approach and disembarkation was stealthy as befits a commando-style raid, once ashore they rampaged through the town beating drums and blowing trumpets, seeking to cre-

ate panic amongst the terror-stricken inhabitants, mostly women and children. Their tactics were successful, for the mayhem started a panic scramble towards the gate of the castle into which the Governor had barricaded himself. Denied entry and with 300 Turks at their heels, at least 26 were suffocated in the crush at the gate. The rest of the raiders simply concentrated on plundering the town

and collecting hostages; 63 women and children were eventually taken back to the ships.

Their appetite sated, the raiding party withdrew under the cover of a small reserve force who had busied themselves looting on the southern side of the Rock. In four hours they were re-embarked, but instead of making the traditional fast getaway they spent no less than three days rowing up and down in front of the town in an orgy of triumph, plundering the odd merchant ship which from time to time appeared in the bay. They were ostensibly waiting for the hostage money for their captives, which indeed the Spanish were trying to put together. But this rash behaviour was to contribute to their downfall, for all the time a Spanish squadron under Bernardino de Mendoza was hurrying to the rescue. Bernardino eventually caught up with them near the island of Alboran and decisively defeated the Turkish galleys. Caramani was killed and Ali Hamat and over 400 hostages were taken: they were eventually exchanged for the captives from Gibraltar. As a bonus

The Line Wall ending in the South Bastion was constructed during the reign of Charles V.

The South Port Gate was built by Charles V in 1552: the weathered arms above the arch are of Spain and Gibraltar. The left hand gate was opened in 1883.

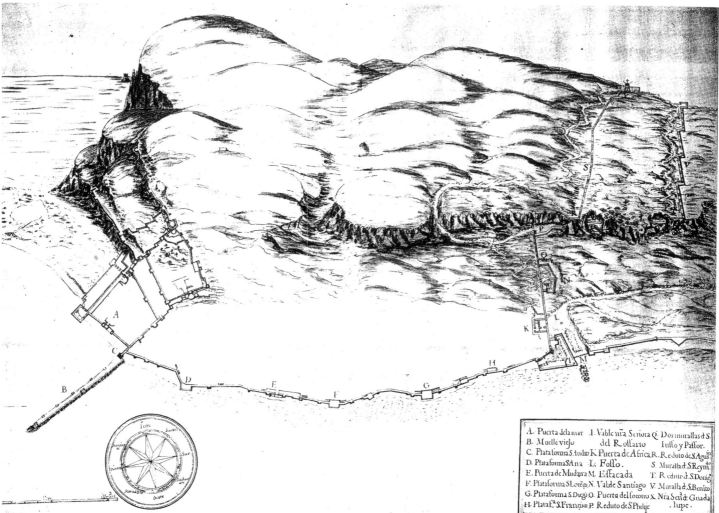

A. Puerta dela mar   I. Vable nra Seniora Q. Dos murallas d S.
B. Muelle viejo   del Rossario   Iullo y Pastor.
C. Plataforma S. Andres K. Puerta de Africa R. educto de S Agus
D. Plataforma S Ana   L. Fosso .   S. Muralla d S Reym
E. Puerta de Mudqura M. Estacada .   T. R educto d S Doming
F. Plataforma S Lorenço N. V al de Santiago V. Muralla d S Benito
G. Plataforma S Diego O. Puerta del socorro X. Nra Señd Guada
H. Platafª S Francisco P. Reducto de S Philip   . lupe .

This plan of Gibraltar is from a series by Luis Bravo dated 1627. This is one of the earliest depictions of Gibraltar.

750 Christian slaves were given their freedom. Honour was saved, but that a band of renegade pirates could cause such damage and panic in one of the main military outposts of Spain should have been a salutary warning to King and Gibraltarians alike. Some effort was made to improve the defences, particularly to the south of the town and along the seafront. Indeed the South Bastion bears the same date as Caramani's raid and, if correct, shows a very prompt response. The following years saw the building of Charles V's wall up the Rock from the Bastion and the South Port Gate which was protected by a glacis and drawbridge. A very good idea of the fortifications at this period can be gleaned from a remarkable series of plans and drawings prepared for the King by Don Luis Bravo in 1627.

*   *   *

The next one hundred and sixty years of Spanish rule of Gibraltar were not marked by dramatic sieges or pulsating battles. The Turks made a brief and unsuccessful sortie into the bay in 1558, and from time to time individual forays plundered the surrounding hinterland and took away a few captives for ransom. But these pinpricks, irritating though they were, no longer seriously threatened the security of the town, and the Turkish threat diminished, even if it did not finally disappear, after the Battle of Lepanto in 1571. More worrying was the decline of the commercial prosperity of the town stemming from the run-down of the maritime trade. The Granada silk industry which traded through Gibraltar was suppressed after the Morisco* revolt of 1568 and the shipyard, which was mostly manned by Moriscos, suffered a major setback after

* Moriscos were Moslems who had converted to Christianity, usually under compulsion. In the same way, Jews forcibly converted were known as Conversos or Marranos.

1609 when they were expelled altogether from Spain, incidentally providing a major boost to the Barbary pirates who had by then become the scourge of the Mediterranean. More significant in the decline of the commercial importance of Gibraltar was the rise in trade with the Americas which was concentrated on the rival ports of Seville and Cadiz.

However, although the commercial importance of the town was declining through the later years of the sixteenth century, this period saw the dawn of a more important role for Gibraltar, that of a naval base influencing strategy in the north and south Atlantic as well as the whole of the Mediterranean. The New Mole, on the site of the present dry docks, was begun in 1620 and completed under the direction of Philip IV in 1660. At its head was a tower, generally known as the Torre del Tuerto although this may be a misreading of 'Puerto'. From being a stepping-stone to Africa, Gibraltar was to become a guardian of the Strait, an east-west axis as opposed to the north-south axis which had been predominant since the departure of the Romans. Thus far only the navies of Spain and their surrogates the Genoans, the Portuguese and the Turks (superseding the Arabs) had played a role in the seas around Gibraltar. Henceforth they were to be joined by those of France and the Netherlands, and above all by England. To comprehend the development of Gibraltar in the latter part of the sixteenth and the seventeenth centuries requires therefore a brief account of the ever-changing interests and alliances of the great maritime powers of western Europe throughout this period. It is a long and complex story with many strands and motivations and I will try to concentrate here mainly on those aspects which had some repercussions upon Gibraltar.

Although Henry VIII and Charles V had their differences, these largely centred on the latter's role as Holy Roman Emperor rather than in the context of his Spanish kingdom. In the brief reign of Mary Tudor (1553-58),

Charles V's wall was continued up to the saddle of the Rock by his son Philip II.

cemented by her marriage to Charles' son Philip (later Philip 11 of Spain) and the reversion to Catholicism, relations between England and Spain became more harmonious although an underlying distrust never disappeared. This hesitant cordiality, however, vanished completely with the accession of Elizabeth 1 in 1558 and the increasing hostility between the two countries never entirely subsided until they became allies against Napoleon in the nineteenth century. There were three main reasons for this estrangement. Firstly, and of greatest importance, was the antagonism engendered by the revolt in the Spanish Netherlands and its impact on English trade. This came to the boil in 1559 when Philip abandoned the country for the more congenial soil of Spain leaving the Netherlands as a Spanish Viceroyalty to be governed solely for the material benefit of the fatherland. This economic animosity was exacerbated by the second source of contention – religious differences. There was a genuine spiritual zeal behind most of Philip's foreign activities which manifested itself in England in the support of the claim of Mary Queen of Scots to the English throne. Papal aspirations, as personified by a crusading Philip, generated a real fear in the minds of England's Protestant rulers and led to a fervid and at times almost paranoid hatred of the Spaniard and all his perceived devious machinations. Despite her external adventures, however, Spain was in many respects an inward-looking country at this time: the Inquisition was at its most powerful and the concept of 'limpieza' – purity of blood – was an insidious and divisive force within the church and state.

A third cause of the developing antagonism was the rivalry over trade with the New World. Portugal and Spain had undoubtedly stolen a march on the other states of Europe by the speed and efficiency of their acquisition and exploitation of the west coast of Africa and Central and South America. However genuine the missionary element of the conquistadors, there can be no doubt that it was old-fashioned greed which provided the main spark: Pizarro was quite clear in the aims of his conquest of Peru – 'I have come to take away from them their gold,' he brazenly declared. Bernal Diaz, a soldier in Cortes' expedition, was equally forthright – 'We came here to serve God and also to get rich'. But if commercial acquisitiveness motivated the Spanish, it was matched by the first English seamen and traders who sought to gain a share of the riches. Trading activities soon gave way to piracy, and piracy tacitly supported by government soon led to war. The culmination of this rivalry, as every schoolboy knows, was the defeat of the Spanish Armada in 1588 – it marked the beginning of the end of the 'Golden Age'.

The English navy had rarely sought to confront Spain in the Mediterranean before the Armada, but in 1590 ten armed merchantmen encountered and severely mauled 12 Spanish galleys in the Strait forcing them to withdraw to Gibraltar for repairs. This highlighted one of the deficiencies of the Spanish fleet, for whilst like the other European navies they had developed the broadside sailing vessel for Atlantic waters, they still depended upon the cumbersome galley for the inland sea. It was also the reason why they were comparatively unsuccessful in combatting the piracy which had become endemic in the Mediterranean after the defeat of the main Turkish fleet at Lepanto. In 1607 an encounter in the Bay of Gibraltar between a Dutch fleet under Admiral van Heemskerk and Spanish galleys left the latter routed with 3000 Spanish dead for little loss except the death of the Dutch commander.

The successful depredations of the Corsairs of the Barbary Coast encouraged a renegade English sailor, John Ward, and a Dutch pirate, Simon Dansker, to set up after 1604 an elaborate pirating operation under the patronage of the Bey of Tunis. For a few years this was outstandingly successful, mainly at the expense of the Venetians, but Ward overreached himself in 1609 and his fleet was destroyed in the harbour of Tunis. Ward himself escaped to France where he was joined by Dansker, and for a short time relative peace reigned in the vicinity of Gibraltar. But such were the potential spoils it was not long before the Corsairs, European as well as Muslim, were as active as ever in the Mediterranean and the importance of Gibraltar as a naval base grew accordingly.

During this same period James I was negotiating a Spanish bride for his son Charles and relations between England and Spain seemed to have improved. The reconciliation did not last long. The marriage negotiations ended in embarrassing humiliation and the anti-Spanish feeling in England reached a new pitch of intensity. Various plots were hatched, some involving that virulently anti-Spanish Elizabethan gallant Sir Walter Ralegh, to support either Savoy or Venice in their little local wars with Spain, but nothing came of an ambitious proposal for Ralegh to capture Genoa. The pirates meanwhile, despite occasional reverses, were not restricting their activities to Catholic merchantmen, and the English Levant trade was suffering as much as the Spanish and Venetian, leading to a general desire among all the maritime nations, despite their differences, to put an end to their depredations.

This requirement became the official ploy for the next English foray into that sea. Six men of war and 12 armed merchantmen under Sir Richard Mansell were despatched to the Mediterranean in January 1620, ostensibly to hunt down pirates, of which they did a little, but in reality to act as a strategic threat to Spanish interests should the current anti-Spanish hysteria in England turn to war. It was an early example of 'gunboat politics'. As England and Spain were officially at peace, and because the latter had a strong vested interest in any action against the Corsairs, Mansell was allowed to victual in Gibraltar although England turned down all offers of cooperation from the suspicious Spanish to help in the suppression of the pirates. For most of the year Mansell cruised in threatening inactivity near the Spanish coast, capturing few pirates and failing to secure the release of the many English subjects allegedly held in captivity in Algeria. Nevertheless, this seemingly ineffectual operation had two important consequences: English sailors were acquiring valuable intelligence on the ports and waters of southern Spain, and the Spanish were at last provoked into making substantial improvements to the fortifications of Gibraltar. It was about this time that Philip III commissioned the 44 watch towers which ringed the coast from Portugal to the River Guadiaro, many of which remain today and can be seen, in varying states of repair along the coast road between Gibraltar and Malaga. Gibraltar's own watch tower, which became known as the Devil's Tower, on the east side of the isthmus was demolished in World War II to improve the field of fire from the North Front.

Mansell's expedition of 1620 was followed by a far larger and formidable sortie into the waters of southern Spain five years later. England was still not at war with Spain even though relations had further deteriorated: Charles had been finally rebuffed in his Spanish match and bore his malice as though a jilted lover. Instead he had contracted a marriage alliance with Henrietta Maria of France and forged a treaty with Holland. The new expedition was of 90 ships, with 10,000 soldiers and siege artillery: it was led by a soldier, General Sir Edward Cecil, Viscount Wimbledon, who had no knowledge of the sea. Although Spain was not at first specifically named as the recipient of this powerful force, everyone knew for whom it was intended. It was given three secret objectives: to destroy Spanish ships, to intercept the Spanish treasure fleet on its annual return from Hispaniola, and to capture a port. Its composition clearly indicated that the last of these was the predominant aim.

The Wimbledon expedition is particularly interesting from our perspective because it was the first time that England had given formal expression to a desire to capture Gibraltar. Furthermore, it differed from previous naval forays because the intention, of at least some of the participants, was not merely to loot, destroy and withdraw, but to capture the Rock with its fortifications as intact as possible and to maintain it as a naval base. England was beginning to realise that control of the sea guaranteed control of the arteries of commerce and power. The mercantilist theory was by no means new, but the most effective method of achieving commercial supremacy was now gradually becoming clearer, and England was moving hesitantly into the van of those countries which were in succeeding centuries to dominate an imperialist world.

Of those ports considered for attack when the fleet lay off Cape St Vincent on the 20th of October 1625 – Lisbon, Cadiz, Sanlucar,

Puerto de Santa Maria, Malaga and Gibraltar – the last was undoubtedly the greatest strategic prize, and a few of those engaged in the debate clearly recognised this. But it was well known that the defences of Gibraltar had been improved and that further strengthening had been in progress since Mansell's visit five years earlier. It was concluded that the defences were too strong for Wimbledon's force and it was decided instead to mount an old fashioned raid of plunder on Cadiz. By no means for the last time, this ended in dismal failure in an orgy of drunkenness in the many wine stores of the Bay of Cadiz. As Wimbledon bitterly exclaimed, 'If the King of Spain will defend his country, let him but lodge wine upon his coasts, and he may overthrow any army with it'. These were to prove prophetic words. The Wimbledon expedition was a complete failure in all its aims and was justifiably widely condemned upon its return. How it would have fared if it had made the attempt on Gibraltar we cannot know, but it appears that the Rock was capably defended and a significant, if numerically smaller, Spanish fleet, was close by. Furthermore, the English soldiers were reputed to be the lowest form of rogues and vagabonds, and winter was approaching bringing with it siege conditions which would have tried even the best soldiers available. It is not difficult to conclude that an attack on Gibraltar at this time might well have proved a disaster, but at least it would not have been drowned in the bodegas of Andalusia. The threat nevertheless was sufficient to stimulate Philip IV into another burst of frenzied activity to improve the fortifications on the Rock. Unfortunately these exertions were to lapse after 1627 when the threat of war with England subsided.

*   *   *

In the eighty years since the siege of 1540, Gibraltar's commercial decline had been counteracted by its increasing use as a naval base. It was now a more or less permanent haven for one or more squadrons of Spanish naval ships and the Strait and the bay had increasingly seen both English and Dutch men of war, either engaged in actual hostilities, or in wary manoeuvring whilst the major states of Europe prepared for the next round of the almost incessant wars of reli-gion and dynasty which marked the seventeenth century. For the next thirty years or so, however, England drifted out of the equation, for Charles I had enough difficulties in trying to sustain his position at home without indulging his Spanish vendetta. Spain's fortunes were also on the wane, sapped of its strength by increasingly weak and corrupt leadership, the ongoing revolution in the Netherlands, and the Thirty Years War in the heartlands of Europe which left the German states in disarray for two hundred years and destroyed Spain as a front-ranking world power for ever.

In Gibraltar it was plague (or perhaps typhoid fever) rather than war which beset the population in 1649. Something like 1500 people died, almost a quarter of the population, but it also fostered the legend of the Hermitage of San Roque which was supposed to preserve those penitents who sheltered within its walls. In the same year Charles I was beheaded and the rule of the major generals began in England: it also led to a resurgence in the status of the navy and it was not long before the fleet was once again scouring the waters around Gibraltar. The first occasion was in 1650 when Robert Blake, an erstwhile general turned sailor, passed through the Strait in pursuit of Prince Rupert – whom many regarded as a better sailor than general – with the few surviving Royalist ships. They met their end near Cartagena off the eastern coast of Spain.

The kaleidoscope of changing affiliations saw England at this time opposed to France and Holland, and therefore friendly with Spain. William Penn, another converted general, used Gibraltar for supply and repair the following year when he patrolled the Strait in a successful action against French and Dutch shipping. This amicable arrangement did not long survive and the circumstances of its going give good justification for the tag of 'perfidious Albion'. There were of course many influential people in England who were unhappy at any rapprochement with Spain. Religious differences and commercial rivalry, and in particular the craving for the riches of the New World, soon persuaded Cromwell, that arch Protestant, to conceive a devious plan to capture Hispaniola. Known as the 'Western Design', it determined that Penn was to sail secretly to the

Caribbean whilst Blake took a major force to the Mediterranean, ostensibly to seek out the Corsairs who were still troublesome in the area. Once word on the Indes fleet leaked out, Blake would immediately sail back through the Strait and blockade Cadiz to prevent the Spanish fleet sailing to oppose Penn. As a bonus they would seize any Spanish treasure ships which came their way. The deception worked perfectly, indeed Blake was made welcome in the ports of Cadiz and Gibraltar, and it was from the latter that he sailed in May 1655 to take up his appointed station off Cape St Vincent. Penn failed to take Hispaniola but captured Jamaica instead, and Blake returned to England in the winter albeit without any treasure. Not surprisingly, Spain declared war on England in February 1656.

Blake returned to the area again that year with an even stronger fleet of 49 warships and a force of some 10,000 soldiers and marines under General John Montague, later to achieve prominence as the Earl of Sandwich. Cromwell was convinced of the value of capturing an outpost on the Spanish coast to maintain a permanent naval presence in the area and Gibraltar was at the top of his list. Montague actually made a reconnaissance of Gibraltar, but concluded that it would require a sizeable land force of up to 5000 men which Cromwell could not provide. However as Blake and Montague had more than this number immediately to hand, it is clear that they were not confident of their ability ashore, and past experience in the Spanish peninsula suggests they may have been right.

Developments within the rest of Europe ensured that Anglo/Spanish relations were relatively quiescent in the succeeding generation. The demise of the New Model Army and the Carolingian restoration demanded a period of consolidation in England. The navy which had seen a resurgence of strength and efficiency under Cromwell declined under a parsimonious parliament which now controlled the purse strings. But the rise of Louis XIV in France and the Habsburg/Bourbon rivalry ensured that warfare on the continent reached new heights of intensity and expertise. The declining Spanish power militated strongly against their seeking conflict with England to add to

their difficulties and it was not until 1693 that Gibraltar again became the focus of naval rivalry. This time it was England and France who were the contestants, with Spain as a near passive onlooker.

A Royal Navy fleet assembled off Ushant to protect a convoy of 400 merchant ships bound for the Mediterranean. The threat was the resurgent French navy under Admiral Tourville who was thought to be in Brest. The convoy with an immediate escort of only 13 English and Dutch ships under Admiral Sir George Rooke safely negotiated the Bay of Biscay, but to their complete surprise came face to face with Tourville with a vastly superior force as they rounded Cape St Vincent and headed for the Strait. Rooke decided he had no option but to order the ships to scatter, a decision for which he was later condemned in the same way as Admiral Pound when, with less justification, he ordered the Arctic Convoy PQ17 to scatter in July 1942. In any event, the consequences were just as disastrous as in 1942: 50 merchant ships were sunk and 27 captured, the rest headed in panic for the nearest Spanish or Portuguese ports. Some reached Gibraltar with 4 of Rooke's warships, hotly pursued by the French. The merchant ships sheltered behind the New Mole while the 4 men of war took station outside to give them whatever protection they could. Twenty French men of war bombarded the ships and the town for nine days, often with considerable success, and 19 merchantmen were sunk by French fire ships. The French only withdrew when they ran out of ammunition. The survivors were not impressed by the help they had received from the Gibraltarians, but this is perhaps understandable given their past experience of the English.

There remains just one more aspect of the growing English interest in the area which needs to be mentioned. Charles II's Portuguese bride, Catherine of Braganza, brought with her as dowry the ports of Tangier and Bombay. Given the English interest in a base in the Strait, the acquisition of Tangier seemed a significant bonus, all the more welcome because it had been acquired without confrontation with Spain. Some additional fortifications were constructed and a permanent garrison installed. Nevertheless it was not easily defendable and was subjected

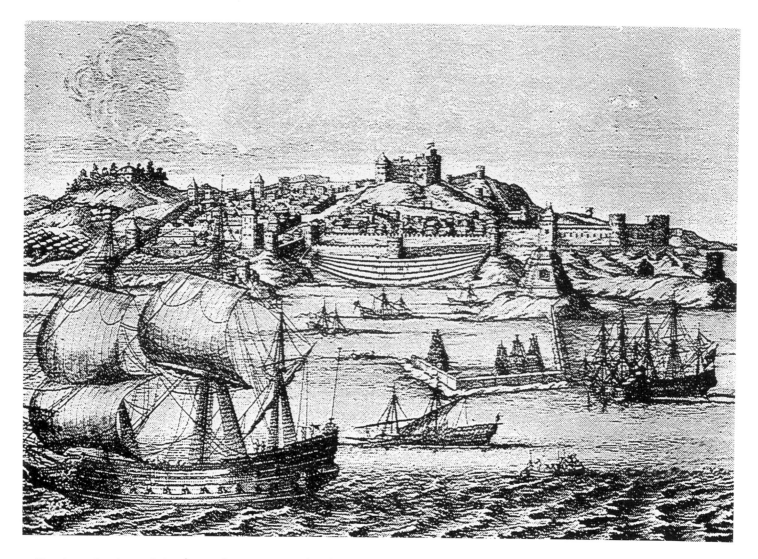

Tangier under the English, from a contemporary print.

to frequent attacks by the Moors, often inspired by France, Spain and even Holland. However, it was financial stringency and a not unjustified reputation as a hotbed of popery that led to the Government deciding to withdraw its garrison in 1683, some of the troops actually passing through Gibraltar on their way home. Nevertheless, the question arises – could England have improved its overall strategic posture by building up Tangier as its guardian of the Strait, thus removing any interest in Gibraltar? The answer is probably no. It must be recognised that the need for a base at all in the Strait was only a minority view at this time, as will be seen by the frequent

attempts Britain made in subsequent years to relinquish its hold on Gibraltar. The latter in any case was a far more effective and secure base than Tangier. The difficulties that both Spain and France have faced in maintaining any sort of foothold in Morocco and Algeria in this century suggest with hindsight that Britain was probably prudent to relinquish its interest in Tangier, even if it was done for the wrong reasons.

But in 1683 it was not to know that within thirty years England would have acquired the more important prize of Gibraltar, and it is to that seminal event that we must now turn.

5 GIBRALTAR FOR THE HABSBURGS 1704–13

WHEN PHILIP IV died in 1665, little remained of the legacy of Spanish power and prestige in Europe. His 4-year-old heir, Charles II, was adjudged weak and feeble-minded and unlikely to live long. The great dynastic powers of Europe immediately began to manoeuvre both to procure the patrimony of Spain and to pick up the scraps of Empire. Charles, nevertheless, was an inconveniently long time dying, acquiring two wives over the years, but proving incapable of consolidating upon his good fortune by producing a son.

The two main players in the territorial struggle in Europe were the Bourbon King of France, Louis XIV (1643-1715) and his cousin and brother-in-law, the Holy Roman Emperor, Leopold I of Austria-Hungary (1658-1705), the eastern arm of the Habsburg dynasty. Among the lesser players, the Electors of the Central European states, Poland, and the multitude of German princelings were generally uneasy and often disloyal subordinates or allies of the Habsburgs. Russia, harassed by the Ottoman Empire, was still feeling her way in Europe; and Sweden, although patronised by both sides, was more interested in Russia. England was preoccupied with the 'Glorious Revolution' of 1688, but with the Stadholder of Holland, William III, on the throne, could hardly ignore the volatile balance of power on the continent. The Dutch, capitalising on their aptitude for maritime commerce and warfare, had emerged as one of the more important of the smaller powers. Other bit players were Savoy, Portugal – always eager to profit at the expense of Spain – and indirectly, Turkey, which was continually twisting Leopold's tail in the east. These then were the powers which became increasingly involved in the diplomatic manoeuvres which inexorably led to the War of the Spanish Succession, and to Great Britain's unexpected acquisition of Gibraltar at the Treaty of Utrecht in 1713.

The wolves gathered at the door as Charles II, an epileptic, stuttered towards death at the early age of 39. Exhausted by a century of almost incessant warfare, none of the main participants was overly enthusiastic to recommence hostilities if a suitable carve-up of the still considerable Spanish Empire could be arranged. There were three possible candidates for the vacant throne, all nephews or grand-nephews of the Spanish King. The strongest contender genetically was the French Dauphin, the son of Louis XIV, but also in the frame were the Archduke Charles, son of Leopold I, and Joseph-Ferdinand, Prince of Bavaria, who had the great advantage of being neither Bourbon nor Habsburg. Although not counting for much in the power houses of Europe, he was also Charles' preferred choice.

England and France conspired in the First Partition Treaty of 1698 to divide the spoils. Joseph-Ferdinand would get Spain, but her Italian possessions would be divided between France and Austria – England's reward would be a continuing balance of power within Europe. However, this cosy arrangement was soon spoilt by the untimely death of the heir in waiting, Joseph-Ferdinand. Undeterred, William III and Louis went back to the negotiating table and in June 1699 produced the Second Partition Treaty by which Archduke Charles would have Spain, but in return France would obtain the whole of Italy. This was not well received in the English Parliament or the Hague and, more surprisingly, unacceptable to Leopold, emboldened by the conclusion of war with Turkey now to lay claim to the whole Empire. However, any chance of this agreement prospering was quickly stifled in Madrid when the long suffering Charles dropped the bombshell of a new will by which he bequeathed everything to the Dauphin's second son, Phillipe duc D'Anjou, and then promptly died.

This was too much for Louis' uncharacteristic restraint so far. He not only accepted the will, at which there is little doubt that his skilful ambassador in Spain, the Marquis of Harcourt, had connived, but also made a series of provocative gestures which made war inevitable. None of the other participants in the diplomatic game was prepared to see the Bourbon dynasty abolish both the Pyrenees and the Alps at a single stroke, and the installation of duc Phillipe in Madrid as Philip V of Spain, after more fruitless political manoeuvring, prompted the Emperor, England and the United Provinces to declare war formally on the twin Bourbon monarchies on 15th May 1702. Leopold had in practice been fighting Louis in Italy since the previous autumn; and Queen Anne was now on the throne of England after the death of William III.

The main arena of the War of the Spanish Succession was of course the mainland continent of Europe encompassing Marlborough's historic victories at Blenheim, Ramillies, Oudenarde and, less convincingly, Malplaquet. Encouraged by the Whig faction in Parliament, this was a novel departure for England which had not engaged in a major continental campaign since the days of the infant Henry VI. However, the more conventional maritime strategy espoused by the Tories was by no means neglected, for in many quarters the war was seen as a continuing struggle for the mastery of the Indies and the Mediterranean as much as a contest for the throne of Spain. Indeed, the very first action of the war was an unavailing attempt to confront a French fleet off Corunna which led to the court martial of its commander, Rear Admiral Sir John Munden.

A much larger Anglo/Dutch amphibious force under Admiral Sir George Rooke and his nominal superior commanding the land force, James Butler, 2nd Duke of Ormonde, sailed from Spithead on 19th June 1702. Its primary objective was the capture of Cadiz,

now, following the decline of Seville, the centre of the South American trade. The assault on Cadiz was an unqualified disaster. Diminished by the internecine quarrelling of its many commanders, it finally ended in an orgy of drinking and looting in the *bodegas* of Puerto Santa Maria, still some six miles by sea from Cadiz. That Rooke and Ormonde were saved from the same fate as Sir John Munden was due only to their higher political and social status and a somewhat fortuitous, albeit successful, encounter on their way home with the Spanish Indies *flota* in the harbour at Vigo.

It was not until 1703 that the Grand Alliance turned its attention to the Mediterranean and the Iberian Peninsula leading to the formulation of a new war aim, the physical removal of Philip V and his replacement by Archduke Charles who was carried to Lisbon with Rooke's fleet. The key factor in this development was the adherence of Portugal to the Grand Alliance which opened up the back door to a land invasion of Spain. In the Mediterranean Admiral Sir Cloudesly Shovell, a more resolute and innovative commander than Rooke, led an ill-equipped fleet on a largely abortive sortie to Toulon, but which at least helped to persuade the Duke of Savoy to abandon his allegiance to Louis and join the Grand Alliance.

Action in the Peninsula at last got underway in 1704. On land there was extensive but inconclusive skirmishing between the Franco/Spanish forces under James FitzJames, the Duke of Berwick, and the Alliance, largely composed of the Portuguese and Dutch under the ineffective Duke of Schomberg. Berwick is an interesting character, the natural son of King James II and Arabella Churchill, he was thus the nephew of the Duke of Marlborough who held him in high regard. Later in the war he was opposed on the Alliance side by the Earl of Galway, a French Huguenot refugee, leading to the conflict of French forces led by an Englishman opposing English troops commanded by a Frenchman. Such are the bizarre occurrences of war!

Also in 1704, Rooke accompanied by Prince George of Hesse-Darmstadt, who had previously been Governor of Catalonia under the Habsburgs, attempted an amphibious operation against Barcelona. Rooke's support was noticeably unenthusiastic, the expected Catalan support did not materialise, and Darmstadt's force of 1200 English and 400 Dutch marines was too small to inflict any damage on a stout defence. Once again an Alliance expedition had ended in ignominious withdrawal. Rooke's extended credit was further undermined when he missed a chance of intercepting the French fleet off Toulon in June. The English Parliament as well as King Pedro of Portugal and the Archduke Charles were all becoming increasingly restive: Rooke needed an early success if his reputation was to be salvaged.

*   *   *

Admiral Sir George Rooke (1650-1709) was the second son of Sir William Rooke of Canterbury. He had a broad, but not noticeably distinguished, career as a sailor starting with the Battle of Sole Bay against the Dutch in 1672. He attracted wider attention when in command of the 50-gun *Deptford* at the Battle of Bantry Bay in 1689 for not supporting the beleaguered army ashore in Londonderry. He was often criticised in Parliament for his irresolution, although this was an occupational hazard usually more dependent on political faction than the record of events, and he progressed steadily through the naval ranks to command the combined English and Dutch fleets by 1700. A lifelong Tory, he obtained a seat in the House of Commons for Portsmouth in 1702. By the time of the assault on Gibraltar he was 54 years old; taciturn, demanding, cautious, of uneasy temper, and suffering painfully from gout. Although he enjoyed a battle, he was sometimes a little reluctant to be drawn into one.

Admirals at this time usually carried secret orders which were markedly different to those circulated to their allies, thus causing inevitable confusion and misunderstanding. But these orders themselves were often wide-ranging, ambiguous or even contradictory. Gibraltar was one of the targets contained within Rooke's secret orders, and although its strategic value had been recognised since at least the days of Cromwell, few within England or the Alliance regarded it as of quite the same importance as, for example, Cadiz or Port Mahon in Minorca, the finest natural harbour in the Mediterranean. Its main value was as an observation post from which to monitor the passage of the French and Spanish fleets between the Atlantic and the Mediterranean. But not possessing a good natural harbour or a hinterland capable of supporting a fleet, it was not regarded as a suitable long term base for the Royal Navy.

Rooke held a council of war on the 28th of July 1704 on board his flagship the *Royal Catherine*. With no artillery or troops except the marines, Cadiz, Port Mahon and Barcelona were quickly ruled out as potential targets, and there is no record of any disagreement to the selection of Gibraltar as a suitable alternative. There was no doubt that Rooke was embarking on this exercise on behalf of the Habsburg throne: his personal directive from Queen Anne instructed him 'to pay the same obedience to the King of Spain [Charles]... as you would to myself', and the council of war explicitly stated that 'it [the attack on Gibraltar] was to reduce it to the King of Spain's obedience'. Rooke was familiar with the port from 1693 when fighting on the Spanish side and it was not thought that it was well defended. This was indeed true: under the governor Don Diego de Salinas, the permanent garrison of little more than 50 was supplemented by a militia and volunteers, variously estimated as numbering between 250 and 400. There were 50 old cannon facing the sea approach and about 120 in all, some either unusable or unmanned. Salinas quickly made a plea for help to the Marques de Villadarias, the Captain General of Andalusia: it went unheeded. The Alliance force was overwhelming, 69 ships of the line supported by 16 frigates and with 1800 marines and sailors supplemented by an unknown number of Catalans, perhaps as many as 400, as well as disaffected Spanish officers.

The land attack was led by Prince George of Hesse-Darmstadt. Darmstadt has attracted little attention from military historians, but he was a very capable soldier and tireless administrator. He was a younger son of the Duchy of Hesse whose Landgraviate was constituted in 1567 in the area around Frankfurt in Germany. His military career was founded in the hard school of the Balkan wars and, as a cousin of the Queen of Spain, he had been appointed Viceroy in

Catalonia. A devoted Habsburg, he was predictably soon dismissed by Philip V, but retained a strong following in Catalonia. He was killed in the assault on Montjuich near Barcelona the year after the capture of Gibraltar

The unequal contest began shortly after noon on Friday 1st August when Darmstadt with about 2300 troops was put ashore on the isthmus at Puerta Mala with some grenadiers masquerading as engineers and armed with crowbars and axes to dismantle the Land Port. Salinas boldly dispatched a small force of cavalry to intervene, but they were quickly sent scuttling back behind the walls leaving one trooper dead. Darmstadt dug in close to some old windmills within musket range of the walls and, abiding by the normal conventions, dispatched a messenger to the Governor demanding his surrender and threatening dire retribution should he choose not to do so. Surveying

Rooke's fleet, by now arrayed in the bay, Salinas must have recognised the hopelessness of his position. Even so, after consulting the city council, his response seems stronger on bravado than realism, intimating that 'they would defend Gibraltar with their lives while there was a single shell remaining in the town that could be fired in its defence'. Sadly, there were far too few!

Despite overwhelming numerical superiority, the lack of artillery would have made an attack from the isthmus a lengthy and costly affair. But the artillery was to hand in the fleet. The bombardment was entrusted to Rear Admiral Sir George Byng, a most capable sailor who eventually became an Admiral of the Fleet, but is less well known to history than his son, Admiral John Byng who fifty three years later was executed at Portsmouth, after a scandalously rigged court martial, for failing to save Minorca from the French. Byng's squadron consisted of 11 ships of the line to which Rooke added 5 more plus a Dutch contingent of 6 ships, a total of 1490 guns of which half could be brought to bear on the town and the foreshore defences at any one time. The light offshore wind and shallow draught meant that the ships had to be laboriously warped into position, and this took all of the next day (2nd August). During that night Captain Edward Whittaker of the *Dorsetshire* captured a French 12-gun privateer within the Old Mole which had been shelling Darmstadt's position outside the Land Port.

At midnight 3 Dutch bomb ketches of shallower draught than the ships of the line had commenced firing incendiary shells, called 'carcases', but the main bombardment began at dawn and lasted for about six hours, firing more than 15,000 rounds. Rooke ordered a ceasefire after two hours, but Byng showed that a blind eye was not unique to Nelson. There was some desultory return fire but few hits although the flagship, the *Ranelagh*, suffered damage to its mainmast. The town as well as the two moles and the south bastion were targeted and the whole area was soon wreathed in smoke making it impossible to discern what damage was being caused. Most of the town's inhabitants fled when the shelling began and the women and children congregated at Europa Point. As the smoke cleared after the guns stopped firing at noon, it was seen that although the town was little damaged, there appeared to be a breach in the defences of the New Mole.

There were two landing parties, one authorised and one not. Captains Jumper of the *Lenox* and Hicks of the *Yarmouth* who were nearest the New Mole immediately launched their longboats and quickly established themselves ashore. A little later the main landing party of 3000 sailors and marines under Captain Whittaker landed to the south of the Mole in Rosia Bay. In the meantime an incident had occurred which is still the source of some controversy. The Torre del Tuerto at the head of the Mole, which the Spaniards had used as a magazine, suddenly blew up leaving 40 of Jumper's party killed and 60 injured. Some reports indicate that it was deliberately detonated by the defenders, and some credence may be given to this by the deliberate firing of Fort

Leandro near the Old Mole. On the other hand an English account by Dr Pocock, chaplain of the *Ranelagh*, suggests that the fort was deserted and that it was the carelessness of the sailors who were searching it with lighted tapers which caused the explosion. Whatever the truth, it resulted in by far the largest number of casualties in the whole operation.

Another controversial incident occurred when warning shots were fired at the women at Europa Point who unaccountably started to return to the town when the shelling stopped. A few were accidentally killed although the Spanish version has the English sailors plundering the women and their possessions. Certainly the shrine at Europa Point was desecrated and its image of the Virgin tossed over the cliffs. The women were subsequently put under guard and no more incidents occurred. Pocock later reported some plunder and desecration in the town, but there is no doubt that Byng did his best to counter this inevitable concomitant of early modern warfare.

The assault soon lost momentum after the setback of the Torre del Tuerto. Whittaker with 300 seamen advanced along the seafront to a bastion, the Santa Cruz Battery of 1627 (now Jumper's Bastion), and raised a standard. There has always been a somewhat esoteric argument about the flags raised during the capture of Gibraltar and their later significance. It is really of little account: although an integral part of the Grand Alliance, individual formations carried their own standards which practically

Europa Point was the usual refuge for civilians during sieges of Gibraltar. Only Caramani, the Turkish corsair, attempted a landing in this area during his raid of 1540.

Admiral Sir George Rooke (left) and Admiral Sir John Leake. These paintings by Michael Dahl, a Swedish artist working in London, epitomise the stylistic formality – even in facial features – characteristic of this type of portrait in the early 18th-century. (National Maritime Museum)

were still intended as a mark of identity rather than as a symbol of sovereignty. Whatever flag was raised in any individual location, there can be no doubt, as we have already seen, that Gibraltar was captured on behalf of King Charles III of Spain.

Leaving small guard detachments ashore, Byng withdrew his seamen and Darmstadt, who had by now taken control of the Old Mole, sent a further demand for surrender allowing Salinas only 30 minutes to reply. The latter asked for an eight-hour truce, which was implicitly granted, and consulted his city council. Their deliberations cannot have been very contentious for the fortress was clearly lost, and at dawn on the 4th of August two emissaries rode out to negotiate the terms of surrender. However, they brought no written proposals and Darmstadt clearly thought this was a ruse to gain more time. Accordingly he sent Captain Fox of the Marines with written terms adding that if they were not accepted by noon and the landward gate handed over, the defenders could expect nothing less than unconditional surrender. Salinas dallied no longer and the terms were quickly agreed. They were not ungenerous: the garrison, except for French subjects who would become prisoners of war, would be allowed to march out with their colours, three cannon and supplies for six days. Although any other civilians who elected to remain must

swear allegiance to Charles III, they would retain their rights and privileges as they had existed under Charles II.

All bar about 70 of the 4000 inhabitants elected to leave, crossing the isthmus with whatever possessions they could carry and seeking shelter over a wide area of Andalusia. They had been promised by their priests that the French would quickly retake the city and most doubtless believed this. Many settled in San Roque and the museum there has many mementoes of this troubled period; the town was granted formal recognition by Philip V in 1706 as 'My city of Gibraltar in the fields'. Others travelled as far afield as Ronda and Malaga. On the following day Darmstadt made his formal entrance with a salute of 21 guns and declared the city Spanish – Habsburg rather than Bourbon.

The capture of Gibraltar was widely acclaimed by Rooke's Tory friends in England, but the news was soon overtaken by Marlborough's triumph at Blenheim on the 13th of August. The capture of Gibraltar was certainly no great feat of arms: the city was doomed to surrender as soon as it was recognised that Villadarias could offer no help. Although Berwick severely criticised Salinas, there was little more he could have achieved. That Gibraltar was defensible was clearly shown by later events, but it required a much larger, better armed and trained garrison than Philip had provided, as well as a source of supply by sea, and thus the protection of a fleet. The allies suffered 60 seamen killed, the majority in the Torres del Tuerto explosion, and 216 injured. Spanish casualties probably amounted to no more than 60. There were inevitable arguments about who would garrison the captured territory, but in practice it was largely an English force which assumed the responsibility. It was quickly to be put to the test.

The immediate French reaction to the loss of Gibraltar was to dispatch the Mediterranean fleet from Toulon to effect its recapture. Rooke had already put back to sea and watered at Ceuta, leaving Darmstadt with 1000 marines to garrison Gibraltar. The French meanwhile under the Comte de Toulouse had anchored off Malaga and the two fleets came to grips on the 24th of August. The fleets were almost identical in size and fire power although the Allies had the advantage of the very light winds. On the other hand, some of Rooke's ships were low on ammunition after the bombardment of Gibraltar, and the French fleet, newly out of harbour, was in better condition. The action was hard fought and although no ships were sunk, damage and casualties on both sides were high. Rooke said: 'It has been the sharpest day's service that I ever saw'. Although both sides claimed victory, the French more vociferously, the result is best described as a draw. It had, however, one positive consequence, like the Germans after Jutland, the French fleet in this war never sought again to confront the English fleet. Rooke had returned to Gibraltar by the 30th of August and departed for England a few days later. The Battle of Malaga was Rooke's last battle: acclaimed too highly by his supporters and put forward as the equal of the national hero Marlborough, he was destroyed by his Whig opponents and died embittered in 1709.

*   *   *

Darmstadt, always a man of vision, saw his foothold in Gibraltar as a door to Andalusia, perhaps even eventually to Madrid. But this was an idle dream unless he received a massive intake of troops from Portugal, and these were never likely to be forthcoming as the Alliance prepared for a major thrust towards Ciudad Rodrigo. The loss of Gibraltar was received with dismay in Madrid and Versailles and Louis himself in a letter to Philip urged its immediate recapture, or at the very least the prevention of the enemy penetrating any farther inland. All was not well, however, in Philip's kingdom. He was a weak man dominated by his wife, Maria Luisa, despite her tender years (she was only 15 at the time), and the court was riddled with intrigue and incompetence. Notwithstanding the French King's entreaties, Berwick was unable to support Villadarias and recovering Gibraltar devolved upon him alone with no offensive support from the French fleet.

Although his vision was focused on Madrid, Dartmstadt's realism ensured that he concentrated his efforts on putting his defences in order. Much to their disgust, Rooke had left 2300 marines at Gibraltar when he returned to England in September, and together with the Catalans, a handful of sailors and Spaniards, the garrison totalled about 2700. Its seaward defence was in the hands of a Squadron commanded by Admiral Sir John Leake, but the ships were currently in Lisbon having their keels careened. Supply was one of the main longer-term concerns and Darmstadt initiated a long-running arrangement with Morocco to supplement that which could be sent from Lisbon. The fortifications, already crumbling, had hardly been improved by Byng's bombardment, but reinforcing the landward approaches was the main priority. Despite his chronic shortage of money, Darmstadt, using the sometimes less than enthusiastic marines, set to with a zeal which had often been missing throughout the years of Spanish control. He first of all inundated from the sea the low lying land to the north of the Rock, leaving just a narrow causeway across the isthmus – roughly where the modern road bisects the runway. He placed his batteries on the two sides of the rectangle between the San Pablo (later North Bastion) and the Round Tower with the San Pedro Bastion (later Hesse's Battery) in the angle by the Land Port Gate. The Old Mole was also strongly defended by the Devil's Tongue Battery.

Villadarias had failed to support Salinas in the earlier battle because he had sensed, with some justification, that Rooke's assault would fall upon Cadiz rather than Gibraltar.

The fortification above the Land Port gate below the rock face, now known as King's Lines, was first laid out by Prince George of Hesse-Darmstadt.

He now acted with commendable speed, for having lost Gibraltar the honour of Spain was at stake. By the 24th of August his advance guard of 600 cavalry and 500 foot was encamped beside the bay and the main force was in place by the 3rd of September, even before Rooke had left for England. He had 40 guns and 12 mortars. He was at first optimistic, but his spirits slowly sank as bad weather, desertions and lack of progress sapped the morale of his troops. King Louis had ordered the French fleet from Toulon to deliver reinforcements and supplies to intensify the siege and these arrived in the Bay of Gibraltar on the 4th of October. They were unshipped without difficulty as the Royal Navy was still refitting in Lisbon. The reinforcements were disappointing, only 2000 men and an Irish engineer, Colonel Richards. The French Admiral, de Pointis, made no attempt on Gibraltar itself, although it was a relief to Darmstadt when he departed for Cadiz three weeks later where his orders were to intercept any English resupply ships. He left just 6 frigates in the bay.

In Lisbon, Leake, a modest and energetic sailor, was increasingly fretting at the time the dilatory Portuguese were taking to prepare his ships for departure. But the good news was that Rooke on his return to England, true to his word, had persuaded the Admiralty to send reinforcements for the relief of Gibraltar and a modest Dutch force of 5 ships was already on its way. In Gibraltar also the tension was mounting: a Spaniard had been caught communicating with the enemy and hanged, and two other Spanish officers were suspected of disaffection, one of whom was eventually executed. There was also an on-running dispute between the commander of the marines, Colonel Fox, and Henry Nugent, an Irish adventurer who had long been in the service of the Emperor and whom Darmstadt had appointed as Governor on 6th August. It ended only when they were both killed early in November. Perhaps such tensions are inevitable in an enclosed environment like Gibraltar, but it did little to promote Darmstadt's energetic efforts to secure the garrison. By the end of October the 6 French frigates were stationed in the bay beyond the Old Mole and the first Spanish batteries had commenced their bombardment. It was Rooke's battle in reverse, but the French could command nothing like the fire power that had been available to the English admiral.

Villadarias' task was not easy. The isthmus was totally without natural protection and siege trenches had to be laboriously dug in soft sandy soil to position the guns. The defenders on the other hand had the advantage of natural as well as man-made defences and superior elevation for their guns. Connecting the Land Port curtain wall and the Round Tower 200 yards to the north was a slighter wall with a trench, later called the King's Lines, running along a natural platform in the cliff face. It provided flanking fire against any enemy approaching the gate from the isthmus. The capture of the Round Tower was a prerequisite therefore for an assault on the Land Port. Even the weather was kind to the defenders, the autumn rains proving particularly virulent that year, washing away the Spanish lines almost as quickly as they were constructed.

Admiral Leake at last managed to escape from Lisbon on the 6th of November and on the way south dispersed or captured the shadowing force de Pointis had left at Cadiz. Villadarias was well aware that his best chance of success lay in an assault before Leake's relieving force arrived and he made an ambitious plan to launch a three-pronged attack. An assault on a breach already made in the Land Port wall would be coordinated with an attack up the steep eastern side of the Rock and a landing of 3000 troops on the New Mole and at Europa Point. Alas for the Marquess, the Royal Navy arrived, like the cavalry in a good Western, in the nick of time and the major part of his plan had to be abandoned. Nevertheless, he pressed ahead with that part of the plan which entailed an attack up the eastern face of the Rock with 1500 men. On the night of the 11th of November Colonel de Figueroa, with an advance party of 500 men and guided by a Gibraltarian refugee, Simon Susarte, scaled the face of the Rock, reaching the Little Saddle undetected, and descended to St Michael's Cave to await the main body. They waited in vain; the main party never arrived and after leaving their refuge they were spotted, leading to a very sharp battle in which as many as 200 Spaniards were reported killed; Figueroa and the survivors were captured. It was a gallant attempt, but it would have needed exceptional good fortune to succeed without the support of the other two elements of the planned pincer attack. There is some evidence that a probe was also made towards the Land Port curtain, but if so it was ineffective.

Encouraged by this success, Darmstadt proposed a sortie outside the walls to force the Spanish lines. Leake was less enthusiastic; he could not spare the men to support a garrison already depleted by sickness and shelling and there were growing indications that de Pointis was planning to bring his fleet out of Cadiz to attack Gibraltar from the sea. Leake's squadron was of course nothing like as strong as Rooke's combined fleet and the limitations of the Gibraltar anchorage were demonstrated on the 4th of December when a fierce easterly gale damaged several of his ships. He decided to stand off to the west to await developments.

By the turn of the year Darmstadt's position was looking much more secure. Thanks to the efforts of Tory supporters in London, 3000 fresh troops had arrived in Lisbon of

The eastern face of the Rock climbed by Colonel de Figueroa's small force in 1704. To the right is the later water catchment area.

The Devil's Tongue Battery, so-named because it was the scourge of Spain, was constructed on the Old Mole in 1704.

which 2500 were to be sent on to Gibraltar. On the 10th-December they left the Tagus under the command of Brigadier-General John Shrimpton of the 1st Foot Guards along with 400 Dutch troops. De Pointis' fleet intercepted them off Cape Spartel, but although the *Roebuck* and four transports had to return to Lisbon, the majority reached Gibraltar safely, trebling Darmstadt's effective force to about 3000. Darmstadt proposed that Shrimpton should become Governor, but the Government in England would accept no responsibility for the administration of Gibraltar and Shrimpton received a temporary commission serving Charles III of Spain. This clearly indicates once again that England had no proprietary intentions regarding Gibraltar at this stage.

Conditions on the other side of the line meanwhile were deteriorating rapidly. Although more French troops were starting to arrive, relations between the two allies were poor and food, clothing and ammuni-

tion in very short supply. Desertion was still rife and those recruits arriving were described as 'mere boys...fit for nothing but to work as labourers'. Villadarias' original strength of about 10,000 was now reduced to 3700. The heavy rains had inundated trenches, fostered sickness and debilitated morale. Villadarias' frequent reports to Madrid were redolent with gloom and despair. Shelling of the enemy lines continued sporadically but had little effect. It required a great weight of shot, even if it could be projected accurately, to destroy solid fortifications. There were sporadic sorties from both sides, but none in sufficient strength to achieve more than marginal results.

In the third week of January 1705 General de Thouy arrived with another 4000 mostly French troops and Villadarias decided to make one more attempt to take the Rock. He was perhaps stimulated by the news that he was to be superseded in command by the new overall French commander in Spain, Marshal de Tesse. At dawn on the

7th of February 900 grenadiers and 100 dragoons, supported by 1000 Spanish infantry in the rear attacked the Round Tower and the lines of communication to the batteries higher up the hill at the Soto del Lobo. The defences had been caught by surprise at watch change and the French occupied the Round Tower and the King's Lines for about an hour before reinforcements from the town under the command of the Huguenot Colonel Moncal pushed them back with heavy losses. The assault against the adjoining communication trench by 300 grenadiers soon stalled. The attack might still have prospered if the Spanish infantry had come forward, but this they failed to do and General Thouy, after about 30 minutes' very sharp fighting, elected to withdraw. It was the last serious attempt against the town although sporadic action continued for some time.

Tesse arrived two days later with another 3000 French troops, but immediately concluded that the town could not be taken from the land. The key, as it always had been, was de Pointis and what remained of the French fleet. Leake had returned to Lisbon with his fleet for revictualling and careening over this period leaving only a modest guard of two frigates. It was de Pointis' last opportunity to influence events in Gibraltar and he failed to grasp it. Leake, energetic as ever, sailed from Lisbon on the 10th of March with 35 ships including 4 Dutch and 8 Portuguese, which according to Leake proved more hindrance than help. He was about to put in to Gibraltar after an uneventful voyage when he spotted 5 French ships of the line stealing away through the Strait. He gave chase and eventually came to close quarters off Marbella. It was a mere skirmish, 3 French ships were captured and 2 run ashore: the residual French fleet of 7 ships scuttled off to Toulon. The French fleet was to play no more part in the siege, in any case it had achieved very little, and with that any continuing Franco/Spanish action was untenable. On the 12th of April King Louis formally ordered the siege to be lifted and, although a Spanish blockade nominally persisted until the end of the war, it proved a passive imposition.

Although the French blamed the Spanish and vice versa, it was really the inability of de Pointis to make any significant contribution from the sea which doomed the siege to failure. As de Tesse recognised, the fault lay more in lack of resolve and coordination in Madrid than upon de Pointis himself, although he seemed to be singularly lacking in drive or offensive spirit. On the other hand Prince George of Hesse-Darmstadt emerges with considerable credit: his optimism, energy, courage and resource saw the garrison through a difficult period until the tide turned in 1705. Darmstadt was ably abetted by Admiral Sir John Leake who, although never called upon to fight a major action like Rooke at Malaga, showed exemplary zeal in the support of the garrison. Furthermore, perhaps aided by some luck which all good commanders deserve, he twice managed to appear on the scene with his squadron at just the right moment to relieve a critical situation.

*　　*　　*

Gibraltar played no further active role in the War of the Spanish Succession, although it was increasingly to play a part in the politics of its conclusion. On 2nd August 1705, almost exactly a year to the day since its capture, the Archduke Charles arrived in the town to be acclaimed King Charles III of Spain, the first slice of Spanish territory he could truly call his own. Darmstadt departed for Catalonia with two British regiments and the Catalans and Spaniards, leaving the English and the Dutch to garrison the Rock with two regiments each under Major General Shrimpton as Governor. Gibraltar was not well served by its governors over the next few years; peculation was endemic and the defences were neglected. Of significance for later developments was the migration of civilians back to the town to provide all the many services that a resident garrison requires. These included some 300 Spanish as well as a mix of Jews, Moroccans and other European races, thus launching the cosmopolitan nature of the Gibraltarian population of later years.

The war in Spain ebbed and flowed over the next few years. King Philip was twice ejected from Madrid but recovered it with the help of good French generalship. One significant gain for Britain (as it had become after the Act of Union of 1707) was the capture of Minorca in 1708. On the continent of Europe, the successive victories of Marlborough and Prince Eugene were becoming increasingly costly and strategically less decisive and the war began to drift into stalemate. Louis XIV clearly wanted to bring it to a close and the Grand Alliance was becoming ever more fragmented: Marlborough fell from favour in 1711 as the peace faction prospered. However, the excessive demands of the Habsburgs kept breathing new life into the war when it might have drifted to a close.

There was no formal change in the status of Gibraltar until 1713, but there were groups in England, strongly supported by the British Resident in Portugal, Sir John Methuen, who believed that as it had been captured by the English, it should remain British as a spoil of war. The equal claim of the Dutch to a share in the spoils was conveniently ignored. Although the arguments advanced were often of a military perspective, the underlying reasons were mainly commercial. Gibraltar was seen as the gateway to the Levantine trade, a convenient base for sheltering and supplying the mercantile fleet and a location from which the activities of competitors might be controlled. The argument was not supported by the Admiralty who saw the limitations of the harbour and the potential cost of upkeep and defence as far outweighing the strategic benefits. Port Mahon, which dominated Toulon and had a far better anchorage, was a much better proposition. Although the Royal Navy might be accused of a lack of foresight, Gibraltar did not have any overwhelming strategic advantages. The Rock did not control the Strait – whole fleets could creep through unnoticed in the right conditions – and even if a potential enemy was spotted, no land-based gun had anything like the range to challenge it. Control of the Strait, therefore, required not only the presence of a sufficient naval force in Gibraltar, but of overriding importance, the right weather conditions to weigh anchor and escape the bay. When the wind was in the wrong direction, the fleet was as impotent as a guard dog incarcerated in a kennel.

In 1711, however, an event occurred which changed for Britain its whole approach to the war. Emperor Leopold had died in 1705 and been succeeded by his eldest son Joseph. But on 17th April 1711 Joseph also unexpectedly died and his younger brother, Archduke Charles, erstwhile King Charles III of Spain, inherited the whole Habsburg Empire. This was no more satisfactory to Britain then had been the earlier prospect of a united Bourbon dynasty. War weariness was now reinforced by dynastic imperatives which quickly led to an accommodation with an exhausted France to conclude a peace. The Grand Alliance soon collapsed as bilateral negotiations between France and Britain settled the terms of peace. The Dutch, their bargaining power much reduced by war, were literally blackmailed into removing their troops from Gibraltar and Philip coerced, much against his wishes, into relinquishing Gibraltar and Minorca to Britain. King Philip V was recognised as the legitimate ruler of Spain, but the British obtained, for what it was worth, agreement from Louis that the thrones of France and Spain would never be united in a single ruler. The agreement was sealed in the Treaty of Utrecht of 1713 to which the other powers soon had to adhere.

It is sufficient to say at this stage that Gibraltar was ceded to Britain at Utrecht. But the actual wording of the Treaty will have to be examined more closely later, for its interpretation is still at the heart of the differences between Spain and Britain today.

6 A PAWN IN THE BALANCE OF POWER 1713–79

IT WOULD BE AN exaggeration to suggest that Britain acquired Gibraltar by accident, but if the War of the Spanish Succession had ended in the way intended by the Grand Alliance at the outset, Gibraltar would have been an integral part of the Spanish kingdom of the Habsburg Charles III. In the event, the untimely death of Emperor Joseph and a widespread apathy among the contestants augured for peace; and Britain, whose main interest was in maintaining some semblance of a balance of power, picked up the useful scraps of Gibraltar and Minorca. It may be that the British Government intended from the outset to use Gibraltar as a bargaining counter, for in the next sixty six years before the Great Siege they attempted to barter the Rock for more attractive acquisitions, or even merely to regain the 'status quo ante', on no fewer than seven occasions.

Why is it then that the territory which appeared to be such a fundamental part of Britain's Imperial power base in later years should have been regarded so lightly at the outset of the eighteenth century? The main reason is probably the dramatic change that occurred in British politics with the accession of the Hanoverian dynasty in 1714. After the revolutionary upheavals of the previous century and the heady days of Queen Anne came the sober stability of the Whig oligarchy and a constitutional monarch who, although not without influence, was rarely seen and regarded with little affection by his subjects. The reign of the first two Georges was relatively speaking an era of tranquillity between periods of intense agitation and radical innovation. The pressing desire of ruling authority was peace in Europe and the establishment of a political environment conducive to the enjoyment of property and trade. The ownership of Gibraltar was inevitably destined to be contentious, and to solid, parsimonious Whig politicians did not seem to justify the cost and aggravation. It is, nevertheless, ironic that another aspect of the early Hanoverian period, the emergence under the influence of John Locke of 'public opinion' should consistently thwart the Government's efforts to divest itself of its unwanted colony.

There were other more immediate reasons why the retention of Gibraltar did not seem to be of overriding importance at the beginning of the eighteenth century. The Mediterranean Sea itself was not so important to Britain at this time: there was no Suez Canal and there were no Imperial possessions on its borders. Furthermore, the importance of the Levant as a trading *entrepot* had declined significantly as interest had veered towards the New World and to India and the East Indies. It is true that there was the need to keep an eye on the French fleet, but this could be done more effectively from Minorca of which Britain always sought to retain control. On the reverse of the coin was the cost of maintaining a garrison, for whilst an attack across the isthmus would always be difficult, the possibility still had to be countered. Furthermore, almost everything that the garrison needed had to be brought in by sea as there could be little prospect of obtaining much from Spain. There was also the need to maintain a sufficiently large naval presence to deter the much easier option of attacking Gibraltar from the sea, either by bombardment or landing a force on the south-westerly beaches. Spain could mount such a surprise raid from its secure port of Cadiz little more than a hundred miles away whilst the Gibraltar anchorage as we have seen was far from ideal. Finally, an inactive garrison always tended to be unruly and this would be exacerbated within the confined limits of Gibraltar. It is perhaps not surprising that the Government and the Navy, always strapped for money and resources, did not look upon their acquisition with unmitigated approval.

There could be little doubt that Spain would contest the possession of Gibraltar. Philip V had suffered most from the Treaty of Utrecht which his grandfather had forced him to sign, and although the loss of his Italian possessions may have strained his purse, the loss of Gibraltar touched his heart. It has continued to inflame the passions of Spaniards ever since and many of the arguments which are deployed today were first brandished in the years after 1713. But at first there was the problem of the Jews and the Moors which the Treaty required should be expelled from Gibraltar. The Jews, who were mostly merchants, supplied a valuable need for the garrison, and they also lined the pockets, if not of the absent Governor, certainly of his resident deputies. (The governors in this period tended to reside in Britain leaving a deputy and the military commandant actually to run the fortress.) Whilst the Government in London continually exhorted the deputy governor to expel the Jews, only lip service was paid to this in Gibraltar.

There were also religious problems. The garrison at this time consisted of about 1500 soldiers plus their dependants who would mostly be practising Protestants. But the civilian population was predominantly Spanish and Genoese, some 400 of each, who would almost entirely be Roman Catholic and who under the terms of the Treaty were allowed freely to practise their own faith. It was not clear whether their jurisdiction lay with London or the Bishop of Cadiz, and whilst the local hierarchy strongly supported the former, the Government in England ruled in favour of Cadiz. This led to innumerable confrontations which continued to flare up for more than a century.

Controversy also raged over the extent of the territory ceded to Britain by the Treaty. An early military requirement for land beyond the walls equal to two cannon shot was lost in the eventual wording of the Treaty which meant that the Spanish regarded as theirs the ground right up to the line of fortifications. The unspecified military requirement itself was open to question, for a cannon shot could be interpreted as being as little as 250 yards – point blank killing range – or as much as 2500 of a gun at maximum elevation whose shot would be almost spent at the end of its trajectory. The military in Gibraltar, not unreasonably, required some breathing space in front of the walls and as early as 1713 occupied the Devil's Tower and a windmill which were within one cannon shot. They claimed that these were an integral part of the defences of Gibraltar ceded by the Treaty. There is substance to this argument, for it was generally accepted (even by Spain in other circumstances) that a fortress had a kind of prescriptive right over its immediate environs for its legitimate security, rather like the doctrine of territorial waters. The British would claim, and still do, that this did not need to be specifically spelt out in the Treaty. Eventually a *modus vivendi* was tacitly accepted that the tower and the mill would remain unoccupied by both sides, leading to the concept of the neutral area which remained a source of contention into modern times. In practice, each side has occupied its own half of the no-man's land between the main lines of the fortifications.

All these grey areas impinged upon a general clause which stipulated that Britain's right to the territory was dependent upon her observing the terms of the Treaty. In all three of the areas discussed above were ample grounds for dispute, and Philip was determined to seize upon any loophole that offered the opportunity of regaining his lost domain. The British Government on the other hand had no wish to go to war again with Spain, particularly over Gibraltar, and tended therefore to be more conciliatory than those in authority locally might have wished. As often happened when communications were so protracted and supervision difficult, there developed a dichotomy of interests tending to pull in different directions. It was enough to persuade the Government to dispose of Gibraltar if a suitable reward and a face-saving deal with Spain could be engineered.

There was one area which offered a possible solution to this problem, but we need to

delve a little more deeply into European history to see its implications for Gibraltar. Philip V had married in 1714 an Italian princess, Isabella Farnese, who had been recommended by the French connections in Madrid as a quiet, compliant girl who would be receptive to their designs to entwine the thrones of Spain and France in defiance of the Treaty of Utrecht. In the event, in the long tradition of Spanish queens, she proved to be anything but malleable – 'imperious and aspiring...a perfect mistress of dissimulation' was one later description of her character. She dominated her weak and vacillating husband and gained control of the Government by inserting as chief minister one of her compatriots from Parma, Cardinal Alberoni, a brilliant, devious, loyal, but over ambitious servant. Isabella recognised that her infant son, Don Carlos, would be unlikely to inherit the throne of Spain as Philip already had two sons of his first marriage. (In the event he did in 1761 as Charles III.) She therefore sought to establish a dynasty for him and her younger son in Italy which had, in effect, been carved up between Austria and France at the Treaty of Utrecht. Although Philip was pledged to retrieve all of Spain's possessions lost at Utrecht, in practice everything hinged on the recovery of at least a decent patrimony in Italy – something to which the greater signatories of Utrecht would be unlikely to accede.

The war over, the diplomatic manoeuvring began in earnest with General James Stanhope, the Secretary of State, adopting Britain's traditional role of trying to conduct the orchestra. In foreign affairs Stanhope was a man of considerable ability and vision, for Britain had few friends within a Europe which seemed dedicated to strife. To general surprise Philip distanced himself from the French and the latter, after the death of Louis XIV in 1715, became more amenable to a rapport with the British. The Habsburg Emperor, with the Russians and the Turks snapping at his heels, was happy to conclude an agreement with Britain which guaranteed the neutrality of Italy. Spain was incensed, for this directly conflicted with her interest in the area even though Stanhope protested that agreement with Austria did not preclude friendship with Spain. Britain was also negotiating an alliance with the United Provinces and France and accordingly invited Spain to join them in a quadruple alliance. If successful, this would nicely have wrapped-up the 'concert of Europe' for the foreseeable future allowing Britain to get on with the more congenial task of making money out of the burgeoning world trade. In order to join this entente, however, Philip would have to renounce any claims to Italy, and this he was unlikely to do with his wife and Alberoni looking firmly in the other direction. This impasse prompted the first British offer to concede Gibraltar as a carrot to Philip to join the alliance.

Although the Whigs in power would have been content to dispose of Gibraltar, Parliament, the pamphleteers and the public, as well as the Tories, had begun to develop a curious affection for the place. Thus the offer to Philip had to be made in the utmost secrecy, not only to approach Philip round the back of Isabella and Alberoni, but also to prevent an outcry at home. A devious scheme was hatched whereby Spain would mount a show of force against Gibraltar and the Lieutenant Governor would be secretly told to surrender. It was to be of no avail and the proposed quadruple agreement was eventually concluded as the Triple Alliance without Spain as the participants watched with mounting dismay the latter's preparations for war.

It was not known where the expected

James Stanhope, 1st Earl Stanhope by Sir Godfrey Kneller. (National Portrait Gallery)

Spanish blow would fall, but neither Gibraltar nor Minorca was in particularly good shape to resist an attack. Gibraltar now had no more than 1100 soldiers to service the garrison and only 14 days' supplies. But the assault did not fall on Gibraltar or Minorca: Alberoni had his eyes firmly fixed on Italy and in 1717 he annexed Sardinia with little difficulty. The following July he turned his sights on Sicily and invaded Palermo. Scorning any further subterfuge Stanhope initiated a diplomatic procedure, later commonplace but at this time unprecedented, by hurrying to Madrid in person to offer Gibraltar to Alberoni if he would call off his assault on Sicily. But the land battle in Sicily was going well, and despite the likelihood of having to face hostility from all the other major European powers, Alberoni was sufficiently confident to rebuff the offer – after all Gibraltar hardly compared with the glittering prizes of Sicily, Naples and perhaps Tuscany. In fact Alberoni's confidence was misplaced, for even while Stanhope was in Madrid, although not yet known there, Admiral Byng was inflicting a humiliating defeat on the Spanish fleet at Passaro. In retaliation Spain seized the possessions of all British residents and recognised the Pretender as James III of England. It was a provocation too far and both England and France declared war on Spain at the turn of the year.

England's old adversary in the War of the Spanish Succession, the Duke of Berwick, was now on the British side and made substantial gains in the Basque territories, and a projected raid by the Duke of Ormonde on Ireland was dispersed by a storm. However, England's old allies from the last war, the Catalans and Valencians now in exile in Portugal, saw the war as an opportunity to re-ingratiate themselves with Spain and hatched a plot to capture Gibraltar. Initially all went well, a request to be allowed to use Gibraltar as a base for attacking Spanish ships was agreed, but the plotters only intended to use this as a pretext for seizing the town itself. Their intention was to try to bribe the Deputy Governor, Colonel Stanhope Cotton, and to render the garrison inert with a free gift of captured Spanish wine. Given the past record of British governors and soldiers in the area, it was not quite

such a far-fetched scheme as it appears today. However, the rebels were not likely to be able to withstand the retribution when the garrison sobered up, and so they needed a force of Spanish troops on hand to take over at the opportune moment. It was at this stage that their plot came to the notice of London and Cotton was warned accordingly. The Spanish troops gathering on the isthmus dispersed.

It was soon clear to Alberoni that the war was lost and in October 1719 he sued for peace. Spain had missed a clear opportunity to regain Gibraltar, either by conquest or negotiation, in a vain quest for greater glory thanks to the aspirations of the Queen and her enthusiastic Italian minister. Alberoni was dismissed and Philip now agreed to join the Triple Alliance providing that Gibraltar was ceded to Spain. Even if Stanhope had wished to agree, and there is little doubt that he did, Parliament could not have been persuaded to relinquish Gibraltar in the flush of victory. It was beginning to acquire for Britain the same sort of emotional attachment that it has always held for Spain, and which has been mirrored again in recent years in the Falkland Islands where any strictly rational appraisal might have considered disposing of them before 1982. Stanhope's dilemma was acute, for at stake was the Triple Alliance, which had never been popular in France, and was now again coming under pressure to unite the thrones of Spain and France. To Stanhope Gibraltar seemed a small price to pay for peace and he again explored the possibility of a sale or exchange to make the deal more palatable. His reward on his return to London was a hail of invective from the anti-government press which had blown up Gibraltar to the status of the very linchpin of the British Empire.

His opponents gained a considerable propaganda advantage when it was learned in London that a Spanish force was gathering in the Campo under their foremost general, the Marquis of Leyde. It was assumed without hesitation that they were destined for Gibraltar and feverish activity ensued both to reinforce the small garrison and to stoke up anti-Spanish feeling in Britain – never difficult. In fact Leyde was destined for Ceuta which was under strong Moorish pressure at the time, but the jingoism aroused really ended for good any genuine attempt to return Gibraltar peacefully to Spain.

In February 1721 Stanhope died and thus precipitated what may be regarded as the first of modern governments, the ministry of Sir Robert Walpole who appointed his loyal brother-in-law Charles Townshend Secretary of State. Townshend did not possess the vision of Stanhope who was prepared to concede much, including Gibraltar, in the quest for a stable peace. Whilst in future Britain might talk of relinquishing Gibraltar to Spain, it had no real intention of doing so. The following years saw a bewildering exchange of treaties, but the trend was ever towards renewed hostility between Spain and Britain and the focal point was now invariably Gibraltar.

The first rapprochement was between France and Spain in March 1721 in which, in a secret clause, France promised to bring unceasing pressure upon Britain to return Gibraltar to Spain: cracks were already appearing in the balance of power which Stanhope had so painstakingly constructed. The next round went to Britain, if only by deception. Philip was persuaded to ratify a treaty in June 1721 which restored Britain's trading privileges in the Indies on the personal written promise of George I that he would return Gibraltar unconditionally to Spain subject to the 'consentement de mon Parlement'. Clearly Philip and his advisors had a mistaken impression of the malleability of the British Parliament, for by this stage there was little chance they would ratify this deal, and Walpole and Townshend were only too well aware of this.

For two years Philip apparently persisted in the belief that he had regained Gibraltar, but the tension slowly returned and incidents between Spanish and British merchantmen only served to heighten the discord. In 1725 the balance swung in favour of Spain when the Queen's new favourite, a Dutch adventurer by the name of the Duke of Ripperda, negotiated a treaty with the Habsburg Emperor which allegedly contained secret provisions to assist in the recovery of Gibraltar. Philip protested that friendship with Austria did not preclude an accommodation with Britain – an ironic reversal of Stanhope's position a decade

before. Townshend seized the opportunity of reneging on George's promise of 1721 and also concluded the League of Hanover with France and Prussia. The major states of Europe seemed again to be manoeuvring into a position from which war was inevitable. In fact, when the confrontation arrived it evolved only into a low-key war between Britain and Spain and, apart from some minor hostilities at sea, was fought directly over the control of Gibraltar.

*   *   *

War became inevitable after an unusually acerbic exchange of letters at the end of 1726 between the respective ambassadors and the governments to which they were accredited. Philip had already summoned a Council of War at which the experienced Villadarias, who had conducted the siege of 1704/5, adamantly declared that the capture of Gibraltar was impossible without support from the sea, and after Byng's victory at Passaro Spain had no effective navy. He was supported by other experienced military commanders and engineers. But such circumstances will usually throw up some ambitious and confident young blood who will defy reason in the quest of glory, and the Count of Las Torres admirably filled the bill. It was of course the response that Philip wanted to hear and Torres was soon putting together a motley collection of indigenous and mercenary troops. There were 30 battalions of infantry of which only 11 were Spanish, and 700 cavalry about half of which were mercenaries. Of the balance, the majority hailed from the Netherlands or Italy, but there were 4 battalions of Irish troops, ever ready to support the lost causes of the Jacobite Pretender.

Gibraltar was as usual poorly garrisoned at the outset with both the Governor, Lord Portmore, and his deputy, Colonel Clayton, absent in England. But the Commander in Minorca, Brigadier Kane, had been deputed to keep an eye on the situation and sent more than 400 soldiers from the island to supplement the regular garrison of about 1200. The Government in London had also reacted with unusual zeal and dispatched 3 regiments of troops under Clayton, now Brigadier, which arrived in mid February. By the 1st of May the garrison had been stiffened by the appearance of its absent

One early development in the British occupation was the creation of Willis' Battery above the Moorish Castle of which Queen Charlotte's Battery forms part.

Governor, and more substantially by 4 more regiments, bringing the defenders' strength to more than 5000 infantry with 135 mortars and 60 guns, some of which were survivors of the old Spanish garrison. The 400 Spanish civilians were expelled by Brigadier Kane. Most important of all were the 14 ships of the line under Admiral Sir Charles Wager which ensured that the garrison was kept supplied, ruled out any possibility of an attack by sea from the south, and provided useful supplementary artillery.

Torres' approach was leisurely, hampered by the appalling roads which made the transportation of cannon exceedingly difficult. Even so, by the end of February he had some 17,000 troops and about 90 guns in his forward area around San Roque. Almost from the outset his effective force declined rapidly as desertion and sickness added to those killed or wounded in action. On the 21st of February 1727 Torres moved labourers and siege tools into the disputed area on the isthmus and began the slow and tedious

business of driving trenches and parallels towards the fortifications and preparing the earthworks for gun batteries. In the absence of a declaration of war, a polite exchange of letters between Clayton and Torres failed to resolve the impasse and on the afternoon of the 22nd the British began to bombard the Spanish labourers from Willis' Battery high on the Rock and from the Devil's Tongue Battery on the Old Mole. The penultimate military siege of Gibraltar had begun.

The defending artillery had the benefit of elevation and a secure base for their cannon. The Spanish on the other hand had to sap forward to get within range and to construct a platform and defences for their guns as best they could in the open sandy ground. The wet and windy weather did not help, filling the newly dug trenches with blown sand and water almost as quickly as they were excavated. Furthermore they were subjected to flanking fire from some of Wager's ships which had left the bay and moved round to the eastern side of the isthmus. It is not surprising that Torres made only slow progress and suffered many casualties whereas the defenders suffered more from drunkenness and disease than enemy shot.

Nevertheless, by the 21st of March Torres had guns in position to commence a ten-day intensive bombardment of the defences which caused considerable damage. The main problem from the defenders' viewpoint was insufficient manpower to repair the fortifications and to remount the guns as well as to transport and prepare ammunition, and at the same time post the necessary guards to raise the alarm in the event of a surprise night attack. The Jews, one of the original sources of contention, were forced into unaccustomed manual labour and a request by some of them to be evacuated to Morocco was soon stifled when Brigadier Clayton agreed only to release them to the besieging Spanish. The British made no attempt to employ the standard defensive tactic of making surprise sallies against the forward guns: they had no need to risk casualties, the wet weather which set in with a vengeance in April was doing the work for them.

The biggest problem for the attackers was Willis' Battery above the Moorish castle and the Spanish made one spirited attempt to undermine it. Under cover of darkness they infiltrated a group of sappers into a natural cave underneath the battery and attempted to excavate a gallery in which they would explode 400 barrels of powder. The defenders could hear the work going on, but because of the overhanging rock could do little about it despite lowering a man in a basket to investigate. Unfortunately, the miners had stumbled upon the hardest strata of rock on the peninsula and had made little progress when the siege ended.

One attempt at a sortie by the defenders was unsuccessful. At dusk on the 28th of April two parties, each of a sergeant and ten men, sallied forth in an attempt to lure the Spanish from their trenches. The idea was that as soon as this happened they would speedily retire leaving the guns to wreak havoc on the enemy troops in the open. Unfortunately the guns opened fire prematurely, it was alleged because the gunners were drunk, and the Spanish, correctly suspecting a trap, remained securely in their fox holes.

On the 7th of May the besiegers made their final attempt to dislodge the guns with a massive bombardment. At first they achieved some success and 16 of the 24 guns on the Old Mole, the most vulnerable of the defensive positions, were dismounted, as well as all but two in Willis' Battery. But most of the damage was repaired overnight, with guns remounted or replaced. On the 15th Torres tried a new tack. He sent an emissary to Lord Portmore tacitly inviting surrender by suggesting that the Spanish artillery had barely even begun its onslaught, and indeed some 1500 shells fell on

The north-east face of the Rock near Forbes' Quarry. Top right is the entrance to the Spanish gallery intended to undermine Willis' battery in 1727.

The Land Port Gate was destroyed in the siege of 1727. Its successor is still a busy thoroughfare into Casemates Square. (Gibraltar Heritage Trust)

Gibraltar on that day alone. But it was the bluff of a desperate man, and Portmore knew it. Few casualties were suffered and it has been suggested that more were killed by the bursting barrels of the old commandeered Spanish guns than by direct enemy fire. At the end of the siege, thanks to Wager's ability to resupply the garrison, there were more guns operational than at the beginning.

About 11 days later the defenders recognised that the intensity of fire was diminishing: Torres had played his last card. His guns could not stand the strain of incessant firing and he was running short of ammunition which could not be brought forward fast enough on the treacherous roads. Philip too realised the game was finished, the Austrians were withdrawing their support

and a 'preliminary' truce had been concluded in Paris at the end of May. The shelling dragged on in desultory fashion for another month before, on the 23rd of June, one of the Duke's Irish contingent, Colonel Lacey, advanced from the Spanish lines with a flag of truce. So confident were the British that the offer was initially spurned, but the following day a truce was agreed at San Roque and the thirteenth siege was over.

Like most defeated commanders, the Count of Las Torres has received little credit from historians. But this siege was a lost cause unless the defenders had displayed crass negligence. With no naval support Torres only had two possible chances of success: to storm the fortress before the defences could be put in order and the garrison reinforced, or to batter the guns into submission by an intense bombardment. Having missed the first opportunity, whether or not through his own lethargy is difficult to determine, he tried his utmost to achieve the second. At the beginning of the final bombardment he came close to success, but the resources of the defenders who held almost all the advantages were too much for him. As well as spirit he showed some ingenuity in seeking to construct a parallel right under the walls where the British guns, which could not be depressed, would have been ineffective, and in trying to mine underneath Willis' Battery. The final casualty figures are instructive: the best available figures suggest that the Spanish lost about 2400 of which 700 were killed and 900 deserted. The comparable British total was only a little over 300 of which about 100 were killed and only a handful deserted. Torres' biggest mistake was to undertake the task in the first place: Villadarias was undoubtedly right, this place could only be taken from the sea.

By comparison with most medieval sieges, conditions for the defenders were almost benign. Water was plentiful and food sufficient; fresh meat and vegetables were available from Morocco, albeit at prices that only the more wealthy officers could afford. Wine was too freely available for the good of the troops and had to be rationed. The garrison was hit by an outbreak of disease which was probably yellow fever, but the death rate, at least while the siege persisted, was minimal. Discipline was fierce such that a deserter if caught could consider it a privilege simply to be hanged. Two Moors accused of collaborating with the enemy were executed and their flayed skins displayed on the town gates from which the soldiery cut pieces to send home as souvenirs. The 'ladies' of the town did not escape either if their services were in any way considered inadequate, some being committed to the stocks or to the whirligig, a sort of revolving birdcage in which the unfortunate victim was spun by volunteers for hours at a time. Life in a British garrison of the eighteenth century was never easy.

*   *   *

Although the truce ended the fighting, it did not bring agreement between Britain and Spain any closer. The Spanish troops did not at first withdraw from their advanced positions and Gibraltar was effectively blockaded by land. It was also soon clear that Philip had repudiated at least some of the conditions agreed by his ambassador in Paris. There is some reason to believe that Walpole may still have been content to see the return of the territory to Philip, but that was out of the question given the hostile mood of Parliament and public opinion. Philip was passing through one of his periodic moods of depression and Isabella

A magazine in the Hanover Battery in the North Defences, probably built in the 1720s.

Farnese, intransigent as ever, made the running on the Spanish side. Spain held two useful cards: one was the possession of an armed English merchantman with a £2-million cargo seized off Vera Cruz and the other was the secret letter from George I of 1721 implicitly conceding Gibraltar to Spain. This latter, which had become public knowledge, threatened to spell disaster for the Government in the feverish climate pertaining in London. However, Isabella's main interest was still in obtaining Tuscany and Parma for her offspring and it was through this avenue that agreement was eventually reached.

A peace conference was convened at Soissons in June 1728 which rambled on for months with little progress. The British, recognising the ambiguities of the provisions of Utrecht, were reluctant to discuss Gibraltar at all. Furthermore, they were not helped by their erstwhile French allies who had shrewdly recognised that there could never be peace between Britain and Spain whilst the Gibraltar question remained unresolved, and that the fall-out could well be beneficial to France. From time to time both sides attempted to raise the stakes by apparently making preparations to renew the war. In the end a treaty seemed possible which would satisfy Isabella's interests in Italy and studiously avoid any mention of Gibraltar. This time the British Parliament was not satisfied; they wanted to see an 'unqualified right' to Gibraltar included within the agreement and William Stanhope (brother of the former Secretary of State and a former ambassador to Spain) was dispatched to Madrid, with the promise of a peerage if successful, to obtain a secret codicil to this effect from Spain and the return of George I's incriminating letter. Predictably, he was unsuccessful but got his peerage just the same – the price of discretion? The treaty was eventually signed at Seville in November 1729.

In 1730, therefore, the situation was exactly the same as before the siege – Gibraltar was held under the contentious Article X of the Treaty of Utrecht. There was even a temporary thawing of relations when British troops were sent to Gibraltar to reinforce the treaty provisions in respect of Spain's right to Tuscany, but the border soon clanged shut again when this little difficulty was resolved. The main source of dissension, which was vigorously conducted by the ambassador in Madrid, was the Spanish claim to occupy and fortify positions in the so-called neutral zone. The Spanish began to construct a wall with fortifications at a distance of 1400 yards from the Rock, which by one definition was more than the two cannon shot previously considered adequate, but which had now been overtaken by a British demand for 5000 yards which was said to be two cannon shot at maximum elevation. This was the beginning of the 'Spanish Lines' which was to play such a major part in the Great Siege fifty years on, and signs of which are still visible at the eastern end. In the cold light of hindsight the British demand must be considered excessive, probably contrived more to quieten the voluble and jingoistic majority at home than as a realistic negotiating stance.

*   *   *

The half century after the siege of 1727 was relatively quiet in military terms for Gibraltar and this allowed the town both to develop commercially and to be placed on a sounder base administratively. But the international scene was far from quiescent as balance of power politics replaced the religious and dynastic conflicts of earlier centuries. The alignment of powers remained fairly stable: Holland and Britain generally allying with Austria against France and Spain. But Spain was a declining force in the balance, continuing to retrogress in economic and military terms throughout the century and suffering from vacillating leadership until the advent of Charles III in 1761.

In the early years, the governors continued to exact their dues from trade to the detriment of both merchants and government until greed and envy inevitably led to their individual downfall. But as the century progressed, and particularly under the governorship of General Sir Humphrey Bland (1749-54), the administration was put on a sounder and more honest footing. The population settled down at around 6000 of which three quarters consisted of the garrison (nominally 3000) and their dependants. Of the rest, Genoese and Jews made up the bulk of the population, the former occupying most of the menial trades whilst the Jews

had cornered the shopkeeping and business interests. The governors, with little success, did their best to attract a solid, respectable Protestant citizenry, but there were few rewards in trying to raise a genteel family in a tightly constrained garrison in which drunkenness flourished along with other vices to which soldiers are susceptible. Other religions in the civilian population were tolerated and even a synagogue was accepted, a clear breach of Utrecht. Such restrictions as existed for other sects, for example regarding the ownership of property, were easily circumvented.

The War of Jenkins' Ear between Britain and Spain in 1740 was a silly affair entered into by a weak Government in response to the worst form of public hysteria. It did not affect Gibraltar, but in 1746 Philip began to formulate another plan to capture the territory. He died, however, before anything came of this and the earlier passion for Gibraltar of his widow, Isabella Farnese, had abated after she had attained her aims

for her sons in Italy. Philip was succeeded by a son from his first marriage, Ferdinand VI, who was interested only in peace and generally managed to maintain neutrality against the blandishments of both France and Britain.

The Seven Years War (1756-63), a conflict of mercantile and imperial rivalry, was a much more serious affair, but still did not impinge directly on Gibraltar. At the outset France captured a weakly defended Minorca by a clever deception which led to the court martial and dismissal of the Governor of Gibraltar, General Thomas Fowke. Admiral Byng (the son of the admiral who participated in the assault on Gibraltar in 1704) was directed to go to the support of Minorca, but on passing through Gibraltar was relieved of his embarked regiment of Royal Fusiliers by the Governor because his own garrison was under strength. Although Byng engaged a superior French fleet off Minorca, he did not attempt to relieve the beleaguered Port Mahon, the only part of

A brass cannon made by Bowen in 1758, now in the Alameda Gardens.

Minorca still under British control. Byng was shot for incompetence, in the famous words of Voltaire *'pour encourager les autres'*, and Fowke suffered as well in one of the most infamous examples of dissimulation engaged in by any British government.

The relative importance of Minorca and Gibraltar in the eyes of the Government now became very evident. That great war minister, the elder Pitt, instructed the ambassador in Madrid in carefully-worded but unmistakeable terms to open negotiations with the Spanish Government to exchange Minorca for Gibraltar. The plot was that the Spanish would recover Minorca from the French by force of arms, hand it over to the British and obtain Gibraltar in return. It was hoped by this subterfuge to circumvent the inevitable outrage of Parliament and public. Perhaps a Philip or Isabella Farnese might just have been tempted, but all Ferdinand wanted was peace: he was in any case moving closer to France, but in the event remained neutral.

In the early stages, Minorca apart, the war was going well for Britain. Victories in Canada and India as well as at sea boosted Pitt to a Churchillian esteem in the eyes of an aggressive public. The Mediterranean fleet under Admiral Sir Edward Boscawen was refitting in Gibraltar in August 1759 when intelligence arrived that a French squadron of 12 ships was passing through the Strait. Boscawen gave chase with the only 8 serviceable ships available to him and caught the French off Lagos in southern Portugal. He captured 3, burnt 2 and damaged others: although not a major victory, it was indicative of the immense superiority of the Royal Navy in the eighteenth century which was to culminate in the epic triumphs of Nelson just a few years later.

The death of George II in 1760 brought Pitt's career to a halt and the war drifted to an unsatisfactory conclusion. The advent a year later to the throne of Spain of Isabella's son, Charles III, who hated and mistrusted Britain as deeply as his mother, led to Spain entering the conflict. The only outcome, however, was the loss of Florida, and Britain in any case regained Minorca from France at the Treaty of Paris at the conclusion of the war. Gibraltar was again not mentioned in the Treaty – the ambiguities of Utrecht were best kept under wraps. But with a hostile king on the throne of Spain, it could only be a matter of time before Gibraltar was thrust back into prominence. After an uneasy peace for sixteen years war again erupted in the Mediterranean and this time Gibraltar was to endure the most famous moment in its history – the Great Siege of 1779-83.

7 THE GREAT SIEGE 1779-83

DISCONTENT HAD BEEN simmering in the American colonies for some time before open rebellion erupted in 1776. At first the other European powers remained passive, smugly enjoying Britain's little local difficulty. But as it gradually became apparent that all was not going well on the American continent the other Imperial nations decided to pick up whatever crumbs might fall from the British table. France was the first to declare war in 1778 and intervene in North America, but her Bourbon ally Spain was more hesitant: after all it would not create a favourable perception in Spain's own American possessions if she was to be seen supporting rebellious subjects. Furthermore, Charles III was piqued that Spain had not been consulted before her ally pronounced for war. But the temptation of regaining Gibraltar whilst Britain was otherwise engaged was too much for Charles and in June the following year he decided to follow suit, but with the limited aim of recapturing his lost territory. Ironically, Spain's best chance of gaining the Rock had already passed in 1766 when the defences had been inundated by a massive storm and flood, and a request by the local commander to take advantage of the mayhem had been rejected by the King.

The pattern of Gibraltar's fortifications had been set in the earlier part of the eighteenth century, but Britain was fortunate in having a skilled and dedicated military engineer drafted to this outpost in 1761. Colonel (later Major General) William Green, of Irish descent, had seen service with Wolfe in Canada and was a gunnery expert as well as an engineer. He combed every inch of the fortifications and concluded that although the northward defences were generally satisfactory, there were serious deficiencies in the

Line Wall facing the sea. In 1769 he had his plans for improvements approved in London – not without difficulty – and initiated his most spectacular achievement, the building of the King's Bastion, that massive bulwark which still stands facing Queensway today. Its casemates were built to hold 800 soldiers but frequently accommodated many more. But perhaps Green's most significant contri-

Major General Sir William Green was mainly responsible for the formidable fortification of Gibraltar before the Great Siege. A copy by S.C. Smith of an original by George Carter. (By permission of the Officers of the Corps of Royal Engineers)

At Parson's Lodge Battery guns were concealed from view behind a rock face to provide a warm welcome to any enemy ships which might seek to enter Rosia Bay. The platform was constructed some time after 1704 and the guns displayed at present date from about 1750.

bution to military evolution was the raising of the Soldier Artificer Company. It was customary hitherto for the manual work associated with fortifications to be undertaken by civilian labourers until Green recognised that using serving soldiers subject to the constraints of military discipline could be more effective. His ideas led indirectly to the amalgamation of the sappers and miners into the corps of the Royal Engineers in 1856 which

until then had been an officer only formation. Green remained in Gibraltar throughout the siege and was promoted Brigadier General in 1781.

By 1779 the defences were formidable. The narrow causeway approaching the Land Port Gate was made even less accessible by the Inundation, first constructed by Hesse Darmstadt, and now watched over by Bayside and Forbes' Barriers. At the eastern side of the isthmus was the Devil's Tower. These were more outposts than a serious element of the defensive scheme. Beyond the Inundation was a glacis, a mined slope leading up to the gate itself. Adjacent to the gate below the old Moorish zigzag wall stood the Prince of Hesse's Bastion, flanked by the King's, Queen's and Prince's Lines, stepped at two levels on platforms cut out of the rock. Immediately above the Moorish Castle was Willis' Battery, the most formidable of the gun emplacements facing north. Green's Lodge Battery stood higher still. A cannon was eventually manoeuvred onto the summit

The King's Bastion was the main fortification on the Line Wall facing the sea.

of the Rock itself, called Rock Gun Battery, with a wide field of fire which not only had great symbolic value, but could actually reach the main Spanish camp. Down by the water-side was the Grand Battery, and to its west the heavily-fortified Old Mole with the Devil's Tongue Battery which could cover both the isthmus and the sea approaches.

Running south from the Old Mole along the Line Wall was a succession of batteries – North, Montague's, Prince of Orange's, King's and South – with a curtain wall in between making use of the old Spanish walls where these were still serviceable. In 1779 the Line Wall directly overlooked the sea. From South Bastion, Charles V's Wall ran up to the saddle in the middle of the Rock, breached only by the narrow South Port Gate, itself protected by a ditch and glacis. Immediately above and commanding the bay with 13 guns was Flat Bastion, built by the Spanish in 1552 to replace the African Gate and still looking as imposing today even with a house sitting incongruously on top. The Line Wall contin-ued south beyond South Bastion past Ragged Staff Wharf (named after the emblem of Charles V) as far as the New Mole, now totally erased by the modern dry docks. Along this stretch and beyond to Rosia Bay were yet more batteries to protect the sea approaches, the most formidable of which was adjacent to Rosia Bay and now called Parson's Lodge Battery. The defences culmi-nated at Windmill Hill, guarding against any approach from the south. Round the corner of Europa Point to the east was the impene-trable natural barrier of the rock face. Most of this impressive array of fortifications can still be seen today.

Colonel Green had transformed Gibraltar from a formidable stronghold into a near impenetrable fortress. It needed only a com-petent commander, an appropriate garrison and a naval shield to ensure its continuing impregnability. In 1779 the first two require-ments were adequately met, but the garrison never had the sustained support from the sea which we have already seen on so many occa-sions was a fundamental prerequisite for its survival. This of course mainly stemmed from the many worldwide commitments which faced the Royal Navy at this time, but also from continuing equivocation within govern-ment as to the value of retaining Gibraltar.

General George Augustus Eliott (1717-90) would have been a remarkable man in any age, but in the context of the eighteenth century military hierarchy he was probably unique. The seventh son of a Scottish baronet, he was in his sixty second year when the siege began. Much of his original-ity must have derived from his education at the University of Leyden, the French Royal Engineer Academy of La Fere and at Woolwich. He had already served with the Prussian Army before entering the Life Guards and being wounded at Dettingen. He later commanded with distinction a cavalry regiment in the Seven Years War and as deputy to the Duke of Albemarle in Cuba. After a brief spell in Ireland, the threat of war with Spain led to his appointment as Governor of Gibraltar in 1776. His military career was thus varied and profound, but it was his personal character which distin-guished him from the conventional military officer of the age. Austere and frugal in his habits – his adoption of a vegetarian and tee-total lifestyle would alone have distanced him from most of his colleagues – he was a firm but compassionate disciplinarian who identified himself with his soldiers of all ranks. An indefatigable worker, he required only four hours' sleep a night. Such a man might find it difficult to get along with his more hedonistic officers and indeed his rela-

Major General Robert Boyd was Eliott's deputy during the siege, eventually becoming the Governor of Gibraltar in 1790. (National Portrait Gallery)

tions with his worthy but rather more conventional deputy, Major General Robert Boyd, were often strained. Although not always popular, few commanders could have inspired such respect by his spirit and wise leadership, if not always approval for his spartan life style and mania for work. Above all, he was the ideal soldier for the hazards and privations which were about to descend on Gibraltar.

Estimates of the size of the garrison vary, but about 4600 seems the most reliable figure consisting of 5 British and 3 rather smaller Hanoverian regiments. There were slightly more than 3000 civilians in the town in 1779, but this number fell significantly as the siege progressed and the privations increased. The naval element under the uninspiring Admiral Duff was very small – one 60-gun ship, the *Panther*, 3 frigates and a sloop. The size of the Spanish forces is difficult to gauge accurately, but upwards of 14,000 by September 1779 seems to be the best estimate. They were assembled near San Roque at a site today called El Campamento, the Spanish for camp. To their front was the Spanish Lines, a fortification about a mile in length extending from Fort St Philip in the west to Fort St Barbara in the east and lying across the north of the isthmus a mile or so from the Land Port Gate.

The strategy and tactics adopted by the Spanish to capture this near impregnable fortress were at times incomprehensible and often incompetent. It was not that Charles approached the task lightly or underestimated the difficulties. As far back as 1774 the military academies had been directed to devote all studies to those relating to attacks on fortified places by sea and land. Gibraltar and Minorca were clearly at the forefront of Spanish thinking long before hostilities commenced. At the outbreak of war, Floridablanca, Charles' chief minister, conducted a competition for ideas on how Gibraltar might be captured: some were conventional, others weird and wonderful. They included plans to poison the atmosphere, building an adjacent mountain even higher than the Rock, dissolving the Rock by attacking it with huge syringes full of vinegar, and pouring drugs on the inhabitants from a giant balloon. One of the more subtle and sensible strategies was for France and Spain to mount a massive invasion of England whilst her forces were preoccupied in America, out of which Gibraltar would fall. Fifty thousand troops were assembled at Le Havre and St Malo for this purpose but nothing came of it. In the end the Spanish opted for a conventional blockade of Gibraltar to starve it into submission.

*   *   *

Despite the hostility in Madrid, relations between the garrison and the local Spanish had been cordial before war was declared. Officers regularly hunted and shot in the Cordilleras as guests of the Andalusian grandees and Eliott had actually been across to the mainland on a courtesy visit to General Mendoza, the Spanish commander, only two days before passage across the isthmus was forbidden on June 21st, 1779. There was no frontier as such, only two barriers at Bayside and Forbes – more or less where the Sundial is today – manned by advanced guards and giving rise to the modern Ceremony of the Keys. This did not presage an immediate outbreak of hostilities and nothing much happened for nearly three months. Eliott made good use of the respite to continue work on the fortifications, a task which never ceased throughout the siege, and to level the sand dunes on the isthmus which would have provided cover for snipers. The British, however, could see intensive work going on in the Spanish Lines and occasional shots were fired by both sides at ships which came too close.

At a Council of War on September 11th, Eliott decided that the Spanish preparations warranted a little discouragement, and as the sun arched above the sea on the following morning the first serious shots were delivered. According to one chronicle, in true British style the first round was ceremonially ignited on Eliott's command 'Britons strike home' by a Mrs Skinner, a junior officer's wife, which was the signal for all the guns in the North Defences to launch a furious barrage. Most of the rounds fell well short of the Spanish Lines. Lieutenant General Don Alvarez de Soto Mayor had by now taken over command of the Spanish forces and Admiral Antonio Barcelo had implemented his blockade. This was the key to the Spanish strategy, for if Gibraltar could be totally cut off from resupply it must surely fall. On paper his forces were overwhelmingly superior to those available to Eliott: 9 ships of the line carrying a total of 304 guns supplemented by 37 smaller ships, both sail and galley. Barcelo was confident; he was reported as 'riding most magnificently in his flagship, exulting over a people shut up like poultry in a coup. He is so vain and so possessed with the prospect of our capitulating that he has ordered all officers under his command to wear the keys of the Straits, tied with a ribbon upon their bosom'.

Resupply, particularly of food, was indeed General Eliott's main concern. A small ship heading for Gibraltar had already been escorted into Algeciras by Barcelo's customs patrol. The dispensing of food within the garrison was not particularly well handled and a constant source of contention throughout the siege. Instead of instituting a collective system of purchase, pricing and distribution, Eliott allowed the freemarket system to reign supreme. The result was that prices rose dramatically from the outset, hoarding and profiteering were rampant, and inequalities arose which led to distrust, dishonesty and inevitable disaffection. Whilst Eliott himself could never be accused of benefitting from this unrestrained capitalism, it opened the door to corruption and to accusations from the lower ranks, including

the junior officers, that they were starving in the midst of plenty for the privileged. In fact, although there were undoubtedly periods of shortage, sometimes severe, Barcelo's blockade leaked like a sieve throughout the siege. There was universal concern regarding when the next major resupply fleet would arrive, but small privateers and traders continually crept into the harbour with much needed food, particularly fresh fruit and vegetables.

The other and interrelated problem of a fortress under siege is discipline and morale, even if the situation in Gibraltar was not perhaps as acute as for those entombed within the restricted walls of a castle – it was at least possible to move people to the southern end of the peninsula which was for the most part relatively free from bombardment. Although they had a modicum of 'personal space' to obtain some respite from the mental and physical rigours of war, it was difficult nevertheless with upwards of 7000 people, many of whom were interned for the whole three and half years of the siege, to retain the allegiance and maintain the spirit of a diverse population of soldiers, dependants and civilians of many races. That the situation in Gibraltar remained notably stable throughout the siege must be largely attributed to the leadership of General Eliott. There were of course outbreaks of indiscipline, occasionally quite serious, but a careful blend of rigorous punishment and compassionate understanding soon quelled any serious signs of trouble. The example set by Eliott himself – he once lived on four ounces of rice a day for eight days to prove it could be done – was an inspiration to his subordinates which did much to contain their occasionally flagging spirits. Desertion, that scourge of medieval armies, was low. This is perhaps not surprising as escape was not easy – one successful deserter across the isthmus was pursued by 1143 rounds of shot at his departing posterior. On the other hand, more surprisingly, there were frequent deserters from the Spanish side, mostly Walloons, who provided valuable intelligence on the state of play in the enemy camp. It was another example of Eliott's wise regime that after interrogation he allowed the deserters to mix freely with the garrison where he judged their rumour mongering would be beneficial.

The bust of General Eliott in the Alameda Gardens is on the site of his headquarters during the siege.

Admiral Sir George Rodney, a copy by Bullock of a painting by Sir Joshua Reynolds. (National Maritime Museum)

As soon as it appeared that the war would start in earnest, most of the civilians and some of the army barracks were moved out of the range of enemy guns towards Europa Point. The streets of the town were ploughed up so that the soft surface would absorb the plunging fire, and prominent landmarks such as steeples and towers were dismantled so as not to provide ranging marks for enemy gunners. The Governor set up his headquarters in a tent outside the walls on a mound near the Red Sands, today marked by his bust in the Alameda. He also had a tent above Willis' Battery, still known as Governor's Lookout. At night he either returned to the Convent or to a bombproof shelter in Poca Roca Cave. It is believed that Mr Churchill used this same safe haven during the Second World War. General Boyd remained in quarters within the King's Bastion.

Spirits sagged as the food became scarce – only eight weeks' reserve was recorded in October and the staple diet was fish and flour – but the arrival of a British privateer, the *Buck* of Folkestone, which successfully evaded Barcelo's patrols raised morale. Although the quantity of sustenance they brought in was minuscule compared with the size of the garrison, the arrival of a privateer was a psychological lifeline to the beleaguered inhabitants. In the absence of enemy fire gardeners were still working the grounds outside the walls in the neutral area and additional plots were cultivated on every spare foot of soil on the slopes of the Rock.

After the brief flurry in September the 'phoney war' returned. It may be that the Spanish were undecided how to use the troops they had assembled, but it is more likely that at this stage they still intended to starve the garrison into submission. The furious activity in the Spanish Lines may therefore have been intended mainly for show and to keep the British on their toes: it at least had the benefit of keeping the troops employed, for their camp was already beginning to suffer from disease as the winter rains arrived. At last in early January the Spanish opened fire on the outworks, forcing the Gibraltarians to abandon their gardens and the Genoese their fishing. But it must also by now have been obvious to Soto Mayor that the blockade was by no means watertight. The occasional small cargo ship was still finding its way into port when weather conditions were suitable and in the New Year news arrived, with a brig bearing flour, that a resupply convoy was on its way.

Admiral Sir George Rodney did not only bring with him much needed relief when he arrived on January 19th, but also the news that he had fallen in with a Spanish fleet of 11 ships near Finisterre of which 6 had been captured or destroyed. The *Fenix (Phoenix)* of 80 guns together with three others of 70 each were brought into Gibraltar with the captured Spanish Admiral, Don Juan de Langara. Prince William Henry, the future William IV, was a midshipman with the fleet which greatly impressed Langara – 'Well does Great Britain merit the Empire of the sea when the humblest stations in her Navy are supported by Princes of the Blood'. He was not to know that the Prince in question was better fitted to be a midshipman than King of England! Although a convoy like this could bring in dry rations, there was still an urgent need for fresh fruit and vegetables to hold the scurvy at bay, and so it was an added bonus when a small ship from Tangier slipped in under cover of the fleet with oranges and lemons.

It was by now woefully apparent that the Spanish strategy was not likely to succeed, for Barcelo could only sit tight in Algeciras and watch this manifestation of British naval power at work. Rodney also landed another battalion of 1000 men which had been intended for Minorca and who were immediately quartered in the casemates at King's Bastion to replace troops who had succumbed to scurvy. Some of the women and children sailed with the fleet when it left on February 13th, for smallpox had broken out in the garrison in January, claiming six lives a day, mostly children, until it died away in August. General Eliott became extremely unpopular in the garrison when he refused to allow inoculation, a new and to his mind an unproven remedy.

*   *   *

Despite the uplift their arrival had generated, many a tear must have been shed as the masts of the fleet disappeared over the horizon to the despairing salvoes of Spanish guns as the garrison settled down again to the privations of the siege. But they had food for at least a year, ample garrison troops, and after an outburst of fire from the Spanish Lines in December, only 11 rounds were fired in February and not more than 50 in the next three months. This did not, however, deter the British gunners who continued to pepper the feverish activity which was still proceeding in the Spanish Lines. Good entertainment was provided in May when the Spanish staged a mock attack on the Queen of Spain's Chair, a hill about four miles from the Rock. As a dress rehearsal for the assault on Gibraltar under the eyes of the garrison, it was inevitably highly successful.

In June Barcelo launched a well-planned attack on the harbour with 6 fireships chained together; but although it generated a good deal of excitement, even panic, in the end nothing was achieved thanks to prompt action by the Royal Navy who rowed out and towed the burning ships onto the shore near Rosia Bay. The expected coordinated Spanish assault did not materialise; their guns still remained silent – one whole year after the siege had commenced. This was indolent by any standards of warfare, particularly when it was apparent that the blockade, even though it brought some hardship and disease to the garrison, was unlikely

ever to starve it into submission. Indeed, the greatest problem was maintaining the spirits of men who had been keyed up for battle for so long. In this sense Barcelo's little enterprise was a bonus for General Eliott – as active as ever in supervising the continuing improvements to the defences.

There were three possible reasons for the Spanish inaction. The implicit recognition that Gibraltar was impregnable (but which Soto Mayor could hardly openly admit) and the lack of co-ordination between himself and Barcelo were probably significant, but the main reason was that secret negotiations were underway between Britain and Spain to resolve the dispute. The war was not going well for Britain, for in addition to the hostilities against America, France and Spain, a rebellion threatened in Ireland and the Government and the country were disunited. It was on the 6th of April 1780 that John Dunning moved his famous if dubious resolution which was carried in Parliament that 'the influence of the Crown has increased, is increasing, and ought to be diminished'. But the diplomatic activity to resolve the Gibraltar problem was so secret and bizarre that success was remote. The dilemma as ever was that Gibraltar had become such an icon of British esteem that no government, let alone the weak administration of Lord North, could be seen to flinch from its responsibilities. The negotiations were conducted therefore by an Irish priest, Father Thomas Hussey, and a playwright, Richard Cumberland – as unlikely a pair of envoys as Britain has ever produced. The fundamental basis of a deal was that Britain would cede Gibraltar to Spain in return for her withdrawal from the war. But in order to deflect the wrath of the general public when it came out into the open, the detailed terms were so penal to Spain that agreement was always implausible. We need not go into detail regarding the furtive and tenuous negotiations, for they inevitably failed, and it is just as well that the garrison was unaware of them. As it was they attributed the delay to Spanish military incompetence and their morale was accordingly boosted.

After the failure of the fireships Barcelo tried another tactic. Longboats driven by a square sail and oars with a cannon or mortar aboard operated in packs to harass the garrison at night. They were only pinpricks, but their cumulative effect was very wearing on the beleaguered town. At the same time the siegeworks edged forward from the Spanish Lines, subjected to persistent bombardment from the North Defences. Blockade runners continued to arrive with fresh provisions and at least eight broke through the cordon in June alone. A typical cargo was a *settee* from Tangier with 38 bullocks and 80 sheep – others were smaller, but all received a warm welcome. One disturbing development occurred when the wily sultan of Morocco, Mulai Sulaiman, decided to throw in his lot with Spain, thus curbing but by no means ending the supply of fresh food. The siege had reached stalemate and the main enemies in the coming winter appeared to be hunger, disease and boredom. However, as late as October a soldier's weekly rations were reported as 2lbs salt fish (although this soon ran out), 1lb pork and ½lb beef, hardly starvation rations. Scurvy, which could only be held at bay by fresh fruit, was a continual problem, but the smallpox epidemic appeared to be dying away.

Throughout the winter food supplies dwindled and prices rose incessantly, and it is hardly surprising that morale became more brittle, by no means alleviated when beer reached the exorbitant price of one shilling and sixpence a bottle. Although the garrison never reached the point of starvation, this hardly applied to the poorer people of the town. The Spanish were very quiet; indeed, a little more action on that front would have helped to counteract the tedium and hardship. The tension came to a head after the next major supply fleet arrived under Admiral Darby on the 12th of April 1781. Whilst the 100 ships entering the bay as the morning mist cleared was 'one of the most beautiful and pleasing scenes it is possible to conceive', it at last provoked the Spanish to unleash a furious barrage on the town. Once again the inhabitants fled to the south and the shattered storehouses of the merchants revealed vast stockpiles of food and wine. The soldiers, by now on meagre rations, were not surprisingly incensed and embarked on an orgy of drunkenness and rioting that took two days to restrain. One report had a group of soldiers roasting a pig on a fire of cinnamon sticks. Despite this mayhem the ships were unloaded and the fleet departed just a week later. Meanwhile General Eliott set about restoring discipline which had reached its lowest pitch during the last bombardment. Looting was not always profitable: one soldier who had stolen a hoard of watches hid them wrapped in a handkerchief in the barrel of a gun and then fell asleep. The inevitable happened with timepieces showered all over the Spanish Lines.

*   *   *

With the siege now passing its second anniversary, Barcelo was understandably losing patience with a blockade that was patently ineffective, although his gunboats, 'bum-boats' to a contemptuous Royal Navy, wreaked considerable havoc to the south of the town which the artillery could not reach. The bombardment slowly began to subside again although there was hardly a building left standing to the north of what is now John Mackintosh Square. The Spanish had not yet given up the struggle, but they were certainly suffering from mid-term lethargy. Their morale suffered another blow when on June 9th a stray round detonated a major munitions dump by the Queen of Spain's Chair with great loss of life. The Gibraltar garrison on the other hand was suffering very few casualties from gunfire, for at this same time it was reported that only one officer and 62 men had been killed since the bombardment started in April.

It was a long hot summer and by its end gunfire from the Spanish Lines died away almost completely. Only three symbolic shells a day came over from their batteries, irreverently dubbed the Trinity – Father, Son and Holy Ghost. Many of the regular Spanish troops had departed to besiege Minorca and were replaced by militia, clearly ruling out the possibility of a frontal attack. Meanwhile in America the war reached its climax with the defeat of Cornwallis at Yorktown – the heroic defence of Gibraltar had become the sole jewel in a singularly battered war chest. It was perhaps ironic that the sustenance of Gibraltar by Darby's supply convoy had deprived British forces in America of vital support in their hour of greatest need. Furthermore, the end of the war in America released the French to turn their attention towards helping the Spanish –

it led to the eventual loss of Minorca and the final thrust to defeat Gibraltar.

Once again by the late autumn of 1781 the garrison was suffering from a shortage of fresh rations and scurvy was rife. No fewer than 500 were reported to have died and over 450 lay in the Naval Hospital. The incessant work on the Spanish Lines was now taking a more ominous turn as the siege works moved inexorably forward towards the North Defences, and the occasional shell began to reach the southern end of the peninsula. Of particular concern was a battery which threatened the Old Mole and the wharves where the blockade runners unloaded. General Eliott decided to take the initiative for the first time in over two years and launched what became known as the Great Sortie.

On 26th November Eliott ordered that the wine shops should be closed at six o'clock and a force under Brigadier General Ross was assembled after midnight in great secrecy. It consisted of selected regiments and detachments numbering in all 99 officers and almost 2000 other ranks with engineers and workmen in support. Their targets were the advanced gun batteries now only three quarters of a mile from the Land Port Gate. At 0245 they set off from the Red Sands through the shattered town and out of the gate. On the left the advance was detected, but the workmen were able to set their faggots around the batteries which were soon blazing merrily. The artillery spiked 10 mortars and 18 cannon. The centre column was also spotted and fired upon as it passed Forbes' Barrier, but the defenders quickly dropped their arms and fled. Only on the right was there a problem when the Hanoverian columns missed their objective and were fired on by their own comrades in the centre. As a bonus the Spanish duty officer was captured with the keys to the magazines to which powder trails were quickly laid. In little over an hour Ross was able to order the retreat and the whole of the Spanish front line was soon ablaze. General Eliott who had followed the troops incognito as a spectator thoroughly enjoyed himself – 'Look round my boys and view how beautiful the Rock appears by the light of this glorious fire'. A senior Walloon officer, Baron Helmstadt, was captured and the

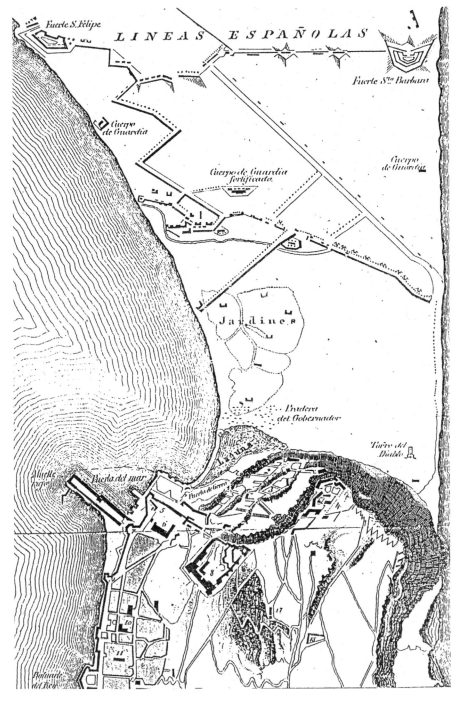

British losses were only 4 killed, 1 missing and 25 wounded. The lines were still burning several days later and it was some time before the enemy even attempted to repair the damage. It was a great success and a considerable fillip to the morale of the garrison.

Baron Helmstadt, only 22 years old, died at the end of December after a great display of chivalrous behaviour from both sides, and his body was ceremoniously returned under a flag of truce following an impressive funeral. Whilst it might seem, and perhaps

The Spanish siege works from a contemporary print. Note the Spanish Lines at the top, the parallels advancing towards the Rock, the Inundation (Laguna) and the Devil's Tower.

was, an example of the courteous gallantry which existed between the officers of both sides, it was also a good propaganda coup of which there were several examples in this campaign, and which Eliott always exploited to the full. The gunboats had now disappeared and with the Spanish guns for the time being silenced, the garrison returned to its regular routine. Whilst food was always scarce, it may seem surprising that the availability of fresh water has never been mentioned. In fact the winter rains were collected in a large natural reservoir within the Rock and piped down to the seafront. It was of good quality and rarely posed a problem. Scurvy, however, continued to cast its black hand on the garrison, particularly in the winter when fresh fruit and vegetables were scarce.

One of the features regularly remarked upon by those who assiduously maintained their diaries during the siege was the constant effort given to improving the fortifications and the accuracy and effectiveness of the artillery. Three aspects deserve particular mention: Lieutenant Koehler's gun carriage, new fusing techniques and red hot shot. Although the elevation of the batteries on the Rock enabled them to outrange the Spanish cannon, there was a particular problem in depressing the gun to allow it to fire at closer range without decapitating its wooden carriage. This problem was solved by Koehler with an ingenious new carriage which allowed the gun to be depressed and to recoil in a groove without moving the whole carriage, and to be swung to one side for loading. Captain Mercier devised a remedy for another difficulty; that of shells burying themselves in the soft sand of the isthmus and dissipating their charge. By experimenting with fuse lengths he managed to produce a shell which would explode in the air above Spanish troops, anticipating the more famous version invented by Colonel Shrapnel and used to good effect in the Peninsular War. Captain Whitham invented the star shell and

A replica of Lieutenant Koehler's gun carriage in Casemates Square.

another innovation was a crude firebomb for setting alight wooden fortifications, heralding the much more important use of red hot shot to be described later. In June the garrison at last had some sort of riposte to the 'bum boats' when they launched 12 gunboats of their own.

*   *   *

The situation in Gibraltar appeared relatively stable during the early months of 1782, the third year of the siege. There were constant complaints about the ever-increasing price of food, but supply ships, official or privateer, arrived regularly and in March four transports brought in another regiment of 700 men. Although the Spanish had restarted their siege works on the isthmus, they were extensively harassed by the North Defences and progress was slow. But appearances were deceptive: Minorca had fallen in February, and with the American war over there was a new spirit of cohesion between the French and Spanish to put an end to this troublesome outpost of Gibraltar. In a gesture of cooperation, all French and Spanish forces were put under the command of Louis de Berton, Count (later Duc) de Crillon who had been Governor of the Campo until achieving fame in the siege of Minorca. The troops available in the Spanish camp had also steadily grown to about 20,000 and were soon to increase to over 31,000.

But the problem remained as disconcerting as ever – how to overwhelm this apparently impregnable fortress. Blockade had proved unworkable and frontal assault across the isthmus was rightly deemed too risky. But whilst the North Defences with their narrow front, the advantage of the rock shield and superior elevation were all but invincible, the man-made western defences offered at least a glimmer of hope. Charles III now turned to another of the ideas, stimulated by his competition mentioned above, which had been devised by a French engineer, Jean Claude D'Arcon. Its aim was to batter the fort into submission from the sea in its most vulnerable sector, the Line Wall, whilst keeping the North Defences under constant threat from the isthmus. If necessary, the breaches formed in the Line Wall could then be stormed by the overwhelmingly numerically superior French and Spanish infantry. So far it was a conventionally tactical plan, but D'Arcon's trump card was to be an unsinkable force of hulks transformed into floating batteries which would be sailed into position close to the shore to mount a massive and unanswerable bombardment against the walls and their bastions.

General Eliott was well aware of what was afoot and the whole garrison watched the arrival from Cadiz in May of 8 shabby looking storeships with tattered rigging – 'fit only for firewood' recorded one chronicler. Later in the month 100 ships arrived and disembarked 9000 men, and hardly a day passed without some sign of feverish activity in the bay including, ominously, the construction of landing craft. D'Arcon was in fact building 10 floating batteries, 4 large hulks would carry up to 21 guns in 2 banks and the smaller vessels between 6 and 11. Even this was eventually exceeded and they finally set sail with a complement of 152 guns and over 5000 men. The hulks were designed to be impervious to fire with the whole of one side covered with rough balks of timber separated from the original hull by a layer of sand, cork and tow. This mixture was to be kept permanently wet by a system of circulating water pipes. The shield was calculated to be sufficient to ward off direct cannon fire, and with a sloping roof reinforced by hides and cordage as a protection against plunging fire, the hulks were regarded as unsinkable. The whole ungainly edifice was kept upright by ballast on the side facing away from the shore. Eliott described them as 'like oblong floating hayricks'. They were to be sailed by jury rig into carefully calculated positions 900 yards from the shoreline and anchored with chains which could not easily be shot away. The two largest were to face the King's Bastion with the rest deployed to the north.

It was such an ingenious plan that it almost deserved to succeed. It suffered, however, from one serious defect – Crillon, the overall commander, did not believe in it. It proved impossible therefore to construct a carefully coordinated plan with cohesive leadership. Crillon was even so terrified of failure that he insisted on being placed under D'Arcon's command – only a Colonel of Engineers – which must be almost a unique phenomenon in military history. Although there was

A lime burning kiln for heating the 'roast potatoes' which played a large part in defeating the floating hulks.

mounting excitement and some apprehension, there was no lack of resolution in Eliott's camp. Two measures were taken, one of which proved decisive in the coming campaign and the other which became Gibraltar's most famed tourist attraction today. It was said to be General Boyd who thought of using red hot shot against the wooden floating batteries, but in fact experiments with incendiary devices had been proceeding for some time with varying success. The shot was heated in iron braziers in lime-burning kilns, and it was a delicate and potentially dangerous manoeuvre to transfer and pack it into the muzzle of the gun sufficiently quickly to take advantage of its unique properties. In this case practice made perfect, and when the time came it was the red hot shot that was to prove the only riposte which the floating batteries could not withstand.

Although his North Defences were already very formidable, General Eliott wanted to place another battery on what was called the 'Notch' about half way up on the north face. Sergeant Major Henry Ince had suggested tunnelling towards the 'Notch' and in May

1782 work commenced. The only tools available were sledgehammers and crowbars with the judicious use of gunpowder. The work had not proceeded very far before it was realised that additional ventilation was necessary and so Ince blasted holes sideways to the outer face. It was soon recognised that these made excellent embrasures and by the end of the siege four more gun positions were available on the north face. Although they were finished too late to play other than a minor role in the Great Siege, a whole new system of communications galleries 659 feet long was completed by 1800 including the famous St George's Hall where Lord Napier of Magdala dined General Grant of American Civil War fame in 1878.

News from England was now very scarce and the presence within the bay of a substantial enemy fleet made relief more difficult. In fact the lack of news was probably propitious, for the Government was again toying with the idea of exchanging Gibraltar for some other Spanish possession. But the fortress and its heroic response to the siege was now acquiring a sort of cult status amongst the population in Britain and no exchange, however attractive , was likely to be acceptable. Instead in July the Government sent General Eliott a message:

'The skill, perseverance and courage which you have shown in this very long and fatiguing siege gives His Majesty's Ministers the strongest hopes that while they are stretching every nerve to send you relief, you will adopt the wisest measures and make the most vigorous efforts to conclude with glory a defence which has attracted the attention and has been honoured with the applause of all Europe... The King has entrusted to your care the important fortress of Gibraltar, one of the most valuable possessions of his Crown.'

Perhaps they didn't even blush!

There had been a steady increase in shell fire from the isthmus towards the garrison in the early months of 1782, but the guns fell silent on June 22nd as they prepared for the great bombardment which would herald the outbreak of the assault. On August 7th a deserter reported that the attack was due on the 25th of that month. On the 15th the defenders were alarmed to discover that the Spanish had built overnight without being detected a sap to within 800 yards of the North Defences. Crillon showed that he too was no stranger to psychological warfare when on 19th August he sent a boat across to Gibraltar under a flag of truce ostensibly on the pretext of delivering letters brought from Madrid, but in fact to announce the arrival of important new volunteers to the Spanish cause – the Count d'Artois, Louis XVI's brother, and his cousin the Duc de Bourbon. There followed an extravagant exchange of courtesies and food hampers, but General Eliott replied in more forthright form on 8th September when a furious onslaught against the Mahon Redoubt in the centre of the Spanish front line, using red hot shot for the first time, caused a spectacular fire and the destruction of several guns. The spectators who had gathered around

The gun embrasures in Sergeant Major Ince's tunnel facing the approach across the isthmus.

San Roque to watch the forthcoming action – for Charles' plans were trumpeted throughout Europe – were appalled as was the Duc de Crillon who launched his long-awaited assault the following morning.

＊　　　＊　　　＊

The firing of two rockets at 0530 on 9th September signalled the commencement of the bombardment from the isthmus. First was a salvo of 60 mortars followed by a cannonade of 170 guns: on occasion there were said to be up to 20 shells in the air at any one time. The fire was mainly aimed at the Line Wall north of the King's Bastion, suggesting that this was to be the location of the attempted breach – 'it was exceedingly warm,' said one commentator. Later in the morning 9 ships of the line sailed in leisurely fashion along the shore line shelling the defences, turning at Europa Point and repeating the medicine. Later in the day gunboats, which normally operated at night, attacked the King's Bastion but were quickly seen off. A second sortie by the ships of the line on the following morning was soon deterred by the use of red hot shot. This premature use of the warships was probably a mistake; it allowed the garrison to fine tune their artillery, and the transparently effective use of the 'roast potatoes', as they were called, did little for the morale of their crews.

The bombardment continued on the succeeding days and it was not until the morning of the 12th that the combined French and Spanish fleet sailed majestically into the bay. There were nearly 50 ships of the line supported by frigates and over 100 gun boats – a less resolute commander than Eliott might have concluded that this was a sufficient display of *force majeure* to allow an honourable surrender. It is unlikely that the thought ever crossed his mind and it certainly did not communicate itself to the men who so far had suffered remarkably few casualties.

As dawn broke on the 13th it was seen from the walls that the floating hulks – 'like so many invincible alligators' – had at last set forth. By 10 o'clock they were in position in a long line about 800 yards off the King's Bastion. There was some panic in the garrison as, not expecting a daylight attack, they had not prepared their red hot shot. The rest of the enemy fleet hovered in the background ready to escort the 300 landing craft prepared to carry the storming troops to the breach in the walls. But the Spanish had also made a mistake in their calculations, or as D'Arcon subsequently maintained, in the positioning of the hulks, and most of their shot fell well short of the red line manning the parapets. Furthermore, the 60 gun and mortar boats which were supposed to support the hulks failed to put in an appearance.

By midday the red hot shot was ready and the artillery duel started in earnest. At first D'Arcon's floating hulks seemed invincible as 32-lb shells were seen to be bouncing harmlessly from the sloping roofs. The bombardment from the isthmus was returned by the North Defences, but every gun which could be resited was turned on the hulks. Eliott was fully aware from where the real threat was coming. The noise and acrid smoke was indescribable as men scurried back and forth from the kilns with wheel- barrows filled with sand, each containing six 'roast potatoes' to feed the inexhaustible appetite of the guns. It was sensed in the afternoon that the enemy fire had slackened, but it was not until nightfall that the first signs of fire were seen on two of the larger hulks. In fact by this time there was a large degree of panic on most of them: small fires in inaccessible areas were slowly taking hold and some of the crews were unwilling to make use of the sprinkler system in case they flooded their magazines or upset the stability of the ships. To compound their difficulties, some of them were now aground on the sandbanks.

As two of the burning hulks exploded, the order was given after midnight to abandon ship. In reality, only two had been terminally damaged by the red hot shot, but Crillon, who remained as contemptuous of d'Arcon as he was jealous of any success he might have achieved, ordered that the remaining hulks should be fired by their crews to prevent them falling into enemy hands. The small force of Royal Navy gunboats under Captain Curtis which had set out to harass the escaping boats ended up performing a major rescue operation, bringing ashore 357 survivors. At dawn on the 14th it was clear that a major victory had been won. It was estimated that 1500 or so of the 5000 manning the floating hulks had died, all of which now lay deserted or sunk. The garrison casualties were fewer than 100 killed or wounded.

The enemy fleet lay supinely at anchor and the landing craft were abandoned.

As the post mortem started, and recriminations were soon rife, it can have done nothing for the morale of the Franco/Spanish force to know that a relieving fleet under Admiral Earl Howe was on its way. What went wrong? It is difficult to disentangle the myriad allegations which were bandied around, but it seems that faults lay more in execution than conception. Certainly there were failures of command, control and co-ordination, and the training of the hulks' crews seems to have been inadequate. Rivalries of national prestige, lack of bold initiative, inborn hostility to D'Arcon's plan – the excuses were endless. But at the end of the debate, the 'invincible' hulks had been disabled or sunk, and although the siege had still a little way to run, in reality the contest was over. When the day of judgment arrived, Eliott's 'roast potatoes' had seen-off D'Arcon's 'alligators'.

Further ignominy followed on October 11th when the *San Miguel* of 72 guns ran ashore in a gale near Ragged Staff Wharf. On the same evening a frigate arrived with the news that Howe with 34 ships of the line and carrying two regiments was close at hand. In the event, however, the fleet was swept through the Strait into the Mediterranean by the adverse wind. Naval mythology has sometimes portrayed Howe's relief of Gibraltar in the Great Siege as a momentous heroic event. In fact it amounted to little more than astute seamanship. On 12th October the British fleet appeared off Marbella and the following day the combined fleet weighed anchor and departed the bay. Eighty vessels, including 44 ships of the line opposed Howe's force of 34. For the next four days both fleets circled, apparently somewhat aimlessly, without coming to action. But Howe had cleverly manoeuvred his fleet to windward of the enemy and on the 18th several ships appeared in the bay including those containing two regiments of reinforcements. His mission accomplished, Howe now took advantage of the favourable wind and set sail for England. There was some disappointment in Gibraltar that he had failed to engage the enemy despite his inferior force. There was in fact a minor skirmish between the van of the French and the rearguard of Howe's departing fleet.

As soon as Howe had departed the French struck camp and withdrew from the siege. The combined fleet retired to Cadiz. The bombardment continued spasmodically from the Spanish Lines and in November gunboats made a spirited but futile attempt to disable the *San Miguel* whose presence in Gibraltar still rankled. Garrison life returned to normal; food was still short, and it was alleged that some of the storeships which came with Howe refused to unload their supplies because the garrison would not pay the prices demanded.

Admiral Earl Howe by Thomas Gainsborough. (Private collection)

Privateers, however, continued to appear with increasing regularity. The refurbishment of the defences continued – Eliott was not a man to rest on his laurels – and the Prince of Orange's Bastion was rebuilt in solid masonry under enemy fire.

But there was an air of unreality about the continuing Spanish endeavours, for it was now clear that the fortress would not fall. An attempt was made to dig a mine under the north-east face of the Rock, although for what practical purpose is not entirely clear. Indeed, the main reason behind the continuing bombardment was its value as a negotiating ploy, for the weakest link in the chain was the Government in Britain which was still trying to exchange Gibraltar for other Spanish possessions in the Indies. George III was reported as saying: 'I think peace in every way necessary to this country, and I shall not think it complete if we do not get rid of Gibraltar'. But the King and Government knew in their hearts that the public would not hear of relinquishing Gibraltar, which was now regarded as though it was nothing less than an extension of the white cliffs of Dover.

On the 14th of January 1783 four guns were mounted in Ince's new gallery, but there was an air of infectious gaiety about the garrison which was not entirely to the taste of the austere Eliott. At last on 2nd February de Crillon sent word by an emissary that a peace treaty had been signed in Versailles on 20th January. As the two boats met, the Spaniards leapt up and shouted, 'Todos amigos, we are all friends'. The siege was over, there was a startling transition from 'noise and confusion to calm serenity'. More supply ships came into the harbour and the price of food fell dramatically. Joy was equally unrestrained on the Spanish side of the line; they too had had enough of this fruitless carnage. On 12th March 1783 the gates of the fortress were formally unlocked after three years seven months and twelve days. The Duc de Crillon and General Eliott entertained each other with ostentatious hospitality and examined each other's fortifications – both were dutifully impressed.

On 2nd April de Crillon departed Andalusia for Madrid, remarkably escaping most of the blame for the debacle. General Eliott and his troops had a ceremonial parade and festivity on St George's Day (23rd April); the band playing 'See the conquering hero comes' as the Governor arrived to be presented with the Order of the Bath by a somewhat reluctant General Boyd. Senior officers dined with the Governor in the Convent and the men enjoyed their pound of fresh beef and quart of wine. The day ended with a grand fireworks display near the King's Bastion.

The statistics of the siege are almost certainly unreliable, but nevertheless give an impression of the intensity of the action. The Spanish were said to have fired 258,000 rounds against the garrison's 205,000, but the latter had many more serviceable guns (663) at the end than when the siege began. The British lost 333 killed, and 1034 died of sickness, 500 of whom had succumbed to scurvy: total casualties were 1729, of which 43 were listed as deserters. The Spanish and French casualties are unrecorded, but were undoubtedly substantially higher. The town lay in ruins, but with its defences still largely intact. General Sir Robert Boyd finally achieved his ambition of becoming Governor of Gibraltar in 1790 and died in post four years later. He was buried, appropriately, in the King's Bastion where he had lived throughout the siege. General Sir William Green, whose meticulous attention to the fortifications had made it all possible, continued with his successful career as a military engineer. He remained in Gibraltar until 1802 and in all devoted 42 years of service to the defence of the Rock. General Eliott did not, as might have been expected, take well-earned retirement, remaining as Governor for another eight somewhat fractious years before finally settling in England as Baron Heathfield of Gibraltar – no reward could be more deserved than the ennobling of this resolute, wise, austere but respected soldier. By now he was a toothless, garrulous septuagenarian, but who would deny that as he stood on the King's Bastion and surveyed the smouldering wrecks of the hulks on the morning of September 14th 1782 that he was indeed 'The Cock of the Rock'.*

* Although some historians have given this appellation to Eliott, it is perhaps more securely attached to General O'Hara (Governor 1795) who kept two mistresses, one in the Convent and one at his summer house at Rosia.

8 A PORT FOR COMMERCE AND WAR 1783–1815

ALTHOUGH THE Great Siege was the last time that Gibraltar faced a direct military assault, the Rock was by no means finished with war. The next thirty years, with the revolution in France followed by the attempt by Napoleon to create the first modern European Union, was a period of great tension, military preparation and planning, and warfare on a scale and intensity to be matched only by the holocausts of the twentieth century. With its expanding strategic importance, it is not surprising that Gibraltar was to play a significant role in the naval and military affairs of the continent.

The tortuous negotiations for ending the war between Britain and France and Spain proceeded erratically throughout 1782.

Britain's hand was weak, for the war as a whole had gone badly with only the heroic defence of Gibraltar and the naval battle of 'The Saints' in the credit balance. A number of conclusions may be drawn from this maze. Firstly, Minorca was always preferred to Gibraltar as a Mediterranean base for, whilst Gibraltar was often on the negotiating table, Britain consistently demanded the return of Minorca which had been lost in February. It follows from this that the British Government was still quite prepared to concede Gibraltar in return for an interest in the Caribbean. Puerto Rico was the favoured prize, but a combination of West Indian islands would have been acceptable. Had it not been for the shrewd and devious

This mortar, made in 1783 by P Verbruggen, presumably found its way to Gibraltar shortly after the Great Siege. It is now in the Alameda Gardens.

skill of the French Foreign Minister, Vergennes, it is likely that a deal would have been struck and the subsequent history of Gibraltar and two hundred years of tension between Britain and Spain avoided. There was even a chance that such an arrangement could have been sneaked past the excitable British public, for the issue of the moment was independence for America which was exercising all minds to the exclusion of almost everything else. But once again France was more concerned to sustain the mistrust between Britain and Spain, for in most other respects these two countries had a concurrent interest in restricting the power of France.

The Spanish ambassador in Paris, the Count of Aranda, was a pronounced Francophile and often conspired with Vergennes to thwart Charles III's steadfast resolve to acquire Gibraltar at any cost. Furthermore, the Spanish position was undermined by the failure of the floating batteries venture in September which became the laughing stock of Paris. Vergennes began to believe that more could be extracted from Britain by Spain forgoing the claim to Gibraltar than by clinging tenaciously to a demand they could not attain by military means. And in the event, this was how the peace was finally obtained, signed at Versailles in September 1783. Britain ceded Minorca and Florida to Spain, but Gibraltar was not mentioned and thus its status remained as defined in the Treaty of Utrecht. Britain had undoubtedly not benefitted from the protracted negotiations and George III was quite correct in thinking that it would be the source 'of a constant lurking enmity'. As for Spain, her defiant posture did not change in the slightest and in 1787 Floridablanca was writing: 'We have given way on the matter of Gibraltar only for the moment. We must get it back whenever we can, either by negotiation or by force if war occurs'. Even now he was planning the next attack on Gibraltar by exploiting a mine which had been started near Catalan Bay before the siege ended and which the British had apparently not located.

The still undefined border between the territories remained closed after 1783 and there were from time to time hesitant negotiations between the two powers. Charles III

died in 1788, his lifetime obsession unfulfilled, and his successor Charles IV, a weak king dominated by his wife Maria Louise, did not bear the same passionate hatred for Britain. The American War of Independence had its backlash in Europe in 1789 with the outbreak of the French Revolution, and the consequences of this dramatic overthrow of the 'ancien régime' was to convulse European politics for the next twenty five years. Its ramifications in Spain have perhaps even today not yet finally run their course.

*   *   *

The twenty years or so after the heroic days of the Great Siege was an unhappy period for the garrison. General Eliott became increasingly querulous and morale slumped. The chief occupation of the soldiers was drunkenness and brawling, and the decadent behaviour of their officers was no better. Lieutenant General Charles O'Hara, who succeeded Boyd as Governor in 1795, kept a good table and two mistresses, but did little to stem the unruly behaviour of the garrison.

Relations with Spain temporarily took a marked turn for the better in 1793. Both countries, for different reasons, were at war with France and the two actually collaborated in an unsuccessful attempt to capture Toulon during which O'Hara, then Deputy Governor, was captured by the French. Among the Republican officers at Toulon was a young unknown artillery officer called Napoleon Bonaparte. The honeymoon did not last for long and by 1796 France and Spain were again conspiring for another attempt on Gibraltar. At first they were quite successful, sweeping the Royal Navy out of the Mediterranean and into the Bay of Gibraltar by the end of that year. Commanding the rearguard of the fleet at this time was another young officer who was to have a close association with Gibraltar over the next few years, Horatio Nelson. In February 1797, however, Admiral Jervis won a crushing victory against a superior Spanish fleet at Cape St Vincent, after which Spain suffered a series of humiliating defeats until a truce was signed at Amiens in 1802. Britain reacquired Minorca in 1798 in a bloodless coup mounted in great secrecy from Gibraltar, but relinquished it finally in 1802 having by then taken control of Malta. With Gibraltar and Malta, Britain was now well placed to control both ends of the Mediterranean, and they remained the fulcrum of operations in this theatre until well after the Second World War.

Gibraltar was thriving throughout this period as a port where few questions were asked regarding the origin or destination of goods. The civilian population, enhanced by immigrants particularly from Genoa where the men were fleeing from conscription in Napoleon's armies, increased rapidly to about 8000 by 1797. A contemporary report said the town 'contains some very excellent houses . . . There is one principal street leading from South Port to Water Port [now Main Street]. All the others are extremely small and narrow. A very good road skirted with trees and parallel to which runs the aqueduct reaches from South Port to that part of Gibraltar called "the South" where there are barracks and an extensive naval hospital. These, with several other buildings, form what may be termed a second town'. It is clear that by the turn of the century the present plan of the city was well established.

Commercial trade was much enhanced by the greater interest now shown in the East Indies after the loss of the Americas. Whilst the Royal Navy was reluctant to use the Bay of Gibraltar as a permanent naval base, the port was in constant use for the refitting and revictualling of ships. Nelson sailed from Gibraltar in HMS *Vanguard* in 1798 on the historic sortie that was to culminate in the destruction of Napoleon's fleet at the Battle of the Nile on 1st August. Jervis, now Lord St Vincent, set up his main headquarters in Gibraltar, taking up residence in St Vincent House in Rosia Bay. The focal point of naval activity moved from the restricted confines of the Water Port to new victualling yards near Rosia Bay and the foundations were laid for the naval dockyard which has continued to dominate the city until very recent times.

But whilst the sailors were unceasingly busy, the unruly behaviour of the underemployed soldiers was a continuing trial. Vincent was unimpressed, as were most of the town's trades people (except for the 90 innkeepers), and in 1798 a shadowy plot was uncovered to hand Gibraltar over to Spain. It appears to have involved Manuel Godoy, Charles IV's incompetent Chief Minister, Jews in Paris and Gibraltar, and recalcitrant Irish officers in the garrison. The plot leaked out, however, and no fewer than 1100 civilians were expelled from Gibraltar for complicity in the conspiracy. Whilst O'Hara was confident that he had quelled the plotting, the Government in London were far less sanguine and decided that discipline in the garrison needed a good shakeup. They were undoubtedly right, but it was not until O'Hara died in 1801 that they were able to put in a stern disciplinarian in Prince Edward, Duke of Kent, fourth legitimate son of George III.

In the meantime, naval action had moved much closer to home when 3 French ships sought refuge in Algeciras in July 1801. Watched by a grandstand of expectant spectators on both sides, Admiral Sir James de Saumarez with 6 ships of the line entered the bay to confront them, but the French ships were protected by the Spanish shore batteries and the first encounter ended in disarray and damage. Soon another French and 5 Spanish vessels joined them in the bay whilst Saumarez's ships were still being repaired in the Gibraltar dockyard. The combined force which contained two ships of 112 guns, the *Real Carlos* and the *San Hermenegildo*, made a dash for freedom on the 12th of July, hotly pursued by HMS *Superb*. In the darkness the much smaller and faster *Superb* caught up with the Spanish ships and sailed between them, firing a broadside into each. In the ensuing confusion the two 112-gun ships engaged each other, collided, burst into flames and sank with the loss of about 1700 lives. The heroic efforts of the Gibraltar dockyard to repair the ships against the clock received a warm commendation from Lord St Vincent, now back in London as First Sea Lord.

On taking up his post the Duke of Kent admirably carried out the Government's intentions, imposing a draconian discipline, the like of which the garrison had never seen before. He placed all but three of the wine shops out of bounds to soldiers and opened 'Canteens' selling weak beer brewed by the British Army Brewery. He also imposed a working day of dawn to half past four in the afternoon: it was a diet of drill, drill and drill again – officers and soldiers alike. Such was the harshness of the new broom that a group of soldiers from the Royal Scots plotted to kill the Duke on Christmas Eve 1802. Unfortunately they took drink first, which was inevitably still available on the black market, and were easily dispersed by the stone-cold sober 54th Regiment (later the Devon and Dorsets). On Boxing Day it was the turn of the 25th Regiment (Scottish Borderers) to get drunk and hatch their own plot, again dispersed by the loyal Devon and Dorsets, this time with death and injury. At the subsequent courts martial, 12 men were sentenced to death and 2 to 1000 lashes. All but three of the death sentences were commuted by the Duke of Kent to transportation. The mutiny had been quelled, but the Government recalled the Duke who was refused a formal inquiry. He retained his title as Governor and salary in absentia for the next seventeen years, but was not allowed to set foot again on the Rock. Today it would doubtless be labelled as a cover-up. Nevertheless, discipline rarely again descended to the depths it had reached during O'Hara's flamboyant but erratic regime.

*   *   *

The fragile truce with France broke down on 17th May 1803. Britain's war aims were limited – the Royal Navy would control the high seas whilst Napoleon would be allowed a more or less free hand on the continent. In pursuit of this policy, Nelson returned to Gibraltar in June as Commander-in-Chief of

Admiral Collingwood's famous message after Trafalgar is remembered in the Trafalgar Cemetery near the South Port Gate.

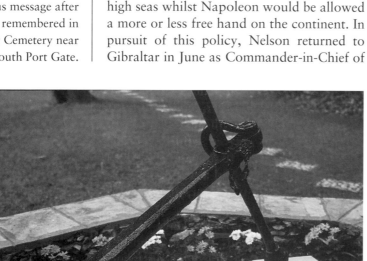

the Mediterranean. He was now flying his flag in the *Victory* and set sail almost immediately to blockade Toulon. Although Spain nominally remained neutral, the atmosphere was generally hostile even though the border remained open for a time.

In 1804 another and more insidious scourge hit Gibraltar. A plague of fever was sweeping southern Spain and the border was closed in a vain attempt to prevent it reaching Gibraltar. It is generally believed now that it was yellow fever which may have come with imported goods from the West Indies, but there may also have been a concurrent outbreak of typhus or typhoid. Whatever the cause, its effects were devastating once it took hold in the confined spaces of Gibraltar. When the epidemic faded away in early 1805 it was estimated that nearly 6000 people had died including 1082 soldiers of the garrison. Even so this left a population of about 9000, which was still larger than that remaining at the end of the Great Siege.

Spain entered the war whilst the fever was still raging, forcing Nelson to impose a blockade of Cadiz and Cartagena as well as Toulon. Napoleon's strategy was to invade England after he had swept the Channel clear of the Royal Navy and he assembled 160,000 troops on the cliffs above Boulogne. In March Admiral Villeneuve slipped unobserved out of Toulon with 11 ships, but was spotted as he made passage through the Strait. The French plan was for the Toulon fleet to join with the French and Spanish Atlantic fleets in the West Indies before sweeping down on the Gulf Stream into the Channel. Nelson, who was in the Mediterranean at the time, was almost a month behind Villeneuve when he eventually reached Gibraltar.

After a fruitless pursuit across the Atlantic, Nelson returned to Gibraltar in July to revictual and gather the latest intelligence. Hearing nothing of value, he returned to England for further consultations with the Admiralty. Villeneuve had also had his problems and, failing to join up with the rest of the French fleet, was unable to make directly for the Channel. It was Admiral Collingwood who made the first sighting of the French fleet as it was entering Cadiz. As soon as this vital information was relayed to England, Nelson immediately set sail from

Although commemorating
the great battle, the
Trafalgar Cemetery actually
contains more victims of the
yellow fever which struck
the town in 1804.

Portsmouth in the *Victory*, assembled his force over the horizon off Cadiz, and waited. Villeneuve left Cadiz on the 21st of October and by the evening his ships had been totally routed off Cape Trafalgar in the most celebrated action in British naval history. The garrison in Gibraltar was well aware of what was afoot, and on the 23rd a civilian boat arrived with the historic message from Collingwood:

'Yesterday a battle was fought...and a victory gained which will stand recorded as one of the most brilliant and decisive that ever distinguished the British Navy... Our loss has been great...but what is irreparable...is the death of the Noble Commander-in-Chief who died in the arms of Victory.'

It was not until a week after the battle that the *Victory* arrived back in Gibraltar. It was a sorry sight, dismasted and under tow by the *Neptune*, and bearing Nelson's body in a cask of brandy. It was suggested that the body should be taken back to England in another ship, but this was anathema to the crew and eventually the *Victory* departed on November 3rd under a jury rig to limp back to Spithead. Neither the French nor Spanish fleet was to offer a serious challenge to the Royal Navy again.

Local relations between the garrison and their neighbours in Andalusia remained surprisingly cordial during the war and it was evident that the latter heartily distrusted their French allies. Nearly 5000 Spanish prisoners from Trafalgar were shipped to Gibraltar and soon exchanged with the

One of the gravestones in
the Trafalgar Cemetery.

The battered HMS *Victory* bearing Nelson's body was anchored in the delightful Rosia Bay after Trafalgar whilst it was prepared for its return to England.

British sailors held in Cadiz. This attitude was in stark contrast to the view from Madrid which remained hostile, and the Lieutenant Governor, General Henry Fox, was alive to rumours of another Spanish attempt to capture the Rock. Their gun boats were still active against unprotected merchant shipping in the bay. But Fox was on good terms with General Castanos, the commander of Spanish troops in the Campo, and the two officers were reported as regularly dining together. When a British patrol was captured near the Devil's Tower, it was returned the following day with apologies from the general for the over-zealous conduct of his subordinates. This local rapprochement was to bear fruit when the situation changed dramatically in 1807. It was around this time that the racecourse, of which we shall hear more in due course, was established on the so-called 'neutral ground' on the isthmus.

*   *   *

After the excitement of Trafalgar, Gibraltar settled down to a relatively peaceful and prosperous existence for a year or two. Although the major threat had evaporated, the French and Spanish fleets still had to be watched in their havens of Toulon, Cadiz and Cartagena, and this led to furious activity in the naval dockyard as ships returned for routine repair and resupply. The civil port also did well as British and colonial goods were transferred to neutral ships, without too many questions being asked, in efforts to breach the blockade which Napoleon had imposed against British goods across Europe. Known as the 'Continental System', it had become the main component of Napoleon's policy to counter the Royal Navy's supremacy on the high seas. The 'System' was more effective than the British Government cared to admit and Gibraltar was a valuable break in the chain.

The military establishment at Gibraltar was now 8 regiments of infantry and 7 companies of artillery who were quartered all over the peninsula. Whilst discipline had improved after the brutal but effective regime of the Duke of Kent, the garrison was still generally underemployed and thus prone to turn to the sublimities of alcohol. One Fortress Order reads: 'The Lieut Governor is much shocked at the shameful drunkenness that has prevailed in the Garrison for these last two days... he cannot allow himself to suppose that British soldiers can be so absurd and unlike men that they cannot have money in their pockets without making a bad use of it'. Well, General Fox soon overcame his surprise and imposed a harsh regime of trial and correction. A punishment of hundreds of lashes was regularly awarded and promptly enforced. Hard labour, called a period of 'blackstrap work' after a brand of cheap wine, was another penalty regularly imposed. The term is still recalled by Blackstrap Cove south of Catalan Bay.

*   *   *

The war moved closer to Gibraltar again after November 1807 when French and Spanish regiments were directed against Portugal which remained Britain's sole ally on the continent of Europe. But Napoleon had a more sinister reason for moving into Spain. Charles IV was deposed by his own militant subjects and both he and his son, Ferdinand VII, were persuaded to meet Napoleon at Bayonne where they both tamely abdicated their claims to the throne of Spain. Their successor was Napoleon's brother, Joseph, then King of Naples. Meanwhile Marshal Murat occupied Madrid and the uneasy alliance between Spain and France broke down into insurrection and eventually open warfare.

The Peninsular War was the beginning of the end for Napoleon's hegemony in Europe; for whilst it was not in itself decisive, it sapped the strength of his Empire and emasculated his subsequent attempt to subdue Russia in 1812. It also led to a period lasting more than a hundred years when Spain and Britain were on more congenial terms, if never exactly intimate, with a consequential reduction in the tension over Gibraltar. Britain made its first move to recover Portugal at the beginning of 1808 when Sir John Moore arrived at Gibraltar with 10,000 troops from Sicily: he was to be joined by another 4000 under General Spencer from England. This would have placed a tremendous strain on the resources of Gibraltar, but in the event the forces did not join up and Moore had already left for Portugal by the time Spencer arrived. General Sir Hew Dalrymple, an amiable but generally ineffective officer who well merited the nickname of 'Dowager', took over from the energetic Fox as the Lieutenant Governor.

The good relationship with the Spanish around Gibraltar now developed by the hour. General Castanos even made tentative approaches at one stage to see whether the Spanish King would be welcome in Gibraltar if he had to flee Spain, although unbeknown to him Ferdinand had already been incarcerated in France with his father. As well as discussions on a concerted strategy, money, clothes and arms began to flow to the self-appointed juntas which were mushrooming in Andalusia. Revolt broke out into the open with the Madrid rising of the 2nd of May 1808, brutally suppressed by Murat, and so magnificently commemorated in two paintings by Goya in the Prado.

Although the rising in central Spain soon suffered a calamitous setback at Rioseco with 20,000 Spanish dead, the emotion generated in the southern part of the country was fuelled by the defeat of General Dupont at Bailen in July when he was encircled by a much larger force under Castanos. It was the first defeat suffered by Napoleon's marshals since Abercrombie's victory at Alexandria in 1801. Paradoxically it did not improve cooperation between the British and Spanish forces as the latter began to think themselves invincible, and they had to suffer a number of humiliating setbacks before Wellington could persuade them that a joint and concerted effort might offer the best chance of success.

In November 1808 Napoleon intervened personally, despairing of the faltering progress of his marshals in subduing Spain. He soon defeated Castanos and chased Sir John Moore's army out of Galicia after the celebrated rearguard action at Corunna in which Moore was killed. Andalusia was ignored in this attempt to subdue the country and again in 1809 when most of the fighting took place in Portugal. However, such was the degree of trust in this area that British engineers helped to demolish the

Spanish Lines in February 1810. A large crowd gathered on the Rock to watch the detonations under the forts of St Philip and St Barbara and some of the stones were used for buildings in Gibraltar: the London Bar in Governor's Parade is a typical example. One wonders whether consideration was ever given to 'turning the forts around' to act as a first line of defence for Gibraltar.

Joseph Bonaparte, known to the Spanish as King Pepe, had by now turned his attention to the south. Seville, Jerez and Ronda quickly fell to the advancing armies under Marshals Soult and Victor and it looked as though Gibraltar might soon be facing its fifteenth siege. The demolition of the Spanish Lines was completed in the nick of time, for an advance French guard reached San Roque a few days later and many of the townspeople fled to sanctuary in Gibraltar. Only Cadiz, Tarifa and Gibraltar of the main towns in the area remained in Spanish or British hands.

A surprisingly relaxed view seems to have been taken in Gibraltar of the approach of the French. A new and energetic Lieutenant Governor, General Colin Campbell, was generous in support of the Spanish cause: he supplied garrisons for Ceuta and Tarifa to allow Spanish troops to pursue offensive operations and dispatched engineering and artillery specialists as well as infantry to assist in the defence of Cadiz. One of the more consistent features of the Napoleonic period was the much greater degree of cooperation and understanding which existed between successive governors and their Spanish counterparts than was ever achieved by Wellington who found great difficulty in identifying with his Spanish colleagues. In fact Campbell's confidence was well founded, for Marshal Soult was too experienced a campaigner to waste resources on an apparently impregnable fortress and concentrated instead on subduing Cadiz and Granada. The former was besieged for two and half years but never looked like succumbing to half hearted French attacks.

Campbell was also active nearer home. In May he sent additional troops to Tarifa to forestall a French attack which was driven off and then retired from the field when it realised it was facing a British garrison. And in October he mounted an amphibious assault on the old Moorish castle at Fuengirola to the south of Malaga. This was a mixed force of 1400 British, Spanish and Hanoverian troops under the command of Major General Lord Blayney. The initial landing was successful, but the French garrison obstinately refused to surrender to a superior force. A second landing closer to the castle on an exposed beach was repulsed and eventually the whole force was withdrawn in ignominy. It was a badly planned venture, poorly led and ill equipped: it was followed by a number of courts martial as the cap of responsibility was hurriedly passed around.

In March 1811 three of the Gibraltar regiments were again involved, this time in the celebrated battle of Barrosa. At the instigation of Campbell and General Thomas Graham, the British commander in Cadiz, the Spanish were persuaded to mount an operation to relieve the port. The plan was for Graham to sail round to Tarifa to mount a flanking attack on the French whilst the Spanish sallied forth from the town itself. Against Wellington's directive to the contrary, the overall command of the operation was taken by the Spanish General Manuel La Pena. The operation started to fall apart from the very beginning when strong winds forced Graham all the way round into the Bay of Gibraltar. The troops were thus somewhat weary when they eventually joined up with La Pena who made the extraordinary decision to retire into Cadiz. Marshal Victor could not believe his luck as he watched the straggling column head along the beach with the British contingent in the rear guarding the ammunition and the baggage train. The British were tramping through a pinewood below the Barrosa ridge when they were fallen upon by two divisions. Graham recognised immediately that the key to the battle lay in the command of the Barrosa ridge on which the French already had a presence. He therefore ordered his light troops to storm the ridge to give him time to deploy his main force. Although losing half their number, they succeeded gloriously, providing that vital breathing space Graham needed to bring his infantry into line. The subsequent march to the ridge was protracted and bloody, but such was the accuracy and ferocity of the British fire that the French eventually retreated. Victor suffered over 3000 casualties to the 1200 lost by Graham. La Pena had made no effort to come to the aid of the British, or even to pursue the French as they fled from the field. It was a battle that should never have happened, at least on these terms, but it was one of the more celebrated and spectacular successes of the Peninsular campaign. The battlefield today is a golf course on the Costa de la Luz.

In 1811 the French again struck south as far as San Roque in vain pursuit of General Francisco Ballesteros who was conducting a successful guerilla campaign across Andalusia. General Godinot from Ronda, however, took one look at Gibraltar to where Ballesteros had retired and decided to take his 10,000 troops elsewhere. He was castigated for his failure by Soult and promptly committed suicide. Soult's main objective in 1811 was to capture Tarifa, but

The Duke of Wellington is commemorated by this bust in the Alameda Gardens, presented by HM Storeship *Weymouth* and erected in 1820.

it was not until December that General Laval appeared before the gates. Tarifa was dependent for its defence upon its old and dilapidated Moorish castle which still stands more or less intact today. Campbell had sent an engineer and an artillery expert to survey the walls, but there was little they could do in the time available to refurbish the crumbling structure. They decided therefore that the only chance of success was to trick the French into attacking one of the gates which, because of its constricted entrance, could be strongly defended. Laval took the bait and the wall adjacent to the defended gateway soon collapsed, as expected, to the French siege train. However, despite their plan apparently falling into place, the British commander, Colonel Skerrett, now suffered cold feet and advocated abandoning the town. The Spanish commander and other British officers were fortunately opposed to this undeniably craven course of action, and General Campbell when he heard of it was furious and ordered the removal of the boats in which they might have made their escape. After an appallingly wet and cold night, two long and bedraggled French columns headed for the breach, now 60 feet wide, which was manned by the Spanish. As they hesitated by the gap they were struck in the flank by a concentrated fusillade from Gough's 87th Foot. It was sufficient to deter the already demoralised French infantry and they retired to their sodden camp. After a few more days of heavy rain Laval packed up and retreated, leaving his spiked guns in the camp. British casualties were negligible.

In 1812 Napoleon concentrated his attention on Russia and the campaign in Spain withered towards a close. Soult intended to have another try at capturing Tarifa, but in July Wellington's victory at Salamanca forced him to abandon southern Spain altogether. In the same month a final raiding force of 5000 French reached San Roque, took one last wistful look at the Rock, and departed. In August the siege of Cadiz was lifted and the French abandoned Seville. Wellington marched imperiously towards the Pyrenees as Napoleon suffered defeat and humiliation in Russia. On the 18th of June 1815 Napoleon's dream ended on the fields of Waterloo. The glory of the Peninsular campaign is rightly vested in England's greatest soldier and his Army of Portugal, but Gibraltar had played a small but significant role in supporting the southern flank of Wellington's vast domain. In doing so, General Campbell and his predecessors played a valuable part in oiling the often prickly relationship with the Spanish, thereby contributing to the hundred years of peace and relative prosperity that Gibraltar was about to enjoy.

9 FROM FORTRESS ROCK TO CROWN COLONY 1815–99

FOR THIRTY FIVE YEARS up to 1813 Gibraltar had been living in the shadow of war. In the Great Siege it was of course in the very forefront of hostilities, but until Wellington finally expelled the French from Spain in 1813, Gibraltar was first and foremost a military fortress, never very far from the roll of drums and the roar of cannon. It was seen as such by the authorities in London as much as it was the *raison d'être* of the Governor and his garrison: it was as a military pawn that the British Government from time to time had sought to return it to Spain in exchange for some real or perceived military or political advantage. The next hundred years were rather different. The fortifications were by no means neglected, indeed the converse is more accurate, but not once was Gibraltar directly threatened by force in this period and the needs of a military garrison increasingly began to conflict with a civilian community which had acquired an impulse and thrust of its own. The Government in London perhaps barely comprehended this transition, but it was nevertheless real and it posed problems and dilemmas throughout the nineteenth century which were sometimes not recognised and frequently went unresolved.

In trying to impose some order and continuity into a complex period, I shall look at Gibraltar after 1815 up to the end of the century under three main headings. Firstly, I shall examine the evolution of the town as a civic entity, to see how the civilian population developed in social and economic terms – how it achieved an identity of its own separate from that of the military fortress. Secondly, I look at Gibraltar's relations with Spain, for this had dominated the political scenario since 1704 and continued to do so, albeit in a much lower key and a rather different way. Finally I shall consider the development of Gibraltar as a military fortress and a naval base. It is, of course, impossible to separate entirely these three strands which interweave throughout this period, but I hope my approach gains sufficiently in simplicity and coherence to justify departure from the chronological narrative used so far.

*   *   *

The civilian population of Gibraltar had expanded rapidly throughout the Napoleonic wars until in 1815, despite periodic outbreaks of the fever, it stood at slightly over 10,000. It had a cosmopolitan composition. The most numerous, although their proportion was falling, were the Genoese who still constituted about a third of the total. But there had been a considerable influx of Spaniards and particularly Portuguese as a consequence of the war. The Jews, mostly of Moroccan origin, were prominent in trade and commerce. Those of British origin formed the smallest of the major groups – about one seventh of the population. The civilian population increased steadily until 1830 when it stood at about 17,000, after which it remained fairly stable until the end of the century. More significant than mere numbers, however, was that as the years passed the population became more settled and static. Whereas at the beginning of the century the majority were alien workers, mainly providing services for the military, by the end of the period nearly ninety per cent of the total were Gibraltar-born citizens. Whilst many of them still worked for the military, Gibraltar was their family home and their official nationality was British.

The economy suffered inevitable decline immediately after the war; naval activity decreased significantly, and no longer were there prizes to be sold at a quick profit or

After the devastation of the Great Siege, the layout of Gibraltar began to take its present form. This is part of the old town below the castle.

Spanish troops to be supplied with arms and clothing. But the recession was short lived, for Napoleon's 'Continental System' stimulated an expertise in shipping agency and brokerage which had gained the confidence of British merchants and manufacturers. There soon developed what would now be known as a flourishing import/export trade as Gibraltar became a distribution point for British goods destined for Spain, Morocco and other ports in the western Mediterranean. Of even more importance was that Gibraltar began to act as a commercial intermediary between Spain and her querulous colonies in South America. A less legitimate trade which also recommended, at first on a minor scale, was the smuggling into Spain of a variety of goods, particularly tobacco. In time this was to become a major occupation but, because it was one of the main sources of contention between Britain and Spain, it will be considered in detail later in the chapter.

In 1815 the population was generally living in congested and squalid conditions. The town had to be almost entirely rebuilt after the Great Siege, but in those troubled times no effort was made to improve upon the maze of narrow and haphazard streets which had characterised the old Gibraltar. In fact, this is not surprising as there was little space available to replicate the elegance in town planning which distinguished new building in 18th-century Britain. In practice Gibraltar had grown, for different reasons, in similar fashion to a Victorian industrial town except that in Gibraltar the wealthy lived cheek by jowl with the poor, for there was no space for the rich entrepreneur to establish his country seat far away from the congestion and squalor. Even so many travellers in the first half of the century commented on the picturesque and colourful aspect of cosmopolitan Gibraltar. It had become fashionable to visit Gibraltar: politicians, poets, pamphleteers and the merely curious passed through in numbers throughout the nineteenth century, recording their impressions in prose and verse.

Nevertheless, improvements there had to be, for the city was regularly hit by outbreaks of the fever or cholera. In 1828, for example, the malignant fever killed 1667, over ten per cent of the population, and of course the garrison was by no means immune from these outbreaks even though they were quartered on the isthmus, on the more open ground of Windmill Hill, or sometimes on ships in the bay. Gibraltar was fortunate in its first Commander after the end of the war. Lieutenant General Sir George Don was theoretically only the Lieutenant Governor as the Duke of Kent remained the nominal Governor until his death in 1820 when he was replaced by General John Pitt, Earl of Chatham. He too, however, was generally absent and Don in effect remained in sole charge almost until his death in 1832. Don was probably the first who saw his role as something more than just the commander of a military garrison. He made improvements in sanitation, water supply, paving and lighting, but a real leap forward in these areas had to wait for the end of the century. He also built the first hospital for the civilian population and laid out the Alameda Gardens. The Anglican Cathedral of the Holy Trinity was built in 1825 and General Don is commemorated by a memorial in the south wall. Indeed, it was during this period that Gibraltar began to take on the general aspect recognisable today.

The increasing prosperity of the civilian elite inevitably generated a desire to have a greater say in the communal life of the town. The Garrison Library, which still exists today in one of Gibraltar's most elegant buildings on Governor's Parade, had become the social and intellectual hub of the garrison. But the military was still a largely self-sufficient establishment, jealous of its privileges, and reluctant to allow the civilians to participate. The latter set up, therefore, their own equivalent institution called the Exchange and Commercial Library. The Committee of this organization, made up of the most eminent men of the town, gradually assumed an unofficial but nevertheless influential voice in civil and commercial affairs which was recognised by most governors until well into the twentieth century. They established a close working relationship with

An austere classical style was adopted for these officers' quarters near Governor's Parade.

The soldiers' quarters at the rear of the King's Bastion were rather more spartan in design.

Shipping in the bay in the 1860s. (Garrison Library, Gibraltar)

the industrial heartland of England, particularly with the Manchester Chamber of Commerce, and even flexed their muscles sufficiently to send delegations to London to present their case against the rulings of the Governor, notably over the question of title to property and later on the implications of attempts to eradicate smuggling. The latter must have required tactful handling in Westminster, perhaps less so in Manchester which had a more realistic approach to local customs.

The cultural life of the town evolved alongside the commercial development. The Royal Gibraltar Yacht Club was founded in 1829, a Jockey Club was formed in conjunction with the racecourse on the isthmus and a theatre was opened by the Duke of Ostrogothia in 1847. The *Gibraltar Chronicle*, still going strong today, had already reached the presses in 1801 and provided a vital function in informing and uniting the civilian community.

A most significant event occurred in 1830 when Gibraltar formally became a Crown Colony and jurisdiction was transferred from the War Office to the Colonial Office. The law in Gibraltar had evolved in a partic-

ularly haphazard way, being at first dependent on Spanish law before the English system was adopted after 1740. The first civil judge was not appointed until 1817, but a Supreme Court was established in 1830 and henceforth the legal system was developed along English lines with appeal to the Privy Council rather than to the Governor. A police force was set up, also in 1830, only one year after the creation of the Metropolitan Police, the first formalised force in Britain. However, the Gibraltar model was rather more of a coordinating agency – it had no constables, only sergeants, in the initial stages – and the enforcement of order within the city remained firmly in the hands of the military. Eventually it developed a more familiar role and the image of the 'English bobby' is of course one of the first aspects of Gibraltar upon which the tourist remarks today.

The post-war boom began to recede after 1830 as the strategic emphasis moved towards the eastern end of the Mediterranean where the Ottoman Empire was in terminal decline. Malta was the main beneficiary of this strategic shift as a consequence of its ideal location in the central basin of the Mediterranean opposite Sicily. Malta also had an immeasurably better natural harbour – always one of the main limitations of Gibraltar in the days of sail. The naval dockyard was run down to a care and maintenance basis and much of the transhipment trade also moved to Valetta. Most of the Spanish colonies were now independent and traded directly with Spain, removing another profitable source of income. The advent of the steam ship – first seen in Gibraltar in 1823 – led to the development of the port as a coaling station, but this barely compensated for the decline in the import/export trade. There was a small surge of activity during the Crimean War (1854-56), but of longer term significance was the opening of the Suez Canal in 1869. This brought a steady increase in the number of ships coaling in Gibraltar and corresponding benefits to the commercial life of the city. Even so, economic activity rather staggered along in a trough until the end of the century which only the threat of war could alleviate.

Governors of Gibraltar throughout the nineteenth century were always British generals, usually with a distinguished background, but of varying energy and expertise. Few made such an impression as Sir George Don whose post of Lieutenant Governor was abolished after 1839, but most were honest and, with one or two notable exceptions, worked harmoniously with the Exchange and Commercial Library. Some were colourful characters, none more so than General Sir Robert Wilson (1842-48). Wilson had a diverse military and political career, but achieved notoriety in 1821 for his part in allowing the funeral of Queen Caroline to be turned into a public demonstration of animosity against her husband George IV, for which he was dismissed the army. Labelled a 'coxcomb' by Castlereagh and a 'madman' by the future prime minister, Lord Aberdeen, it was the latter who was nevertheless instrumental in obtaining his appointment to Gibraltar. His governorship appears to have been less controversial than his early career. As we shall see, acrimony where it existed usually revolved around the issue of smuggling which became the main feature of the economy in the second half of the century.

The recession in legitimate trading continued throughout the nineteenth century and unemployment increased – it was recorded at nearly 8000 in 1871, although this seems an unbelievably high figure given the size of the population. Industry, apart from the rolling of tobacco for the smuggling trade, was very small-scale. Entrepreneurs in both the tobacco and the coaling trade did well enough, but the standard of life for the majority of the population was little better than that in an industrial town in England of the same period. There was no proper sewage system until work tentatively started in the 1870s and the unhygienic lodgings – crowded together within little more than a square mile – were a constant source of disease. The provision of a more adequate sanitation system marked a significant shift in the relationship between Britain and Gibraltar, for it was partly paid for by the imposition of a duty on imported wines and spirits. No longer would the total cost of maintaining the city as well as the garrison fall on the British taxpayer. Water, at least of a good quality, was also scarce and it was not until early in the next century that a reliable supply was provided. Education on the other hand was of an unusually high standard for the Victorian era, for there was not the same opportunity, so detrimental in England, to force children into the factories and mines.

Although Gibraltar was hardly booming economically in the second half of the nineteenth century, conditions were still generally better than in any of the surrounding countries at the western end of the Mediterranean, particularly in Andalusia. There was thus no shortage of immigrant labour to undertake work uncongenial to Gibraltarians. This influx, however, not only led to racial tensions, but also put unacceptable pressure on living space. Steps were taken by successive governors after 1870 to curtail the rights of aliens, and residence permits were required by all those not born in Gibraltar, including British subjects who wished to work and live in the colony. A distinction was created which in effect gave all Gibraltar-born residents a British passport and imposed quite severe restrictions on others. The ramifications of these developments still persist today with the claims for some form of recognition for the Moroccan work force which has largely replaced the Spanish in the more menial jobs.

In some respects the nineteenth century may perhaps be seen as a static period for Gibraltar. Certainly the economy reached a plateau in the first third of the century and then generally stagnated. The Gibraltarian, having experienced a period of prosperity after the war, was reluctant to adapt to the changing conditions after 1840. A good living, even a fortune, was made in some limited areas such as the coaling of the new steamships, but the Gibraltar workman in general was less flexible, and so the low-paid jobs, rather like in Britain after 1945, tended to go to immigrant workers who would have been even lower-paid in their home environments. Indeed such was the reluctance of many Gibraltarians to undertake manual labour that much of the work in the dockyard and on the fortifications was undertaken by Spaniards who travelled daily from a shanty town in La Linea, by convicts imported from England and by immigrants from Malta. Domestic service was also largely in the hands of Spanish women, perhaps one of the reasons why Gibraltar men often took a Spanish wife! Such was the close relationship with Spain that the Spanish language is still the more normal mode of communication for most Gibraltarians today.

On the other hand, the long period of peace after 1815 allowed to some extent an orderly transition towards a civilian community no longer totally dependent on a military garrison. The town began to assume its present shape with an accompanying growth in civic pride reflected in the individually designed buildings and public gardens. The more prosperous inhabitants began to take a greater individual interest in their environment and economic welfare, and looked to the British Government, usually in vain, for a greater share of the responsibility for run-

Casemates Square and the Old Mole in the 1860s. (Garrison Library, Gibraltar)

ning their own affairs. But this had to wait until the next century, for fundamentally Gibraltar ended the nineteenth as it had begun – first and foremost a military garrison controlled by a military governor.

*   *   *

For more than one hundred years after 1704 Spain had maintained an unremitting hostility to the British occupation of Gibraltar. Whilst the French occupation of Spain in 1808 had stimulated an unprecedented degree of cooperation between the two countries in a common cause, it had not erased the underlying resentment that Gibraltar had been extorted from Spain under duress. But the Spain of the nineteenth century was but a shadow of the past. Torn apart by faction, the Carlist civil wars, Catalan and Basque nationalism, revolution and recurring military coups, the country was so unstable that it was quite incapable of mounting any sustained pressure on Britain to relinquish Gibraltar. Indeed, Gibraltar played no part in the mainstream of Spanish politics throughout this period: in Raymond Carr's monumental history of Spain in the nineteenth century, not once is the dispute considered worthy of mention.

Nevertheless, there were numerous niggling little incidents which in more stable times might have again brought the issue into the forefront, and many of these were connected with smuggling. In the wars with Napoleon the imposition of the 'Continental System' had given a quasi legality to smuggling and fostered an attitude of mind among Gibraltarians and Spaniards alike which persisted into the peace which followed. Furthermore, the chains of communication which had been carefully constructed to bring arms and supplies to the Spanish 'freedom fighters' under the eyes of the French intelligence system was the ideal vehicle for less legitimate trade in the post-war years. Many of the guerilla groups in Andalusia remained in existence not only because they opposed the reactionary government of the reinstated Ferdinand VII, but because there was no work available for them in the poor and non-industrialised south. Such groups provided the ideal network for disseminating into Spain the flow of goods which the free trading nations of Europe and the New World were only too happy to supply.

Ferdinand would have liked to create a formal sealed border by rebuilding the Spanish Lines, but he had neither the political will nor the financial resources required, and so contented himself with building customs posts. But the customs officers were easily bribed and did little to stem the flow of merchandise. Furthermore, there was some trade in the opposite direction, for many of Gibraltar's civilian inhabitants had been settled in huts on the isthmus to escape the epidemic of 1814 and were supplied from the hinterland. Troops had also been quartered on the isthmus since 1812: Britain was steadily taking prescriptive rights over the neutral ground which has remained a source of contention ever since.

The concept of the neutral zone is complex and controversial, but certainly in Spanish eyes the British took a further slice out of it in 1854. Another outbreak of yellow fever forced the construction of barracks on the isthmus, an arrangement agreed with the local Spanish commander as it had been in 1814. But this time after the outbreak was over the garrison did not remove its guardposts from the farthest extent of the new building – about 600 yards from the old Spanish Lines. Spain was told officially that this was British territory: there was little that a severely weakened Spain could do other than make a verbal protest.

As the effects of the economic recession began to hit Gibraltar after 1830 the flow of illegal goods into Spain became a flood. Hardware, luxury goods and cotton all found their way into the hands of the wealthier capitalists of the large cities, but the staple of the smuggling industry was tobacco. At one time it was calculated that one ton of tobacco was imported into Gibraltar for every male adult in the town, and clearly the vast majority of this found its way into Spain. General Gardiner, although not perhaps the most impartial source, described it graphically:

'The human beings enter the Garrison in their natural sizes, but quit it swathed and swelled out with our cotton manufactures, and padded with tobacco, while the carriages and beasts, which come light and springy into the place, quit it scarcely able to drag or bear their burdens.'

It puts one in mind of the present day cross-channel trade from the supermarkets of Calais!

Not all the contraband was carried across the land border. Privateers, their boats still armed from the war years, loaded up with merchandise from the warehouses in Gibraltar and carried it to remote bays in Spain where they handed it over to Spanish smugglers. Many of the boats were manned by the Spaniards themselves. It might today have been thought a joint problem, but the 'laissez-faire' governments in Britain saw it as quite legitimate – it was considered Spain's responsibility to control the illegal traffic, or better still reduce duties to the extent that smuggling would no longer be considered profitable. Attempts by Spanish coastguard cutters to intercept the privateers merely revived arguments about territorial limits. In 1826 the Foreign Secretary, George Canning, reiterated the old criterion for British sovereignty as the area 'within the range of the guns of the Garrison'. But with shell replacing shot, a gun on the King's Bastion could now cover most of the bay, and such a definition could hardly be acceptable to Spain. In 1851 Madrid made an apparently conciliatory proposal to consider the isthmus to be neutral ground to be jointly policed and the northern part of the bay to be common waters. It was a chink in an otherwise intransigent position which was brusquely rejected by Lord Palmerston.

At least two governors tried to restrict the smuggling. Lieutenant General Sir Robert Gardiner (1848-55) was of a similar mould to his illustrious predecessor Sir George Eliott, albeit certainly not regarded with the same affection by Gibraltarians. He had often been associated with Gibraltar in a long and distinguished career before his appointment as Governor. He saw Gibraltar single-mindedly as a military fortress with scant regard for its development as a Crown Colony with a life of its own. He not only believed that smuggling was morally wrong, but it corrupted his soldiers who were not above accepting bribes to face the other way when illicit goods were passing through the guard posts. He inevitably came into conflict with the grandees in the Exchange Committee, some of whom were themselves merchants associated with the trade. The Committee took its grievances to the Manchester Chamber of Commerce, who were hardly disinterested as they supplied the majority of the manufactured goods which found their way across the border, and some Lancashire MPs raised the matter in the House of Commons. Gardiner was soon recalled, albeit on another issue: political sleaze is by no means only a twentieth century phenomenon.

In 1876 another distinguished and progressive soldier, General Lord Napier of Magdala, was appointed Governor and immediately sought to curb the tobacco trade. His proposed method, which apparently had Government support, was to impose a tax on tobacco and restrict its export from Gibraltar to boats over 100 tons, thus curbing the small privateer. He faced the same outcry as Gardiner twenty years before and this time it was the Disraeli administration which capitulated. There is no doubt that the Gibraltar economy would have suffered severely if tobacco smuggling had been eliminated, but its very dependence on this trade had distracted the Gibraltarian from more legitimate employment and increased reliance on immigrant labour.

Gibraltar had rather disappeared from public prominence in Britain until the temperature was raised again by General Gardiner after his dismissal in 1855. Doubtless he was carrying something of a chip on his shoulder, but his report, which became a best seller, fairly put the Spanish case and this stimulated some of the more articulate radicals and polemicists, notably Richard Congreve, Richard Cobden and John Bright, to campaign in favour of the return of the Rock to Spain.

From time to time Gibraltar gave refuge to Spanish politicians or revolutionaries temporarily out of favour. It might be going too far to claim that either the colonial administration or the Gibraltarians themselves sought to foment trouble with the Spanish authorities, but it was nevertheless another source of tension. In 1868, Juan Prim, a Catalan general who had taken refuge in Gibraltar, launched one of many military coups when he 'arrived [at Cadiz] from Gibraltar on a boat provided by Mr Bland the English shipping agent'. The rebellion which sought to establish an alternative monarchy was initially successful, but in practice only hastened the institution of a republic which was quick to retaliate by reinforcing the Spanish claim to Gibraltar.

But once again Spain was more absorbed by its own internal problems. The Republican Government was replaced by a constitutional monarchy in 1875 under Alfonso XII, but terrorist outrages and political assassinations still bedevilled the establishment of a stable regime. Relations between Britain and Spain remained at a low ebb, with the former increasingly involved in the scramble for Imperial possessions in Africa. This interest enhanced the importance of Gibraltar as a military base and led to further improvements of the naval dockyard.

Spain too had a colonial obsession of a rather different nature. There had long been separatist demands from Cuba whose economy was dependent on the sale of tobacco and sugar to the United States. This broke out into open rebellion in 1895 and in 1898 the United States declared war on Spain – on both sides it was a war of naked Imperialism which did little credit to either country. Lord Salisbury's Government openly supported the United States which led to further tension in Gibraltar. The Spanish Government began to install heavy weapons round the bay, ostensibly to prevent an American incursion, though that was hardly credible. Britain objected and notes passed between the two Governments in which Britain demanded that no fortifications, temporary or permanent, should be erected within 'a radius of seven geographical miles from the Moorish Castle' – a glance at the map will show that this would be totally unacceptable to Spain. The war in the Caribbean soon ended in a crushing defeat for Spain and at the Treaty of Paris she conceded Cuba, Puerto Rico and the Philippines. Spain had reached the nadir of her fortunes in the nineteenth century, but at least it enabled her to bring the war of words with London to a close by stating that it no longer needed to proceed with the new defences in Algeciras.

Despite these occasional and relatively minor tensions, Britain's relations with Spain throughout the nineteenth century remained on a generally stable and amicable level, and this was particularly apparent in the area around Gibraltar. Spain never relinquished her heartfelt claim on the Rock but was too weak and divided to do anything about it. Britain on the other hand was passing through her most prominent period of Imperial grandeur and self-esteem, and although a few lone voices were raised in Spain's interest on moral or intellectual grounds, the overwhelming emotion in the country was one of excitable self-confidence – it was the era of 'My country, right or wrong'.

*   *   *

The conclusion of the war in Spain in 1813 allowed Gibraltar to return to something like the normal life of a peacetime garrison. Better relations with Spain permitted the officers to indulge in their favoured sport of chasing the fox, eventually leading to the establishment of the famous Royal Calpe Hunt which became the focal point of polite society in the Colony. The ordinary soldiers returned to their favourite pastime of savouring the wine shops and taverns. The size of the garrison fluctuated throughout the rest of the century, but generally remained at its pre-siege figure of about 5000: in addition there would be a shifting population of dependants, although not as many as an army would carry in its tail today. As we have seen, the civilian population tended to grow apart from the military, exacerbated by the rotation of regiments through the colony. The marching and counter marching along the narrow streets and the painfully repetitive cry between guards of 'All's well' throughout the night must have become intensely irritating to the civilian inhabitants. The simmering tensions between the two groups reached their apogee during the governorship of General Gardiner in mid-century, but they were never far below the surface.

Although Gibraltar was never directly threatened during the rest of the nineteenth century, the risk of war by no means entirely disappeared. Tensions in Europe remained and particularly between Britain and France. The scramble for territory along the north African littoral was a constant source of turmoil and Britain and France came close to war in 1830 over Algiers. Pirates were still active in the area at this time and Britain herself had mounted a punitive raid on Algiers in 1816. France decided to take more assertive action in 1830, but this was seen by

Britain as an attempt to colonise the area and strongly resisted. The affair only petered out as a consequence of the revolution in France later in the year. Nevertheless, by 1840 the French had firmly established their position in Algiers and looked to have designs on Morocco and Tunis as well, the continued independence of which was considered a vital British interest. The climax of this confrontation was reached in 1844 when the French bombarded Tangier from which Gibraltar obtained much of its fresh produce. Sir Robert Peel's Government was incensed and the navy was placed on a war footing with the planned transfer of a major fleet to Gibraltar. The war fever faded away, however, when France signed a peace treaty with Morocco in September.

With turmoil on its doorstep, it is not surprising that the fortifications in Gibraltar were not neglected in the aftermath of the Peninsular War. The splendid Naval Victualling Yard just below Parson's Lodge Battery was completed in 1812 to the designs of an Italian architect, Giovanni Maria Rochetti, who did a lot of work in Gibraltar. Its unprepossessing outward appearance conceals monumental arched tunnels on the ground floor with aisled and cubicled storage areas above reminiscent of

Parson's Lodge Battery commands an imposing position near Rosia Bay.

an Arab mosque. It remained in use until 1984 and there are currently ambitious plans to develop it into a maritime museum and craft centre.

In 1830 it was reported that there were no fewer than 550 cannon in the Rock's batteries, about five times as many as at the start of the Great Siege. It was to extend the south mole and to work on the defences that convicts were imported from Britain after 1842: by 1860 there were over 700 of them although numbers started to decline after it was realised that Spanish labour was cheaper and more reliable. The Land Port defences remained much as before with medium-sized cannon along the Old Mole and in the North and Hesse's Bastions flanking the gate, and with batteries echeloned up the zig-zag Moorish wall to the castle. Above this were the guns aligned in Ince's tunnels. Substantial stone barracks to service these batteries were built in Casemates Square which still stand today. The passages which connected the various positions can

be traced amid the agglomeration of modern building. The Line Wall was strengthened and it is along this stretch that we can best see how the fortifications from several periods going back to Spanish times have been utilised in a formidable first line of defence – it would have looked far more impressive when it fronted directly onto the sea. The larger guns were set well back behind the wall in elevated and hidden batteries. In 1884, Gilbard's guide to Gibraltar recorded:

'Every spot from whence a gun can be brought to bear is occupied by cannon, which often times quaintly peep out of the most secluded nooks, among geraniums and flowering plants, while huge piles of shot and shell, some of enormous size, are stowed away in convenient places screened from enemy fire but all ready for use.'

Parson's Lodge Battery is the best place to explore a coastal battery today. This formidable bastion, standing on a narrow limestone dorsal between Rosia and Camp Bays, has witnessed the development of coast artillery over at least three centuries. It is known that a Moorish wall extended across the site towards Europa Point and that this was enhanced during the Spanish period. The battery is first recorded in British times as Parson's Lodge in 1761 although 4 guns were recorded at Rosea(sic) in 1720 and 19 in 1744. The name seems to be an irreverent reference to the nearby hermitage and chapel of St John the Green, both now disappeared. The site was extensively rebuilt in the 1840s to accommodate 8 guns and again in 1872 for three 18-ton 10-inch guns which had a range of 2.6 miles. These were positioned behind a sandwich of armour plate and teak universally known as 'Gibraltar Shields'. Searchlights were the next innovation at the end of the nineteenth century and in the Second World War the site was principally used for anti aircraft weapons and searchlights, and during the threat of German invasion for anti-tank guns as well. The military abandoned the battery in 1956 and work is now in hand under the auspices of the Gibraltar Heritage Trust to transform it into a major tourist attraction.

Nearby, to the north of Rosia Bay, is the so called 'Supergun' or '100-ton gun' in Napier Battery. Designed and manufactured in 1870 by the foremost arms manufacturer in Britain, Sir William Armstrong of Newcastle, it was better known at the time as the 'Rockbuster'. Four of these guns were built originally for the Italian Navy for their new battleships, but the British Government ordered four more, two each for Malta and Gibraltar. The gun weighs 100.2 tons and has a 17.72-inch muzzle loaded rifled barrel. Work started on the site of the old 2nd and 3rd Rosia Battery in 1878 and the guns were installed in 1883: the battery was named after the Governor, Lord Napier of Magdala. The guns were rotated on their mountings by hydraulic power and the 23-man gun crew took up to three hours to prepare each one for firing. But once aligned on the target they could each fire a 2000-lb shell every four minutes which was capable of

The 100-ton gun in Napier Battery.

penetrating 25 inches of wrought iron. The maximum range, however, was disappointing – only five miles – and the gun was not accurate outside of 6500 yards. Range finding was done from a dome higher up the Rock and relayed to the firing positions by telegraph, one of its earliest applications by the Army. The guns were never used in anger, but when practice firings were called, the inhabitants of Gibraltar were forewarned to open their windows and remove fragile ornaments from their shelves. One gun was destroyed when its barrel burst, but the other has been restored and the battery opened to the public.

This whole area around Rosia Bay, with its historical connections to Nelson is a site with tremendous potential for tourist development. Napier Battery is already restored and Parson's Lodge Battery well under way, and if a use for the Victualling Yard can be brought to fruition, it will become one of the most attractive corners of Gibraltar.

The naval headquarters and dockyard had been run down after the end of the Napoleonic wars, but naval ships continued to make regular use of the port. The area north from Rosia Bay and the Red Sands along the waterfront, past Ragged Staff Wharf, and seaward to the New and Old Moles was a bustling hive of activity as ships coaled and revictualled before setting off for distant parts of the Empire, or prepared for the last leg of their run home after perhaps years trading in foreign parts. Photographs of the Roadstead at this time show large numbers of both sail and steam, naval and commercial, sheltering within the bay. It was a collision in Gibraltar harbour in 1891 between HMS *Anson* and an immigrant ship on its way to Australia, the *Utopia*, that led to Gibraltar's greatest maritime tragedy with the loss of 551 civilian lives. But it was not until the last decade of the century that the naval dockyard really began to expand again and that part of the story belongs in the next chapter as we trace the resurgence of Gibraltar as a military base through to its vital role in the Second World War.

10 AS SAFE AS THE ROCK OF GIBRALTAR 1899–1939

AFTER 1813 the main focus of interest in Gibraltar in the nineteenth century lay in its evolution as a Crown Colony and the development of a commercial and a trading base. The essential framework was set then for the debate which has dominated the political agenda since the end of the Second World War – the relationship of Gibraltar to Spain. The growth of a civilian community with a strong affiliation to Britain, but an independent social and economic life of its own, began to parallel the use of Gibraltar as a military garrison. Whereas before 1813 Britain could have relinquished Gibraltar, public opinion notwithstanding, as a military base no longer required, by 1890 the welfare and status of the Gibraltarians had become a small but increasing factor in the balance, until in modern times it has assumed the role of the dominant issue.

But these considerations were far from the minds of the Victorian Imperialists who

The dry docks, now in commercial use, were completed in the early years of the 20th-century during a period of rapid naval expansion in Gibraltar.

Covered slipways at the north end of the naval dockyard.

still saw Gibraltar almost entirely in terms of a military fortress and naval base. This era appeared to be the zenith of the 'Pax Britannica' although in retrospect we can see that the decline of the Empire was already underway. Nevertheless, it was also the period in which the Royal Navy became the supreme bulwark of the nation with the adoption of the 'Two Power Standard' by which Britain maintained a navy equal to the strength of any two of the other major powers. This was initially directed at France and Russia, but it was not long before the race of the Dreadnoughts was being waged with Germany. The expansion ordered by the Naval Defence Act of 1889 led inevitably to the development of the naval facilities at Gibraltar which was ideally placed as a staging post both on the route to India through the Suez Canal and to the south Atlantic and the Cape. We have often noted the limitations of Gibraltar in the days of sail, but the advent of a steam-driven navy somewhat altered the equation. It was now feasible to build an artificial harbour protected against torpedo attack, and this became the aim of the major works which were started at Gibraltar in 1894. The intention was to extend the North and South Moles and fill in the gap between with a detached mole, much

as we see it today. In addition, three dry docks were to be constructed by the South Mole. Labourers came from England and Malta, but the major workforce was recruited in La Linea. Stone was obtained from the eastern quarries and brought through the Rock on a railway in the Admiralty Tunnel opened in 1898.

The dry docks were eventually all completed by 1906 and named by visiting royalty with due splendour, but there was already concern that they would not be large enough to accommodate the new battleships now envisaged. Admiral Sir John Fisher, who in 1903 had become one of the most powerful and dynamic first sea lords in naval history, immediately stationed the Atlantic Fleet at Gibraltar with eight battleships, capable of quickly reinforcing either the Mediterranean or Channel Fleets as circumstances required. From then until the end of the Cold War, the Gibraltar naval base was to play a key role in national, allied and NATO strategy.

It is thus paradoxical to relate that throughout this period of intense development, indeed right through to 1939, an intense debate persisted in Britain as to whether Gibraltar should be exchanged for Ceuta, the Spanish enclave directly opposite

Gibraltar on the north African shore. There can be little doubt that Spain would have looked favourably on such an exchange for at least a part of this period, and the possibility was overtly expressed by General Primo de Rivera in 1917, who as the Spanish dictator from 1923 to 1930 would have been in a position to implement this controversial decision. It was generally the military men who were in the forefront of those wishing to abandon Gibraltar and the politicians and the general public who demurred, although Lloyd George briefly contemplated returning the Rock during the First World War in an attempt to cajole Spain into joining the Allies. The reason for this military 'volte face' was that the landward defences of Gibraltar, which had been virtually impenetrable for centuries, were now embarrassingly vulnerable with the advent of long-range artillery. An enemy from the north could conceal his guns in a variety of sheltered batteries through an arc of almost 180 degrees. It was estimated that a garrison of up to 40,000 soldiers would be needed to take control of a sufficiently large area of the Campo to nullify the threat. It was obvious that a garrison of this size was neither physically tenable nor politically and financially credible.

The case for Ceuta was debatable. In location it was strategically the equal of Gibraltar and it had a better natural harbour. It also had a hinterland which was more easily defended and, a later consideration, ample space for an airfield. In military terms the advantages are clearly discernable: politically, it would have been worse than jumping out of the frying pan into the fire. Throughout the nineteenth century the north African coast was in continual ferment as the indigenous tribes rebelled against both their local rulers and their colonial masters. There were also 50,000 Spanish subjects in Ceuta who would probably be more troublesome to a military garrison than the 20,000 or so Gibraltarians. Spain on the other hand, beset with its own troubles, had been relatively friendly for the best part of a century, and ties between Britain and Spain had been strengthened by the marriage in 1906 of a granddaughter of Queen Victoria to Alphonso XIII, thus establishing the close links between the two royal families which still exist today. Furthermore, there was the general public's emotional, albeit somewhat irrational, attachment to the place – 'As safe as the Rock of Gibraltar' was not just an idle phrase. Finally there was the cost: the millions which had been spent on developing the dockyard at Gibraltar would

The Royal Naval Headquarters in the dockyard built in 1905.

have been wasted and additional expenditure incurred in developing Ceuta. In the end, the whole case revolved around the question – was there a military threat from Spain? History would suggest there was, but realistic analysis in the first half of the twentieth century indicated that the threat was minimal. In all the circumstances, it is hardly surprising that the politicians did not succumb to the forebodings of the military. Nor for once has hindsight shown them to be wrong – Gibraltar served with distinction in the Second World War and it is hardly conceivable, looking along the coast at Algeria, that post-war political problems would not have been at least as difficult at Ceuta as in Gibraltar.

*   *   *

The cordiality between Britain and Spain received another boost in May 1907 and an unnecessary setback the following year. It was by now apparent that Europe was heading again towards conflict. Britain and France were increasingly, if hesitantly, drawing together in the face of German ambition and expansion and in 1907 drew Spain into the entente with a joint declaration. This affirmed that each would hold what it had in the Mediterranean and would consult with the other if circumstances made it desirable; or to put it another way, in the event of war. In return Britain and France guaranteed the Spanish possession of the Balaerics and the defence of her Mediterranean coasts and raised no objection to Spain procuring a small but modern navy.

In 1908, however, a diplomatic gaffe provoked tension. The British ambassador advised the Spanish Government 'as an act of courtesy' that it intended to build a fence along the line of the guardposts in the neutral zone, some 600 yards from the old Spanish Lines. He stressed that this was not a defensive obstacle, being no more than a barrier of steel spikes with barbed wire on top. The intention was to reduce the number of sentries needed to man the guard posts and to inhibit smuggling. The local Spanish authorities saw no serious difficulty and all would doubtless have been well until the ambassador in a subsequent clarification said: 'The line along which the fence will be constructed lies some three feet inside the path formed by the continual passage of British sentries. This...has been for many years and unquestionably still is the British frontier'. This was a red rag to the bull for Spain who soon brandished the Treaty of Utrecht in the British face with its assumption that their territory ended at the Land Port Gate. It was an unnecessary provocation over a minor affair which might have been handled quite amicably at local level. The altercation soon faded away, but this has not prevented its resurrection from time to time in subsequent quarrels.

Much of the diplomatic posturing between the entente nations and Germany was played out in the western Mediterranean in the early years of the twentieth century. Both France and Spain, despite British reservations, had carved out colonies for themselves on the north African shore. For Spain it was a small but important safety valve after the loss of her American colonies and Britain even supported Spain in squeezing a part of Morocco out of the claws of France. Britain's compensation for acquiescing in France's territorial ambition was to be given a free hand in Egypt. No such magnanimity was shown towards Germany which also hankered after colonial acquisitions in the area, and the rivalry came to a head in the Agadir crisis of 1911. The German provocation was faced down, but the war moved a step closer.

*   *   *

Most historians would now agree that the first confrontation with Germany was, sooner or later, inevitable. Kaiser Wilhelm's bellicosity, the German generals' arrogant ambition, and the massive increase in armaments across Europe to which this had given rise could not be contained indefinitely. Nevertheless, the outbreak of hostilities came as a surprise to many and the flashpoint – the assassination of Archduke Franz Ferdinand by a Bosnian fanatic backed by Serb extremists on 28th June 1914 – seemed little enough reason to plunge the nations of Europe into war for the first time for nearly fifty years. But events followed their inexorable course and on August 4th Britain declared war on Germany and five days later the British Expeditionary Force landed in France.

Gibraltar played no major active role in the First World War. Most of the action which took place in the Mediterranean the-

atre occurred at the eastern end, in particular the campaign in Gallipoli. The crucial factor for Gibraltar was that Spain remained neutral. The Spanish population was split with the Liberal left being generally supportive of the Allies and the upper middle classes and the army sympathising with Germany. Spain in fact did quite well out of the war, exploiting her wealth of raw materials and cheap labour. Money flowed in and Madrid became the most important neutral city in Europe.

Within an hour of the declaration of war, a torpedo boat based on Gibraltar stopped the German liner *Emir* in the Strait and escorted her into the harbour. But it was the last hint of excitement for some time as the garrison and the dockyard prepared for the action which never really arrived. Indeed the weather became the main talking point for

the bored population with months of almost incessant rain – 52 inches in a 12-week period at the beginning of 1915 – with one particularly virulent thunderstorm spawning thousands of frogs all over the Rock. Another talking point was the arrest by the Spanish authorities in Algeciras of a German spy posing as a Moor who was attempting to infiltrate into Gibraltar. At this stage the dockyard's main contribution was the repair of the occasional naval vessel damaged in action, but early in 1915 the workforce had to stir themselves as Admiral Sturdee's battered fleet put in for repair on its return from the Battle of the Falkland Islands.

1915 saw a steady stream of hospital ships bringing the wounded from the carnage of Gallipoli, many of whom were too ill to stand the remainder of the voyage back to England. It was partly in response to this

Surveying the Strait – 9.2-inch guns were in place on the southernmost peak of the Rock in O'Hara's Battery during the First World War.

The First World War memorial in front of the City Hall, in course of refurbishment in 1995.

1915 that the aircraft which their subscriptions had paid for had been dispatched to France. This was to be repeated in the Second World War when a Spitfire was presented. But generally speaking the war was passing Gibraltar by although the increased activity in the dockyard was good for the economy. There was some rationing, but most essential requirements were obtainable, albeit at an inflated cost. Although Spain was officially neutral, up to 4000 Spanish workers crossed into Gibraltar daily and few failed to bring with them consumer items unobtainable in the city. Water to support an increased population was the main concern and even this essential commodity was obtained from Ceuta and Algeciras after some delay and subterfuge.

Trouble brewed in the dockyard in 1916. Parliamentary questions were tabled regarding the low pay of locally-recruited dockyard workers who were suffering from the effects of inflation which had increased prices by over fifty per cent. They were belatedly awarded a special war bonus of 'at least one shilling a week', bringing their pay to 15 shillings a week, but it is perhaps not surprising that the much larger complement of Spanish workers, who did not benefit from the bonus, eventually went on strike. The temporary food crisis was alleviated, however, by the Governor of Algeciras who saw to it that supplies of vegetables, bread and fish reached the garrison.

After the dash through the Mediterranean in 1914 of the battle cruiser *Goeben* and her escort the *Breslau* which helped to bring Turkey into the war, the Germans did not deploy a surface fleet in the inland sea. But submarines were regularly used after *U21* first passed through the Strait in April 1915, and they took a steady toll of allied shipping – the troopship *Mercia* was sunk off Gibraltar in November 1915. The battle against submarines was in its infancy in this war and the Allies could do little to detect boats passing submerged through the Strait. But the U-boats also had their limitations and had to spend much of their time on the surface to recharge their batteries and long-distance passage underwater was virtually impossible. From time to time therefore U-boats were discovered on the surface and were twice attacked by guns on Gibraltar –

that Mr Hasluck, a draper of the town, took a leading part in the formation of the Gibraltar Volunteer Corps which carried out guard and picket duties and helped to transfer the wounded from the unloading point at Ragged Staff Wharf to the military hospitals. Money was raised to sponsor the war effort and the population was gratified to learn in the only time they were fired in anger during the war. It was believed at the time that the second attack in June 1917 by the guns of the Devil's Gap Battery had sunk a submarine, but this is unlikely, although it is certain that some stray shells landed in a cemetery near Algeciras.

The success of the U-boats stimulated the introduction of the convoy system which was introduced by a trial homeward run from Gibraltar in May 1917. This system was eventually joined by the Americans and the US Navy established a base in Gibraltar. The U-boats continued to claim their victims, however, and just before the war ended the battleship *Britannia* was sunk off Gibraltar with the loss of over 1000 lives, many of whom died in Gibraltar hospitals from injuries sustained when one of her magazines exploded.

The war ended at eleven o'clock on November 11th 1918 and thanksgiving services were held all over the Rock. By the end of the year American warships left for home and the garrison settled down again to its peacetime existence. Although some assistance had been given to German forces by sympathetic groups in Spain, the stance adopted by the Government was generally beneficial to the Allies. This was particularly apparent around Gibraltar, and the goodwill fostered by successive governors and the activities in Spain of organisations like the Royal Calpe Hunt all bore fruit when the Rock might have been most vulnerable. The fact that Gibraltar made such a significant impact on the local economy, particularly by providing employment for Spanish workers, was also doubtless a significant factor.

*   *   *

The period between the wars was dominated by the Spanish Civil War. Spain had been chronically unstable for well over a hundred years, but for a time Primo de Rivera's generally benevolent dictatorship under a constitutional monarch seemed to have stabilised the political scene. It was a chimera – revolution was seething beneath the surface, nowhere more so than on Gibraltar's doorstep in Andalusia. In January 1930 Primo de Rivera resigned and a year later the King left Spain – The Second Republic was installed and another spell of instability followed with rival factions fighting each other

with increasing ferocity. In such circumstances it had been the tradition in Spain since medieval times for the military to step in to restore law and order and it was little surprise when this occurred in 1936.

General Francisco Franco (1892-1975) commanded the Spanish Army in Morocco and it was here that the revolt broke out in July. But the uprising was not confined to Morocco and there was feverish plotting right across Spain: in very round terms about half the Army supported the insurgents. The Moroccan element was, however, crucial to the success of the revolt – not only were they the elite of the Spanish Army, but they had the most charismatic, political and far-seeing general. By the middle of 1937 Franco was the undisputed leader of the Nationalist movement.

Gibraltar played very little part in the events of 1936-39. Nevertheless, the Gibraltarians had a ringside seat in the first few months as Andalusia was in the front line of the insurrection and the Governor had to play his hand carefully to avoid being inadvertently drawn into the conflict or to embarrass the Government in London. On the 18th of July Nationalist aircraft from western Morocco were seen to traverse the Strait on their way to bomb the Republican barracks at Tetuan and on the same day a steamer escorted by a destroyer entered the harbour at Algeciras to off-load troops. Refugees started to stream across the border into Gibraltar almost immediately and before long 4000 were seeking shelter in the crowded slums, hulks in the harbour and even in the caves on the Rock. Andalusia was almost universally well to the left of Spanish politics – socialist, communist or anarchist – and most of the military commanders, with locally conscripted troops, were not part of the rebellion. But Seville fell almost immediately to an outrageous confidence trick by General Queipo de Llano and as the other commanders were uncertain and indecisive, most of the loyalist fighting was left to the more fanatical militia.

The key to Franco's success in Andalusia was the rapid transfer of the Army of Morocco to Spain, and the movement of about 2000 troops by sea into Algeciras was vital to consolidating the insurgency. However, the bulk of his force was transferred by German and Italian aircraft, the ubiquitous Junkers 52, the first time that this rapid mode of transport had been employed in war. It was a revolutionary development, the lessons of which remained lost on the British military authorities for some time to come. Algeciras, Tetuan and even La Linea were bombed and a Republican militia force took over San Roque before being expelled by the Moroccans. The war came directly to Gibraltar on the 21st of July 1936 when a battleship and three cruisers sailed into Gibraltar harbour without lights. A deputation came ashore next morning requesting coal, but its composition of one petty officer and a group of ordinary seamen alarmed the police and the navy – where were the officers who would normally have been expected to undertake such a mission? The truth was suspected by most, for an order by the Republican Navy Minister for the crews to overpower their officers and take over their ships was common knowledge in Gibraltar. The Navy refused point blank to supply coal and ordered them to leave harbour by three o'clock that afternoon. The civilian merchants said they would supply coal only if the ships' officers were produced. On being told that there were none available the correct inference was drawn and the coal refused. The Spanish ships left at the appointed time. A potential crisis which could well have been embarrassing to a Government determined to sit on the fence had been avoided. Another incident occurred on the 5th August when the destroyer *Lepanto*, damaged by a bomb, anchored by the commercial wharf. The ship was allowed to disembark the wounded and then ordered to return to sea. Later in the day shells from another Republican destroyer landed on the Rock, but this was probably accidental as its target was a Nationalist convoy inbound to Algeciras.

The British Government had a very fine line to tread and was generally successful in maintaining a strict neutrality. There was little active support in Britain for the Nationalists, but a bevy of socialists and intellectuals joined the International Brigade in the Republican cause. In Gibraltar, which was much more concerned with events in its immediate vicinity, there was widespread sympathy for the Nationalists. Gibraltarians were only too familiar with the chaos, anarchy and corruption in Spain to have much sympathy for a Government torn by faction and in-fighting. Later, as tales of atrocities filtered through, their support for the Nationalist cause became more ambivalent. Most of the servicemen based in Gibraltar probably felt the same way, and in their case there was also an inherent conservatism which overcame any distaste they may have felt for overt rebellion. In any event the Spanish Civil War undoubtedly drew the people and the authorities together, if only in fear of becoming embroiled in some way in the struggle. Despite the affinities of many Gibraltarians with Spain, particularly through marriage, the Civil War strengthened their identity as Gibraltarians of British nationality. Another knot was tied in the post-war conundrum.

By the end of August 1936, the Nationalists had gained control of the Campo and the war moved away from Gibraltar. Minor incidents were reminders of the conflict, particularly when the destroyer *Hunter* arrived in the dockyard damaged by a mine off Almeria, and more spectacularly in May 1937 when the German pocket battleship *Deutschland* put in to offload 83 wounded after being hit by bombs. A Communist-directed conspiracy to spread rumours that Nationalist (and by implication German and Italian) guns had been deployed in the Campo facing Gibraltar gained little credence locally, but excited something of a stir in Britain. By the time the war drew to a close in April 1939 thoughts were now concentrated on a much more immediate threat – the likelihood of another war with Germany. Few in Gibraltar could fail to be a little apprehensive about the close links which had developed between General Franco and the Fascist dictators in Germany and Italy – was there a debt which needed to be repaid?

*   *   *

The commercial life of Gibraltar slowly returned to normal after the last convoy departed in 1918. The use of the port by passenger liners and cruise ships increased substantially in the post-war years – it was a port of call for all British ships heading for India and the East and to the Cape, and many passenger liners from Mediterranean

ports stopped at Gibraltar before heading across the Atlantic. But alternative and cheaper coaling facilities were available in ports like Tangier, and when the depression came in the 1930s the coaling procedure at Gibraltar had to be mechanised and oiling facilities provided to compete with the north African ports. Despite the drastic cuts in the armed forces after the end of the war, Gibraltar remained an important naval base, hosting the annual spring manoeuvres of the Home and Mediterranean Fleets.

Although administrative control of Gibraltar still lay firmly in the hands of the Governor, public bodies with Gibraltarian participation gradually evolved of which the Chamber of Commerce and the Sanitary Commissioners were among the most important. Sewage disposal had always been one of Gibraltar's major problems, exacerbated by the overcrowding within the city and contributing to the epidemics which plagued the nineteenth century. A significant improvement in the water supply was provided by the formal opening in 1901 of four reservoirs in the heart of the Rock capable of holding over five million gallons. A plaque close to the Moorish Castle commemorates

this significant advance. The needs of the city and the garrison were still to a certain extent incompatible and as late as 1913 a Governor, General Sir Archibald Hunter, was recalled after complaints that he was out of tune with the civic development of the town. As he had made plain that Gibraltar was to be administered as a 'fortress and not as a commercial bazaar', it is easy to see how the friction arose.

A first step towards internal self government came in 1921 when a constitution for Gibraltar was redefined. Whilst the ultimate authority of the Governor remained largely in being, in practice his powers were circumscribed by the introduction of two new bodies. The Executive Council, chaired by the Colonial Secretary, had local representation as well as administrative and military officials, but of greater significance was the City Council which contained seven elected members and four ex-officio administrative members. It became responsible to the Governor for all municipal affairs and took over such bodies as the Board of Sanitary Commissioners. It at last ended the role of the Exchange and Commercial Library which had been the mouthpiece of the civil commu-

Cruise ships started to visit Gibraltar after the First World War – the pattern continues today with the *Canberra* in harbour in October 1995.

nity for nearly a hundred years. By now the police force established in 1830 had adopted a more conventional role and was supplemented by a Special Constabulary introduced at the time of the flood of refugees at the outbreak of the Spanish Civil War.

The first steps to providing an airfield at Gibraltar were taken during the First World War when a grass strip was provided in the centre of the racecourse on the neutral ground. These experiments came to an end after a BE 2 crashed on the Spanish side of the fence, and attempts to use sea planes from the harbour were not successful. In 1931 a civil company, Gibraltar Airways, was given permission to use the racecourse strip for flights to Tangier, but lasted only three months. Construction of an airfield for military purposes, now known as North Front, began in 1934 – it was not without its opponents from the Army, who used the area for training, and the Gibraltar Jockey Club. Eventually it was decreed that an emergency landing ground only would be available for which one week's prior notice would be required from Fortress Headquarters! In 1936 the Government began to give serious consideration to the building of a permanent airfield at North Front, but such was the bureaucratic and political quagmire, allied with the inevitable objections from Spain, that nothing had been achieved by the outbreak of war.

Life in Gibraltar had been straightforward and relatively prosperous for well over a hundred years before the 3rd of September 1939. The war had been seen coming for some time, but few could have envisaged the upheaval which was to face them over the next few years as once again Gibraltar assumed its mantle as a military fortress first and foremost.

11 LIFELINE TO THE MEDITERRANEAN 1939–45

IN 1939 BRITAIN had occupied Gibraltar for 235 years. At regular intervals, as we have seen, the Government of the day had toyed with the idea of relinquishing the Rock, but for various reasons had never quite resolved to bite on the bullet. Despite the strong emotional attachment of the British people to Gibraltar – it was even seen by some as the quintessential symbol of Empire – it had rarely played an important role in British strategy except, arguably, for the years around Trafalgar. Although there was an increase in activity, the Rock had played no significant part in the First World War and it was in this period that pressure from the military was at its peak to exchange the base for Ceuta. But in 1939 all that was to change – for the first time in its history Gibraltar assumed a vital role in the survival of the British Empire. The reason of course was that, unlike in the earlier confrontation, the Mediterranean became a major focus of the war; and when control of the Mediterranean is important, so too is Gibraltar.

The most important question for Gibraltar in 1939 was the likely reaction of Italy and Spain to the initiation of war by Germany. Would the bonds of Fascism forged in the Civil War hold together in a wider conflict? If they did the war would inevitably spread to the Mediterranean and the security of Gibraltar would be imperilled. And without a secure base at the entrance to the Mediterranean, could Malta or Egypt, or even the Far East be sustained?

The key as always was the attitude of Spain. The advent of long range artillery had transformed the vulnerability of Gibraltar to attack overland and an area of the Campo extending out to perhaps 20 miles would have to be occupied to ensure its survival.

But quite apart from the practical difficulties of achieving this, and Britain certainly had neither troops nor resources to spare in 1940, it would have led inevitably to war with Spain and impel Franco into the arms of Hitler and Mussolini.

General Franco's Spain, however, was in no position in isolation to threaten Gibraltar in 1939; and despite the formal ending of the Civil War in April, guerilla actions still rumbled on in the mountainous regions, particularly in Andalusia. The Spanish press was strongly pro-German and their anger was fuelled by a British press, much of which was violently opposed to Franco and urged that the war against Fascism should be extended to Spain – hardly an attractive proposition in the desperate days of 1939/40. Nevertheless, it was no great surprise to the British Government when Franco decreed at the outbreak of war that all Spaniards should observe the strictest neutrality. But could he be trusted, was there a debt to Fascism that still needed to be paid? In the spring of 1940 defence works facing Gibraltar began to appear in the Campo although British Intelligence rightly concluded that these were defensive in nature; and diplomatically Britain did all it could to establish a friendly relationship with Madrid. Unlike the Spanish military who were predictably pro-German, as were generally the professional classes, the civilian community around Algeciras was on balance sympathetic to Britain. This of course was prompted by the work available in Gibraltar and the food which flowed out from the garrison – each Spanish worker was allowed to take two loaves from the dockyard every day.

Although the Germans and Italians had officially departed in the summer of 1939, large numbers of German businessmen and diplomats remained in Spain to negotiate the acquisition of raw materials and manufacturing contracts. Embedded within this coterie was a solid core of intelligence agents, some of whom were comfortably settled on the sea front at Algeciras or in the elegant ambience of the Reina Cristina Hotel. All was quiet throughout the phoney war, but the fall of France in June 1940 quickly stimulated Mussolini to enter the war before all the expected fruits from the tree were swallowed by Germany. As a diplomat commented, the Italians only wait for the right moment to come to the aid of the victor. The focus of war now moved to the Mediterranean and it was disquieting to the British when Franco declared Spain to be non-belligerent, a subtle and perhaps significant shift from neutrality. Hitler made no overt move towards Spain whilst Operation 'Sealion' – the invasion of Britain – was still feasible, but when the air battle over the Channel was lost his attention turned to the Mediterranean. We know now of course that by this time his mind was mainly focused on Russia, but if Gibraltar could be captured quickly and cheaply, it would be a bonus worth taking.

The British Government was under no illusion that Gibraltar could be defended for long against an attack overland. Indeed there was no fundamental requirement for the Rock itself to be occupied by an enemy. A strong artillery presence in the surrounding hills, backed up by the use of airfields which could be 100 miles or more away, would be quite sufficient to make the use of the dockyard and bay for naval shipping totally untenable – and without the Royal Navy Gibraltar had no value at all. Discussion turned again to abandoning Gibraltar and establishing a naval base in the Canaries or the Azores. On June 17th 1940 Churchill minuted the First Lord of the Admiralty:

'If we have to quit Gibraltar we must immediately take the Canaries which will serve as a very good base to control the Western Entrance to the Mediterranean.'

But what would really have been achieved except war with Spain, the enlargement of the Axis, the undying resentment of Portugal, and the antagonism of most of the neutral nations, particularly in the Americas? In any case control of the gateway to the Mediterranean could hardly be exercised effectively from either the Canaries or the Azores. It was the sort of contingency so often contemplated in war that had little foundation in reality.

Hitler had two options: he could seize Gibraltar with the collaboration of Franco, or he could drive through Spain despite Franco. Clearly the first was preferable and it was to this end that Hitler met Franco at Hendaye on the border between France and Spain on 23rd October 1940.

It was a difficult meeting as the two dictators had contrasting temperaments and no liking for each other. Franco drove a hard bargain in even holding out the prospect of collaboration – large quantities of grain, fuel and the modernisation of the Spanish armed forces were among his more prominent demands. In fact Franco did not want Hitler in Spain any more than he wanted the British in Gibraltar. Furthermore, he was not convinced, even at this early stage, that Germany would eventually win the war. His predominant aim in the winter of 1940 was to sit as tightly on the fence as possible without provoking Hitler to more extreme measures.

German planning for the capture of Gibraltar had been started well before Hitler's meeting with Franco. In July a German delegation led by Admiral Canaris, head of the Secret Service (*Abwehr*), discussed the operation with Franco and surveyed Gibraltar from the balconies of the Reina Cristina Hotel in Algeciras. In August Hitler gave his approval to the Gibraltar operation which was based on Spanish cooperation and envisaged a massive aerial and artillery bombardment before an assault by two infantry regiments, one a mountain unit, and two combat engineer battalions on the north-west corner of the fortifications. It was initially called 'Isabella-Felix' and only reverted to 'Felix' after Hitler's meeting with Franco. The largest problem was the logistics of the operation – it was 800 miles from the French border and the roads and railways were poor. Secrecy was out of the question as all the major rail routes led through Madrid. It would not have been an easy operation even with Spanish complicity

Lieutenant General Sir Clive Liddell (right) hands over as Governor of Gibraltar to General Lord Gort VC. In the centre is Vice Admiral Sir John Somerville. (Imperial War Museum)

– if this was withheld it was probably impossible in any reasonable timescale. The Spanish would have resisted and, whilst their professional army was mediocre compared with the German juggernaut, they had a justifiable reputation for guerilla warfare, and in Andalusia the terrain was ideal for this type of resistance. It has often been said that the army which had overrun Norway, Belgium and France in quick succession would have made short work of Spain: perhaps it would, but I suspect that it would have required rather more holding down than either Norway or Vichy France.

Further attempts were made to cajole Franco, but the longer they persisted the clearer it became that Britain was not in imminent danger of defeat and the greater the possibility of American intervention in the war. Whilst still keeping his options open, Franco slowly recoiled even further from cooperation with Hitler and an intervention by Mussolini was equally rebuffed. The Germans meanwhile had completed their planning and even carried out a rehearsal of the projected operation on a mountain in the Jura which bore a close resemblance to the Rock. Spanish troops had carried out similar training near Estepona. 'Felix' slowly died from December onwards and was formally cancelled in February 1941 – much as Hitler would have wished to occupy Gibraltar, it had to be completed quickly with Franco's cooperation if his greater plan, 'Barbarossa', was to be launched in the spring. In fact Hitler, unlike some of his staff, rarely showed more than mild enthusiasm for the Mediterranean theatre, and any action he did undertake was usually designed to bail out the impetuosity of Mussolini. But there can be little doubt that Gibraltar would have fallen if Hitler had been able to mount 'Felix' with Franco's full cooperation; at the very least its military viability would have been effectively destroyed. It is perhaps ironic that Gibraltar was saved for Britain by the vacillation of Franco, a leader who certainly owed no favours to Britain, and who most probably as a result of collaborating with Hitler would have secured sovereignty for Spain sooner or later. After the end of 1940 the security of Gibraltar was more or less assured, although there was no sense of complacency in the Colony itself.

*   *   *

Winston Churchill talking to the Governor, Lieutenant General Mason-MacFarlane, on the airfield at North Front on 29th May 1943. (Imperial War Museum)

Gibraltar was fortunate in the war years to have a succession of high profile, charismatic and generally able governors. Indeed such was their breadth of experience and ability that it is perhaps capricious to try to categorise them in a few subjective phrases. Furthermore, the relationship between the governors, their deputies and the various senior naval officers in Gibraltar, the latter themselves often at odds with each other, was frequently so acerbic as to cloud the overall picture. The illustrious line began before the war with General Sir Edmund Ironside who, although making little impact when he unexpectedly became Chief of the Imperial General Staff in 1939, set in train the first stages of a review and enhancement of the defences. He was followed by Lieutenant General Sir Clive Liddell, an able administrator, dignified and easy going, but described by his one-time ADC, the actor Anthony Quayle, as essentially a peacetime officer. The same could hardly be said of his successor in 1941, General Viscount Gort VC – formidable, austere, inspirational and pedantic, he showed few signs of the trauma of the British Expeditionary Force and Dunkirk when he arrived in Gibraltar a year later. Gort's favoured mode of transport was the bicycle and it must have been a sight to behold to observe the Governor with a bevy of admirals and ADCs in tow pedalling furiously round the city. He was a popular if demanding master until he moved on to take over the even more critical governorship of Malta in May 1942. His successor Lieutenant General Sir Noel Mason-MacFarlane (Mason Mac) had already served as deputy to Liddell with whom his relationship could hardly have been worse. He was a man of outstanding personality – convivial friend and generous host, or drunkard and womaniser depending upon the viewpoint – he was undoubtedly dynamic, shrewd, courageous and emotional. By turns outspoken, diplomatic, intolerant, sympathetic: he left as strong a mark on Gibraltar as any governor since Eliott. Indeed he was known to the locals as 'Demolition Mac' after his ruthless clearance of buildings, including the historic Devil's Tower, to improve fields of fire. After the war he became a Labour MP, almost entirely it was alleged to revenge a slight by Winston Churchill, but he died shortly thereafter.

The military authorities had not been idle whilst the drama of 'Felix' had been played out. The major requirement still to be resolved was the provision of an airfield.

When war began there were no land-based aircraft in Gibraltar, only three Swordfish float planes of No 3 Anti-Aircraft Co-operation Unit. But within days No 200 Group was formed with its headquarters in the Bristol Hotel to operate the flying boats of No 202 Squadron. Work continued on the construction of a runway, but the possibility of an extension by reclamation work at the west end had not been advanced and it was still theoretically, at least as far as Spain was concerned, only an emergency landing ground. It was just adequate for Bombays and lightly-loaded Wellingtons, but not for the American-built Hudson anti-submarine aircraft which came into service in 1939. In their anxiety not to antagonise Spain, the politicians had been reluctant to pursue the development of a permanent all-weather airfield, and it was not until October 1941 that approval was given for a realignment and extension of the runway into the bay by nearly half a mile. It was at this time that the difficult decision was taken that there would have to be a public road across the runway, still of course a prominent and unusual feature of the airfield today. 7500 tons of rock were quarried from the north face and transported daily as the runway relentlessly penetrated into the bay towards Algeciras. The spoil from the tunnelling operations which were going on at the same time was also put

to good use. By July 1943 it was completed to its full length of 1800 yards. The racecourse, public gardens and sports fields, so beloved of previous governors, had disappeared for ever under a mass of concrete and the impedimenta of a wartime airfield.

Tunnelling for military purposes had a long tradition on the Rock, but nothing matched the scale of the work undertaken during the Second World War. The decision was taken in 1940 to put as many as possible of the support facilities underground. Accommodation, offices, hospitals, storage areas – with heating, ventilation, water and sanitary arrangements to match – were all built in a vast network of tunnels and chambers threading the length of the Rock. To protect the inhabitants from the percolating water, custom-built nissen huts or concrete block buildings were erected inside the chambers. The main thoroughfares, known as the Great North Road and the Fosse Way, run almost the length of the Rock and are still in use today as are some of the operations rooms and storage areas. Enormous caverns, originally designed as food storage areas and tiled accordingly, contain massive electrical generators still in situ today, rusting and unused. In all there are 34 miles of tunnels in the Rock and most were finished by 1943. The bulk of the work was done by four companies of Royal Engineers, mainly

The unusual arrangement by which vehicles and pedestrians cross the centre of the runway is a legacy of the airfield constructed during the war.

Although poorly provided with anti-aircraft defences at the outbreak of the war, Gibraltar bristled with searchlights and Bofors by the time of Operation 'Torch' at the end of 1942. (Imperial War Museum)

consisting of miners and quarry workers, and a Canadian tunnelling company which had perfected a diamond-drill blasting technique. It is unfortunate that it has not proved possible in some way to provide a glimpse of this massive undertaking for the modern visitor, unique in the world today and far exceeding in scale any medieval fortification.

Of the many deficiencies of war materials on the outbreak of war, none was more acute than the shortage of anti-aircraft guns and searchlights. With the defence of the homeland the primary concern it is not surprising that few could be spared for Gibraltar: the meagre ration that was allocated to the Mediterranean was diverted to Malta and Alexandria. Nevertheless, the need for some form of air defence was crucial – the airfield was unready to support fighter aircraft and there could be no guarantee that an aircraft carrier would be available in the vicinity when it was needed. In 1940 anti-aircraft defence was solely dependent on the guns of any warships which happened to be in the harbour, and by no means

all of those could be elevated sufficiently to deal with aircraft. It would probably have proved a fatal deficiency if Hitler had mounted 'Felix' in 1941. As the threat to Britain subsided the situation was steadily improved until by the time of Operation 'Torch' in 1942, Gibraltar bristled with artillery ranging from the large 9.2-inch guns with a range of 20,000 yards situated high on the Rock to batteries of 3.7-inch anti-aircraft guns clustered around the base, and with individual Bofors sited round the harbour as well as on the summits. There was also a mobile regiment which generally reinforced the many embrasures on the North Face which for a time seem to have been seriously neglected.

There were just two resident infantry battalions at Gibraltar as war approached supported by elements of Royal Engineers and Royal Artillery: it will be recalled that at least 40,000 infantry had been thought necessary to control the Campo in the event of an invasion through Spain. The ground forces were strengthened by the formation in March 1939 of the Gibraltar Defence Force which, after the introduction of conscription in 1940, became a self-contained unit with anti-aircraft, signals and other administrative elements. It was the forerunner of the Gibraltar Regiment still in existence today. Air-raid shelters for the civilian population were not neglected with about 12 being constructed in various parts of the city. By 1942 the defence force had been increased to about 18,000 front-line and support troops with 5 resident battalions and a tank squadron.

Security was a continual source of concern in such an open location as Gibraltar. German intelligence agents were scattered around the bay, some living in considerable style in comfortable villas, and at one stage agents even tried to install infra-red tracking stations between Algeciras and Tarifa to monitor shipping in the Strait. These small buildings placed at regular intervals were discovered by a routine Spitfire reconnaissance flight. Although without doubt constructed with Spanish military complicity, this became a little too obtrusive even for Spanish neutrality and the authorities closed down the network after photographic evidence was shown to Franco. Spanish civilians still came across the border from La

Linea in considerable numbers to work in the dockyard – a latent Trojan horse of vast potential which does not seem to have been much exploited. The Gibraltar Security Police was formed in 1938 to counter the threat to security and they generally succeeded in containing acts of sabotage. All inhabitants and workers were issued with identity cards stamped right through with the Gibraltar Crown which would not have been easy to forge. Two saboteurs were arrested and hanged in the Moorish Castle, but not before a bomb had caused a major fire on Coaling Island. One other Gibraltarian agent was hanged in Britain for spying. But this must have been the tip of the iceberg, for the movement of convoys and warships as well as aircraft could not possibly be concealed from the mass of prying eyes in and around Gibraltar.

As might be expected Gibraltar was a hotbed of British Intelligence. But the activities of the various single service and diplomatic organisations do not seem to have been very well coordinated, with their penchant for secrecy inhibiting British operations as much as it confused the enemy. British diplomatic and intelligence sources in Gibraltar had relatively free access to Spain

The Gibraltar Defence Force played a valuable supporting role in the defence of Gibraltar. In recognition of its service a company of the GDF is reviewed by the Governor, Lieutenant General Sir Ralph Eastwood, late in the war.
(Imperial War Museum)

and could keep a careful eye on the activities of the enemy agents who made little pretence of secrecy. It was also a useful route for smuggling escaped prisoners and agents out of France: Basil Embry and Peter Churchill both entered Gibraltar in the boot of a car.

Sir Clive Liddell became Governor in July 1939, and as an ex- Quartermaster General, was well suited to consider the administrative problems of a garrison at war. Contingency plans to evacuate the civilian population were drawn up and implemented in May 1940 when it looked likely that Italy would join the war. Service dependants were evacuated to England, but the majority of the Gibraltarians, at least those without the means to make their own arrangements, were sent to French Morocco. It seemed a close and convenient location at the time without the foreknowledge that France itself would have fallen within a month. Only 3000 men between the ages of 18 and 41 remained who were subject to military service. It was hoped of course that the French Colonies would continue to fight with the Allies, but after Mers-el-Kebir this proved untenable and the Vichy authorities demanded the removal of all evacuees. This was achieved, in appalling conditions, in overloaded merchant vessels which had ferried in French troops who did not elect to join General de Gaulle. Briefly back in Gibraltar, the evacuees were understandably reluctant to move on again and it was only a fortuitous Italian air-raid on the night before the planned move to England that encouraged an orderly departure. Over 12,000 were sent to the UK and most of the remaining 4000 to Madeira and Jamaica. Their story is told in its harrowing detail by Tommy Finlayson in *The Fortress Came First*.

On Gibraltar's reverting to its primary role as a military fortress the Governor decided to suspend the City Council, and from the 1st of January 1941 the brigadier in charge of administration took on the additional task of running the city's domestic services. In the long run this opened the way for a more militant political atmosphere towards the end of the war when the situation was returning to normal. Conditions in Gibraltar were far from satisfactory for those workers who remained. Separated from their families, they could not even look forward to periods of leave in England. Civilians were also barred from service entertainments which, whilst it might have been necessary practically, did nothing to forge harmony and goodwill. Relations between the local civilians and the troops were understandably somewhat strained at times. The average wage in 1939 was only 35 shillings (£1.75) a week and there was no workman's compensation and no death benefits. Housing standards were appalling – doubtless exacerbated by the absence of the housewife in exile. A distinguished economist (F A Hayek) said in a report in 1944 that the minimum wage should be £9 a month, but even many skilled workers in Gibraltar were earning much less than this. Despite these privations the attitude of the civilian workers remained loyally responsive to the Allied cause whilst the security of the Rock still seemed under threat, but once the danger had receded the first signs of civil discontent became apparent with the formation of the Association for the Advancement of Civil Rights which was to become a formidable political force in post-war Gibraltar.

Gibraltar provided a rather different face for the many resident military units. There was no shortage of food and some luxuries were available which had long vanished from tables in Britain. The 'black market' flourished in some commodities as it did in wartime Britain. Many shops in Main Street and elsewhere were changed into 'honky tonk' drinking halls for the troops although female company was predictably extremely scarce. Boredom, as in the Great Siege, was the main constraint on the wellbeing of the troops – 'a bloody military prison full of pubs' was one anguished complaint. Crime, often drink-related, and desertion in the form of illegal and ill-conceived jaunts across to Spain were relatively high. Whilst the officers could cross into Spain for short periods in mufti, organised motor trips for the soldiers were not available until late in the war. For the Governor and the more senior officers, quite apart from their normal duties, there was a constant stream of high ranking visitors – political, royal and military; it would be simpler to compile a short list of those who did not visit Gibraltar during the war than to try to mention those who did.

*   *   *

The advent of war did not touch Gibraltar directly for some time. It was Allied policy to keep hostilities away from the Mediterranean for as long as possible and to this end strenuous efforts were made to keep Spain and Italy neutral. Once the attitude of Franco became clearer, the latter emerged as the more urgent problem. Unlike in 1914, Italy under Mussolini was a potential enemy who had already signed 'the Pact of Steel' with Germany and had substantial forces in Abyssinia and Libya, both plausible threats to Egypt and the Suez Canal. Furthermore, Mussolini had already shown his aggressive intent by the occupation of Albania in April 1939. The British Mediterranean Fleet was based on Alexandria and it was agreed with the French that they would be responsible for the security of the western Mediterranean and the Royal Navy for the east. In the centre was Malta, strategically placed athwart the vital supply line between Italy and her north African possessions. It was at the same time potentially the most important and the most vulnerable of the key naval bases in the Mediterranean. In 1939 the Allies had a comfortable naval superiority except in submarines and little trouble was expected from the modern but untried Italian Fleet. All was soon to change.

The lessons of the First World War regarding the protection of merchant shipping were quickly implemented and the very first convoy with eight ships departed Gibraltar for Cape Town on the day before war was declared. This set the pattern for the rest of the war as convoys formed, reformed or refuelled in Gibraltar and were protected by the resident fleet. But such was the emphasis on the north Atlantic, where merchant shipping losses were already causing concern by early 1940, that the major part of the Mediterranean Fleet was withdrawn to support the Home Fleet. The single aircraft carrier, *Glorious*, was dispatched to the dangerous waters off the Norwegian coast where she was sunk and was later replaced by the Navy's only modern carrier, the *Ark Royal*, which soon became a potent symbol of the spirit of the city and the dockyard alike.

The fall of France and the entry of Italy into the war in June 1940 brought the lull of the phoney war in the Mediterranean to an abrupt halt and placed the balance of forces on an entirely different footing. The Italians overnight had a substantial superiority with 4 battleships (2 building), 19 cruisers, 52 destroyers and 115 submarines. However, the Italians had no aircraft carriers and no radar and were reluctant to fight at night. Indeed, the Italian Battle Fleet was reluctant to fight at all, believing in stark contrast to the British view that a 'fleet in being' posed a greater threat in the longer term than one hazarded in battle. In some respects to compensate for their lack of aircraft carriers, the Italians had substantial land-based air forces which could sweep across the Mediterranean at its narrowest point opposite Tunisia. It could not be known in the middle of 1940 that both the Italian Fleet and Air Force promised more than they were either able or willing to deliver – it was only much later that the jest became prevalent that the best way to view the Italian Fleet was in a glass-bottomed boat. In June 1940, at a stroke, the Royal Navy had apparently lost control of the western Mediterranean.

Initially the First Sea Lord advocated moving the Mediterranean Fleet under Admiral Sir Andrew Cunningham from Alexandria to Gibraltar, but the implications of this withdrawal on the security of the Middle East soon scotched the proposal. Even before Mussolini showed his hand, a decision had been made in May to abandon the trade route through the Mediterranean, so lengthening the voyage from the UK to India by 5000 miles and to Suez by as much again. For a brief period Gibraltar became little more than a minor support facility on the route to the Cape. It was not long, however, before Churchill made the Mediterranean the main focal point of the war – in Corelli Barnett's words: 'Britain, unable in her impotence to slug it out with Hitler, found herself trying to kick his dog Mussolini'. In response to this change of policy a new fleet, called Force H and under the command of Vice Admiral Sir James Somerville, was assembled at Gibraltar. The Force contained some illustrious names – the battleships *Valiant* and *Resolution*, the battle-cruiser *Hood* and the aircraft carrier *Ark Royal* – and it was strongly supported by 2 cruisers, *Arethusa* and *Enterprise*, and 11 destroyers. Its intended role was to provide the lifeline to Malta, but it was often diverted to other tasks, particularly in the Atlantic.

Its first action was just such a diversion and was not only unexpected, but distasteful and controversial. At the fall of France, one of Winston Churchill's most pressing problems was the fate of the French fleet. It was hoped that the admirals would either surrender it into British hands or, better still, continue the fight from the French colonies – whatever happened it was considered imperative that it should not pass into the control of Germany. Today, the operation taken to prevent this is generally considered an overreaction, even a traitorous, betrayal of a recent ally. It did not look quite so simple in 1940 – the abject surrender of France, not only to Germany, but perhaps even worse to a collaborationist Vichy Government, engendered little sympathy in a nation now standing alone against Germany, Italy, and perhaps even Russia.

Despite some misgivings within the Navy Churchill was determined to act; not only was there the practical requirement to emasculate the French fleet, but a need to demonstrate Britain's determination to fight on to the Americans. In Alexandria Admiral Godfroy was persuaded to demilitarise his ships, but at Mers-el-Kebir in Algeria, where the most formidable component of the fleet lay at anchor, Admiral Gensoul refused on the 3rd of July to comply to a wider ranging demand from Admiral Somerville. Throughout an oppressively sweltering day Force H cruised off-shore whilst the minutes of an ultimatum set for 5.30pm ticked away. No positive answer was received and Somerville opened fire – most of the French ships were severely damaged and nearly 1300 French sailors died. Only the battleship *Strasbourg* escaped with a few destroyers under cover of darkness to safe haven in Toulon. It is clear from the surviving signals that Somerville took no satisfaction from his task and it provoked intense French resentment. That was entirely understandable at the time, less so in the cold light of retrospect. The action had two immediate effects on Gibraltar. On July 5th Force H was attacked by the French naval air squadrons from Port Lyautey without damage, but on July 18th four people were killed and 11 wounded by an attack by three Italian SM 82 aircraft. The other impact as we have already seen was the expulsion of the Gibraltar refugees from French Morocco.

In September there was an unfortunate sequel to the action at Mers-el-Kebir which was equally controversial, but for a different reason. General de Gaulle had taken control of most of French Equatorial Africa and hatched with Churchill a plan to extend his base to Dakar in Senegal from where he might hope to influence the far more important colony of French West Africa. It was a dubious enterprise from the outset based on inadequate intelligence, and the Chiefs of Staff were less than enthusiastic in its support by British forces (Operation 'Menace'). For our story, however, the main fact is that nothing was known of this operation by Admiral Sir Dudley North, Flag Officer North Atlantic at Gibraltar. Vichy France was rather better informed and on September 9th dispatched three modern cruisers and three destroyers (Force Y) to reinforce the naval power at Dakar. Admiral North and the Admiralty both had intelligence information about Force Y and it was observed approaching the Strait of Gibraltar by a Royal Navy destroyer flotilla. North was still working on an instruction of the 4th of July that stated: 'If French warships are seen passing through Straits identity is to be reported immediately and no further action taken'. He had no subsequent instructions to the contrary, but much water had passed under the bridge since July which might at least have aroused his curiosity.

North meanwhile had brought the battle cruiser *Renown*, which was the only capital ship Admiral Somerville had available, to one hour's notice to steam and informed the Admiralty in accordance with his standing instruction of July. As Force Y steamed at speed through the Strait on the 11th of September, North took no further action except – an unfortunate gesture as it transpired – to signal '*Bon voyage*' to the French as they passed. There was less excuse, however, for the lack of action in the Admiralty when they learned of Force Y. Unfortunately, thanks to administrative muddle, overwork and an obsessive regard for secrecy, the information did not percolate upwards sufficiently quickly to those who might have taken such action. However, even when a signal was belatedly sent it stated that:

'If French Force is proceeding southward inform them there is no objection to their going to Casablanca but that they cannot be permitted to go to Dakar.'

As the ships put into Casablanca, albeit briefly to refuel, the inference is that no immediate action would have been taken in any case.

Operation 'Menace' was a fiasco, and undoubtedly the presence of the French fleet stiffened the resolve of the Vichy authorities in Dakar which in any case were largely opposed to de Gaulle. As with most military disasters, however, there was inevitably a quest for a scapegoat, and in this case the mantle fell upon Admiral North. He had already upset the Admiralty and Winston Churchill for criticising the Mers-el-Kebir operation and after a prolonged and acid correspondence he was ordered to strike his flag. The argument centred on whether North should have ordered the *Renown* to sea, not whether positive action should have been taken to try to prevent Force Y passing through the Strait. In the subsequent controversy, which was for a long time kept afloat by North himself, opinion has almost invariably come down on the side of the Admiral. Whilst North followed his orders to the letter, he perhaps displayed less initiative than might have been expected of such a high ranking officer: and for one who had already crossed Churchill's path his fate was entirely predictable.

The Mediterranean remained the focal point of the war in western Europe until the middle of 1944 when the emphasis at last moved to France as the Americans had long desired. In September 1941 the first 6 U-boats passed through the Strait into the Mediterranean, and although Doenitz had plans to increase this figure to 60, in the end no more than 25 were ever sent. They were supported by minelayers which entered the Mediterranean through the Rhone waterway. Gibraltar thus became a vital component in the battle to keep the sea lanes open to Malta and thence to Egypt and the Middle East. As we have seen, Gibraltar became the home of Force H and was joined by the 8th (Gibraltar) Submarine Flotilla. The dockyard, modernised and expanded throughout the first half of the twentieth century, at last played that essential role for which its proponents had argued for over two centuries.

The key to the Mediterranean strategy was Malta, although some revisionist historians now consider that the diversion of resources and losses sustained by the Royal Navy in protecting this vulnerable outpost outweighed its strategic importance. Perhaps so, but the efforts of the aircraft, submarines and light naval forces, which could only operate from Malta, in disrupting Rommel's supply lines from Italy in 1941 cannot be discounted at a time when Britain's own forces in that theatre were severely stretched across the Middle East. It is true, however, that after 1941 this theatre was generally supplied round the Cape and convoys in the Mediterranean were more often than not mounted for the sake of saving Malta itself.

But this only became apparent in late 1941 after the second effective intervention of the Luftwaffe. Before this it was recognised that Malta could play an important role in the central Mediterranean in not only monitoring the Italian Battle Fleet, but in reacting sufficiently quickly to attack the convoys which slipped out of Sicily and the southern Italian ports bound for Tripoli and Benghazi. The reverse of the coin was that Malta was only 60 miles from Sicily and thus comfortably within the range of the Savoia Marchetti bombers and their accompanying Macchi fighters. It was thus not considered safe to base capital ships on Malta although light forces and submarines, if their anchorage could be protected by the RAF and the Fleet Air Arm, were an important element in influencing the land battle which raged back and forth across Cyrenaica. In the event, such was the concentration needed to keep Malta precariously secure that the opportunities for offensive action were seriously limited.

The French diversion out of the way, the main role of Force H throughout 1940–42 was to protect convoys running the gauntlet of the Mediterranean and to support aircraft carriers providing a launch platform for fighters flying into Malta. Their area of

A Catalina leaves North Front for a patrol over the Mediterranean in March 1942. The newly developed airfield is on the left in the middle distance. (Imperial War Museum)

responsibility lay from Gibraltar eastwards to the narrow stretch of sea which separated Trapanni on Sicily from Bizerta in Tunisia. It was thought too dangerous for the capital ships to proceed through the Narrows where they could be attacked by Italian bombers from Sicily, and responsibility for the convoy's safety passed to the RAF on Malta and light naval forces until the convoy could be picked up again to the east of the island by the Mediterranean Fleet and escorted to Alexandria. Sometimes the convoys were destined for Malta itself, bringing the fuel, the ammunition and the food which could sustain the island in its strategic role. But as well as providing the sustenance, the convoys were also seen as the bait which would entice the Italian Fleet into battle, for the Royal Navy found it hard to abandon the 'Jutland' syndrome of bringing the major fleets into confrontation, without seemingly fully recognising that almost all of the casu-

alties were being caused by aircraft and submarines.

Immediately after the destruction of the French Fleet at Mers-el-Kebir, Force H was in action again in July 1940 to create a diversion in the western Mediterranean whilst Cunningham ran a convoy from Alexandria to Malta. The main target was Cagliari, an airfield and seaplane base on the south coast of Sardinia. This became a regular task for *Ark Royal* whenever a convoy was being run and the aim was to keep the bombers on the ground whilst the convoy slipped through. Sometimes it was successful, but it was unusual for the convoy to escape entirely unscathed, although fortunately at this stage of the war the Italian Air Force was no more successful at hitting a moving ship than the RAF had been in the North Sea earlier in the war. In August the old aircraft carrier *Argus* transported 12 Hurricanes to a point south of Sardinia where they successfully flew off to Malta. It is a telling reflection on the importance Mr Churchill attached to Malta and his faith in her survival that fighter aircraft could be spared at the very height of the Battle of Britain. A similar operation in November was less successful when 8 of a complement of 12 Hurricanes were lost when they ran out of fuel before reaching the island. In the meantime, the first of the major convoys – Operation 'Hats' – had been successfully run through the narrows in September with little Italian response, as was 'Collar' a couple of months later; although Somerville, who like North had incurred Churchill's wrath, had to contend with an Admiralty Board of Enquiry after failing to pursue an Italian fleet which had made a fleeting appearance.

The war in north Africa had initially gone well with General Wavell driving the Italians back into Libya with heavy losses, but it turned an ominous corner in January 1941 when Hitler transferred the 10th Air Corps from Norway to Sicily. The Luftwaffe proved to be far more successful in attacking shipping than the Italians and losses soon escalated alarmingly. In fact, 1941 was to be a year of disaster for the British forces in the Mediterranean. Whereas the Italians had been seen off after Taranto and Matapan, the Germans provided an enemy of an altogether different calibre. It did not, however, deter Force H from mounting a bombardment of Genoa in February while aircraft from the *Ark Royal* pounded targets on the Ligurian coast and mined the entrances to several ports. After this Somerville took his task force out into the Atlantic to try to intercept German pocket battleships and cruisers on commerce raiding sorties. The 10th Air Corps' main objective was to subdue Malta and the battle reached its climax between March and May 1941. Between April and June Somerville made no fewer than five sorties to deliver a total of 189 Hurricanes to Malta, about half of which flew on to Egypt. Battered and bruised, the fate of Malta hung in the balance, but it did not stop Force H running the important 'Tiger' convoy of tanks through to Alexandria with the loss of only one ship. After that *Ark Royal* was back into the Atlantic again after the *Bismarck* and it was her fighters which eventually crippled the pride of the German Navy by jamming her steering gear. The Mediterranean Fleet meanwhile was thoroughly engaged in the disastrous support of Greece – its troubles relieved only by the success of the Battle of Matapan, the last of the Royal Navy's great fleet encounters.

Gibraltar saw little of Force H at this stage of the war, but it was to the immense credit of the dockyard that it managed to refuel, rearm, resupply and sometimes repair the ships so quickly that they were seldom absent from the front line for long. By the summer of 1941 there was a brief respite in the battle for Malta as Hitler turned his attention to Russia and withdrew his air force from the Mediterranean. For a while Somerville was able to get his convoys through to Malta without too much difficulty. But in November the Germans returned in strength and Force H faced its most critical test yet. It was not, however, the Luftwaffe but Doenitz's submarines which struck the vital blow when on the 13th of November the *Ark Royal* was hit by a torpedo from the *U-81* only 30 miles to the east of Gibraltar. After fighting for her life for 14 hours, the carrier capsized and sank. For two years she had been the main striking element of Force H and a symbol of resistance for Gibraltar as much as for the fleet itself: her loss was a crippling blow to morale at a vital stage of the north African campaign.

Badly mauled in the defence and evacuation of Greece and Crete and the subsequent loss of three battleships, the Mediterranean Fleet was reduced, by the end of the year, to 3 light cruisers and a few destroyers. Somerville at the same time, through losses and damage (as well as the withdrawal of ships by the Admiralty for other duties), had only one old battleship, *Malaya*, an obsolete carrier, *Argus*, and one cruiser. The Royal Navy in the Mediterranean had been virtually annihilated. Rommel was on the borders of Egypt, Greece and Crete had been lost, and only the survival of Malta stood in the credit balance at the end of this dreadful year.

In March 1942 the battle for Malta was renewed with increased intensity. Force H with a new commander, Rear Admiral Sir Neville Syfret, had temporarily departed to escort a convoy to Madagascar which was threatened by the Japanese and replaced by Force W which arrived with the battleship *Renown* and 2 carriers, *Eagle* and the American *Wasp* which was carrying Spitfires for Malta. In the course of the summer *Eagle* and *Wasp*, joined later by the *Furious*, made several delivery runs to Malta which at last began to put the island's defences onto a sounder footing. Eastbound convoys from Gibraltar began again in June and every convoy now faced a bitter battle both against submarines and aircraft. Many merchant ships were lost and some struggled through against tremendous odds. In August Operation 'Pedestal' was mounted with 14 merchant ships and a strong escort, but only 5, mostly badly damaged, struggled into Malta. Among them was the tanker *Ohio* whose heroic and much publicised battle against the odds earned her Master the George Cross. The loss to the Royal Navy was one carrier, *Eagle*, 2 cruisers and a destroyer with many others badly damaged.

Thereafter, the tide began to turn and in November General Montgomery won the crucial battle of El Alamein, whilst at the other end of the Mediterranean a joint American and British force was preparing to crush Rommel in a great pincer movement along the whole length of the north African coast. After an heroic struggle Malta had been saved, but at tremendous cost. Whatever doubts may remain about her overall strategic importance, Malta had become a symbol of the struggle for victory in much the way that Gibraltar had appeared in the eighteenth century: her loss would have struck a psychological blow as great as the earlier loss of Singapore. Gibraltar had played a vital role in this epic struggle for survival and was now about to play a crucial part in the turning of the tide in north Africa.

*   *   *

The Americans were reluctant partners in the war in the Mediterranean. The strain of two years of conflict, almost entirely on the retreat, had convinced Churchill that the Allies should not rush into a second front until the conditions were right. The Americans on the other hand were anxious to get right to the heart of Europe and fretted at the delay which would accrue from nibbling at the 'soft underbelly' so favoured by Churchill and the British Chiefs of Staff. The US Navy in any case would have preferred to wage war in the Pacific where their

The 'Pride' of Gibraltar, HMS *Ark Royal* is listing badly after an attack by a U-boat 30 miles east of the Rock on 13th November 1941. (Imperial War Museum)

giant carrier-dominated task forces had the prospect of a decisive confrontation with Japan. Nevertheless, Churchill finally prevailed at the Washington Conference in June 1942 and the joint British/American landings in north Africa, 'Operation Torch', were reluctantly agreed.

Control of the Strait of Gibraltar was a vital factor in the planning. The Americans (although not Eisenhower himself) were reluctant to commit naval forces in the Mediterranean which might become trapped and would have preferred to land entirely in Morocco and proceed along the coast. But there were solid arguments against this: not only was it a much greater distance from Rommel's main panzer army, still at this stage firmly entrenched on the borders of Egypt, and even more crucially from Tunisia – the key to control of north Africa – but it also risked embarking on a messy confrontation with Vichy Morocco whose acquiescence was at best questionable. Hitler also recognised the strategic importance of Gibraltar and again formed a plan, 'Ilona', to march through Spain to the Mediterranean shore. But Franco was even less enthusiastic than he had been in 1940 – Rommel had not reached the Suez Canal and the Americans were in the war. Whilst the prospect of regaining Gibraltar and enlarging his north African possessions at the expense of France may have appeared superficially tempting, in reality General Franco was beginning to ease himself gently off the fence he had so precariously occupied since 1939. The Allies also went out of their way not to antagonise Spain by ensuring that the integrity of Spanish Morocco was scrupulously observed and that the flow of grain and other essential commodities into Spain was unimpaired. Hitler soon abandoned his plan to take Gibraltar and the threat from Spain was minimal.

In the end a compromise was reached on the landings in north Africa. The main American landing was to be in French Morocco whilst a joint Anglo-American force would land inside the Mediterranean at Oran and Algiers. Gibraltar was a key element in the latter plan as aircraft based at North Front would provide fighter and anti-submarine cover whilst Force H would support the landings and the lines of communication.

More than 400 aircraft were squeezed into the cramped airfield; 200 fighters were brought out in crates and assembled on the spot and Hudsons and Catalinas arrived in numbers to provide anti-submarine patrols. At one time at the height of the battle it was reported that nearly 650 aircraft were accommodated in Gibraltar. General Eisenhower's staff took over operations rooms and offices in the Rock and the General himself arrived on the 5th of November, assuming the temporary role as Allied Commander-in-Chief Gibraltar. Admiral Cunningham was also back as the Naval Commander-in-Chief after a sojourn in Washington. By his own account Eisenhower was far from impressed by the facilities made available in Gibraltar – he described the HQ 'in the dripping tunnels' as the most dismal setting he occupied during the war.

By the 4th of November the bay contained the greatest assembly of ships it had ever seen – no fewer than 160 warships and up to 200 transports and auxiliary vessels. Force H had been strengthened for the task with 2 battleships, the *Duke of York* and *Rodney*, 3 aircraft carriers, *Victorious*, *Formidable* and *Furious*, the battle-cruiser *Renown*, 2 cruisers and 13 destroyers. It was supplemented by the Eastern Task Force with one carrier (the venerable *Argus*), 3 cruisers and another 13 destroyers. The crews had a typical last night ashore, with results at best distasteful to that austere disciplinarian Cunningham, and on the following evening the vast armada put to sea to cover the Algerian landings. The 8th (Gibraltar) Submarine Flotilla deployed boats to cover Toulon, Oran and Algiers. As a timely reassurance, news of Montgomery's success at El Alamein now began to filter through: Rommel was about to be squeezed from both directions.

The invasion convoys sailing directly from Britain throughout late October passed through the Strait on the nights of the 5th and 6th November. By 0400 on the 7th the last ship – the carrier *Furious* and her escort – had left Europa Point astern. The fighters roamed ahead of the convoys but no enemy aircraft were encountered: 63 attacks were reported against U-boats. The greatest problem to emerge was the appalling weather – the worst reported for 25 years with

General Sikorski talking to Polish officers in the grounds of the Convent on his fatal visit to Gibraltar in July 1943. (Imperial War Museum)

13inches of rain – which restricted flying throughout November. All of this activity could not of course have been concealed from the Germans, but it appears that they thought until a very late stage that this was just a larger than usual Malta convoy. A convoy from Sierra Leone, allegedly leaked by British Intelligence to the Germans, enticed the U-boats away from the Strait (for a loss of 13 merchant ships), but leaving the coast largely clear for the invasion convoys.

The landings were entirely successful and although all was not plain sailing – in particular the American reverse at the battle of the Kasserine Pass – the pincer movement eventually forced the Germans and their Italian allies out of Africa altogether by May 1943, rather later than anticipated. Throughout this time Gibraltar continued to support the invasion force and in three months alone around the turn of the year there were nearly 50 convoys passing through the Strait, all of which had to be protected by Force H. Waves of Spitfires and Hurricanes staged through en route to airfields in north Africa as they became available. This support was to continue throughout the subsequent Sicilian and Italian campaigns during the rest of 1943 and 1944.

*   *   *

Of the minor incidents in Gibraltar during the war, none has attracted more controversy than the death in an air crash of the Polish General Wladyslaw Sikorski who had set up a Government-in-Exile in Paris in 1939 when Poland was overrun. The debate around his death was fuelled by the staging at the National Theatre in London in 1967 of a play, *The Soldiers*, by Rolf Hochhuth which suggested that Sikorski had been murdered at the instigation of Winston Churchill to appease Stalin. There were other theories that the aircraft was sabotaged by a German agent or, alternatively, that it was the work of Ivan Maisky, Sikorski's political rival in the tortured affairs of Poland. The Maisky theory was given credence by the fact that he was briefly in Gibraltar at the same time travelling in the opposite direction. But there is no evidence whatsoever that he got anywhere near Sikorski's aircraft – which was guarded throughout – or that he would have the technical knowledge to sabotage it even if such had been his intention. In any case political conspirators of his stature do not usually advertise their presence at the scene of the crime. Nevertheless, there are some contradictory statements and unanswered questions surrounding the accident although this is not unusual in aircraft crashes when the reason cannot be unequivocally determined. The issue was further confused by blatant attempts to use it for propaganda purposes by the Communists in the Cold War after 1948.

The facts briefly are as follows. Sikorski landed at Gibraltar on the 3rd of July 1943 from Cairo on his return from a meeting at Tehran with Stalin to negotiate the release of Polish prisoners held by the Russians and to obtain a political amnesty. His visit was particularly appropriate as there was a floating population of 30-50 Poles in Gibraltar which was at the end of an escape route through Spain. He left just before midnight on the 4th of July in a Liberator converted to carry passengers with an RAF crew commanded by Flight Lieutenant E. M. Prchal, a Czechoslovakian: there were 11 other passengers – a total of 17 with the crew – including two British Members of Parliament, Sikorski's daughter and his Chief of Staff. Eye-witnesses who watched the departure said that the pilot had some difficulty starting the engines – stimulating one of the subsequent theories that sugar had been placed in the petrol tanks – but eventually took off on a very dark night towards the east. The aircraft was heard to climb away, but then the sound of the engines suddenly stopped – there was no explosion. The aircraft was found partly floating about 400 yards off the end of the runway. The only survivor was the captain, Prchal – which led to the bizarre theory that he had engineered the whole thing. Most of the bodies, including Sikorski's, were recovered, as was eventually the wreckage of the aircraft.

The official enquiry eliminated sabotage but failed to come up with a clear-cut reason for the accident. Prchal stated that the start-up and take off were normal and that he climbed to about 300 feet when he throttled back the engines and trimmed the elevator – all of this was standard practice. When he tried to recommence climbing he felt a severe jolt and found the controls jammed solid, the aircraft sank slowly towards the sea as he and his co-pilot wrestled with the controls. When he realised that a crash was inevitable he closed all four throttles and warned the passengers. Prchal was thrown through the cockpit windscreen and badly injured. The wreckage was subjected to detailed technical examination. An air frame fitter subsequently said (24 years later) that he found a jammed socket and chain, part of the elevator trim controls, in the undamaged rear section of the aircraft. The enquiry could not confirm that this had happened before the crash and speculated that loose baggage in the heavily-laden aircraft may have jammed the controls. Alternatively it has been suggested that the pilot may have become disorientated taking off over the sea on a very dark night with no visual horizon. No contamination was found in the fuel tanks.

Churchill certainly had a good reason at this time for seeking to appease Stalin who was stridently demanding the opening of the second front. But it is a very long step from there to entertaining the theory that either he or British Intelligence conspired to kill Sikorski as a sweetener. Furthermore, Churchill was becoming increasingly aware of Stalin's malign intentions for central Europe and had no real incentive to remove one of his potential opponents. There is in fact no worthwhile evidence to support conspiracy theories, most of which are totally based on circumstantial evidence or are patently ridiculous. There were many unexplained aircraft crashes in the war and the possibility that the controls jammed in some way is an entirely credible theory: there was no particular reason why Sikorski should have been immune from such an unfortunate occurrence. Sikorski lay in state in the Roman Catholic Cathedral in a makeshift coffin guarded by his compatriots until his body was taken to England in a Polish destroyer. Many Poles remained sceptical of the British account of the reasons for the crash which has helped to keep the controversy alive if adding nothing to the evidence of its cause.

*   *   *

After the abandonment of Operation 'Felix', the security of Gibraltar was never seriously threatened. Long-range Italian and German aircraft occasionally bombed the city and harbour, but no serious damage was caused. There was, however, one other most interesting attempt, if in the end largely abortive, to undermine the security of the naval base. This was the operation by the Italian Navy to mount underwater attacks against naval ships in the harbour and merchant vessels moored in the bay.

The operation, which persisted throughout the time the Italians remained in the war, was led by Captain Prince Valerio Borghese, a charismatic, fanatically right-wing aristocrat who was eventually implicated in a projected military coup in 1970 and had to flee Italy to Spain. His operations against Gibraltar fall into three distinct phases. The first was based on the submarine *Scire* which was one of two boats modified to carry manned torpedoes in large cylinders fitted onto the deck. The idea was that the torpedoes, called '*Maiali*' (pigs) by the Italians, were carried to the vicinity of the target by the submarine where they could be extracted from the flooded cylinders under water. Driven under its own power and piloted either on the surface or submerged by two 'charioteers' sitting astride, the torpedo carried a 300-kg warhead in the nose which could be detached and secured to the target. The riders would then escape on the torpedo before eventually abandoning it and swimming back to a rendezvous with an Italian agent on the Spanish coast to be smuggled back to Italy. The torpedo had a self-destruct device to avoid leaving behind any evidence as to how the attack was contrived.

The first sortie of the *Scire* in September 1940 was recalled, but the following month the submarine settled undetected on the bottom of the bay near the mouth of the River Guadarranque. On the 30th of October the three torpedoes were launched against two battleships which were reported to be in the harbour. The mission went wrong right from the beginning: one sank after its engine failed and the crews of the other two had to abandon their craft after failure of their breathing apparatus and other equipment prevented them entering the harbour submerged. Two of the crews escaped and reached the rendezvous with their agent, but the third was captured after penetrating within 70 yards of the battleship *Barham*. Unfortunately, their secret mission was exposed when one of the abandoned torpedoes was washed up on the Spanish coast near the Rock. From then on explosives were regularly detonated in the bay to deter further underwater attacks.

It was not until May 1941 that the Italians were ready to mount another mission when the *Scire* once again settled on the mud in the same position as before. One of the torpedoes had an unserviceable motor and so the other two were launched with three-man crews. Again the mission was a failure, for although they reached their targets, merchant ships in the bay, the warheads sank to the bottom before they could be secured. This time the British were totally unaware of the attack and all six crew members returned safely to Italy.

So far three missions and all abortive, but Borghese was refining his techniques all the time and in September 1941 he was at last successful. Two of the crews failed to penetrate the harbour but successfully attached their warheads to merchant ships in the bay. The third breached the harbour defences but was unable to get close to a cruiser, their intended target, and instead attached their warhead to an 8000-ton tanker. At nine o'clock the following morning all three weapons exploded: one small ship was sunk, one so badly damaged that it was abandoned as a hulk, and the third had to be towed to England for repair. Borghese and the *Scire* had even more success at the other end of the Mediterranean when the human torpedoes badly damaged the battleships *Valiant* and *Queen Elizabeth* at Alexandria.

Despite the success of the fourth mission, a new method was adopted for the next series of attacks. A farmhouse, the Villa Carmela just two miles from Gibraltar, was acquired by a Spanish collaborator from which Italian frogmen would carry explosives to their targets in the bay. In July 1942 all was ready and 12 frogmen entered the water each carrying three 2-kg charges. Four ships were damaged and another less successful operation was mounted in September. But clearly such small weapons could not inflict the same damage as the 300-kg charges of the human torpedoes. A compromise was needed by which the torpedoes could be used without the immense difficulties and hazards of bringing a submarine into the bay and the need to return to Italy after each mission for reloading.

The answer was found in the rusting hulk of an old Italian merchant vessel of 5000 tons, the *Olterra*, which had been abandoned and scuttled at the outbreak of war. Borghese, using the cover of a Spanish salvage firm, had the *Olterra* refloated and moored at the outer pier of Algeciras harbour. Under the subterfuge of a leisurely refit the *Olterra* was modified to enable the human torpedoes to be launched through a door cut in one of the holds which could be flooded. The torpedoes were smuggled into Spain disguised as deck piping and the warheads concealed in petrol drums. It is difficult to believe that there was not some collusion with the Spanish authorities, and the British in Gibraltar certainly observed the *Olterra* with deep suspicion. It also lay under the direct gaze of the British Consul in the Hotel Vittoria in Algeciras. Spitfire photo-reconnaissance sorties were even flown to record the work in progress, but British Intelligence did not fully unravel the real role of the ship until after the Italian Armistice.

By December 1942 the *Olterra* was ready for the first mission with 3 torpedoes. The potential targets were tempting to say the least; Force H with 2 battleships and 2 carriers was in Gibraltar. The mission was a disaster almost from the outset. The first torpedo was sunk by one of the explosive charges which were frequently detonated in the harbour entrance and the crew was killed. The second was spotted on the surface by searchlights and sunk by gunfire – its crew was captured. The defences were now thoroughly alerted with searchlights and patrol boats scouring the bay and the third crew decided to abandon the mission. The torpedo made it back to the *Olterra*, but lost one of its crewmen on the way. The British believed that the assault craft had been launched from a submarine. Undeterred, more crews and torpedoes were smuggled into Spain and a second mission was launched in May 1943. This time, concentrating on merchant ships in the harbour, the sortie was far more successful: 2 merchant ships – one American – were crippled and one was sunk. All the crews returned safely. Diving equipment was left by Italian agents on the shore line to suggest the source of the raid.

The final mission was launched on the night of the 3rd of August and warheads were clamped to three merchant ships despite the new hazard of barbed wire draped over the hulls for protection. One crew member was captured but all three ships were damaged. The operation which was now getting well into its stride was only ended by the Armistice in September 1943. In all, the Italian frogmen had sunk or damaged 14 merchant ships totalling nearly 70,000 tons. It had been an extraordinarily bold and courageous attempt to imperil the

By the end of the war the north face of the Rock bristled with embrasures and observation posts even though the threat of a land invasion was small after 1940.

use of the bay and the harbour, and although the small charges were unlikely to have sunk a major warship, with a little more luck they might well have succeeded in disabling one for a sustained period when the Battle of the Mediterranean was at its height.

*   *   *

The hectic days for Gibraltar were mostly over by the end of 1943. The Germans and the Italians had been expelled from north Africa; in May the first unopposed convoy left Gibraltar for Malta, and Sicily was invaded in July. In September the Armistice with Italy was signed by Marshal Badoglio. Admiral Sir Harold Burrough who took over as Flag Officer Gibraltar was able to tell his coxswain on his arrival: 'I've come here for a rest'. Doenitz, in the wake of increasing U-boat losses in the Bay of Biscay, proposed in May that Spain and Gibraltar should be occupied to turn the Allies' flank in the Mediterranean, but a by now chastened and more realistic Hitler replied that it was out of the question. Later in the year Doenitz told Hitler that U-boats were no longer able to pass through the Strait of Gibraltar, although they were certainly exiting the Mediterranean well into 1944.

In 1944 the war was becoming almost a distant memory and in March the evacuees started to dribble back to Gibraltar – children were seen in the streets for the first time for four years. Gibraltar was now of course much safer than London which was enduring the ravages of the 'V' weapons and pressure soon grew for the repatriation to be speeded-up. It was still to be a source of contention until the last refugees returned as late as 1951. On 5th June Gibraltar suffered its last air-raid when 12 Italian torpedo bombers attacked from the south of France: the only weapon to make any impression was a stray torpedo which hit the detached mole and several of the raiding aircraft were lost. The invasion of southern France in August brought a flurry of activity to the airfield when 94 Dakotas were reported to have landed in 79 minutes – a rate of flow on a single runway rather greater than London Heathrow could accommodate today. 202 Squadron with its Hudsons which had borne the brunt of the anti-submarine war were able to depart by September leaving just one Catalina. This was slightly premature as there was a revival of U-boat activity around the turn of the year.

By 1945 the main preoccupations within Gibraltar were no longer military, but echoed around colonial rule, civil rights and local government. This properly belongs to the final, and very different era, for from 1945 for the first time in six hundred years Gibraltar became no longer solely a military fortress.

12 ETERNAL CONFRONTATION 1945-96

THE HISTORY OF GIBRALTAR after 1945 has been overshadowed by the confrontation with Spain. But the period has also seen significant changes in the strategic importance of Gibraltar as a military base and in the constitutional development of the Colony. These three issues constantly interact, and particularly after the 1960s the relationship between constitutional development and the Spanish question become almost inextricably intertwined. Nevertheless, as in my discussion of the nineteenth century and in the interests of simplicity, I shall try as far as possible, despite the disadvantages, to look at these issues separately.

*   *   *

There was only a short period of grace after the war before Gibraltar began to assume a new military role. Its importance as a staging post on the routes to Empire remained although of diminishing significance as Britain divested itself of its Imperial possessions. However, that this role had not totally disappeared was shown with striking force in 1982 when the task force was launched for the recovery of the Falkland Islands. Freetown (Sierra Leone) and the Ascension Islands became the main staging posts, but Gibraltar was a useful back-up base, not least as the repository of some conventional weapons not readily available elsewhere. In using Gibraltar, however, the Government had to bear in mind the sensitivity of Spain on the subject of the Falklands.

But the most important role for Gibraltar came with the deterioration of relations with the Soviet Union and the creation of the North Atlantic Treaty Organisation (NATO) in 1949. The southern flank of NATO was always regarded as one of the areas more vulnerable to Soviet aggression and the latter kept a powerful fleet in the Black Sea. As the Soviet Union developed a 'blue water strategy', the security of the Mediterranean once again came to play an important role in the West's thinking. All seaborne supplies and reinforcements to the southern flank had to pass through the Strait of Gibraltar, and although the greater reach of modern warships and merchantmen reduced the need for staging posts, there was obvious logistic merit in keeping stocks of weapons and other war requirements close to the potential source of conflict. And one great advantage of Gibraltar was the scope and security of its storage capacity. The tunnelling in the Rock was continued with yet more capacious storage halls and operational facilities. However, the fixed defences which had become increasingly obsolete were progressively dismantled: Gibraltar could no longer be defended by guns alone. On the other hand, modern surveillance techniques and new technology gave scope for monitoring even the most silent of submarines which might try to slip through the Strait into or out of the Mediterranean.

The naval base remained the dominant military element although at least one resident British battalion was retained on the Rock until replaced by the Gibraltar Regiment, the successor since 1958 of the Gibraltar Defence Force. A Gibraltar Royal Navy Reserve was created in 1965. The airfield, severely restricted in its potential for development, was of less importance to NATO because the Americans had the major base at Rota just along the coast. However, it was a useful temporary base for Shackleton and later Nimrod maritime reconnaissance aircraft which of course were unacceptable at Spanish airfields. During the heightened tension with Spain in the 1970s, a small detachment of Hunter fighters was

Only the occasional NATO warship now ties up alongside Gibraltar's once bustling quays.

deployed to Gibraltar, but their presence was more symbolic than a realistic deterrent.

The military presence in Gibraltar was slimmed down and the naval dockyard privatised even before the collapse of the Soviet Union. This placed a severe strain on the economy albeit opening up economic opportunities in the longer term. The last resident battalion left in 1991 and air traffic control at the airport was civilianised in 1994 although RAF aircraft still make regular visits. Despite these retrenchments there is still a British military presence in Gibraltar, maintaining an infrastructure which could be expanded again if the need ever arose in circumstances not at present foreseen.

And this is the nub of the problem. All nation states seek to reduce the cost of their armed forces when tension relaxes, and the British Government has a long record of not being slow to take advantage of such changes in the political climate. But as everybody knows and most ignore, the climate can change very rapidly whilst military capacity – even more so in these days of sophisticated and expensive technology – is very slow to respond. The United Kingdom's strategic need for Gibraltar in the late 1990s is no longer readily apparent. With the Soviet threat demolished and surrounded by friendly NATO countries with more convenient and better equipped facilities, the need for a military base on Gibraltar has diminished. Britain no longer has an Empire to protect, but it still professes to maintain a world role – and this was demonstrated as recently as 1992 in the Gulf. It would be a brave, and perhaps foolish person, who would confidently predict that Gibraltar will never again have a military role, and it is therefore prudent that for as long as Britain has an interest in the Rock that at least a basic military infrastructure is kept in place.

*   *   *

Whilst the military men continued to ponder and plan on the future of Gibraltar as a naval and a NATO base, it was far from the minds of the local people except insofar as it remained the economic basis of their continuing prosperity and a symbol of British political integrity. Like those returning to Britain from the trenches of the First World War, the old order could not continue for the evacuees slowly returning to Gibraltar and their menfolk who had stayed at home in the service of the Crown. Democratic freedom, economic and social equality and international order were the bywords of politics in the late 1940s. The constitutional development of Gibraltar, along with the confrontation with Spain, rather than the military criteria have been the dominating issues of the last fifty years.

The evolution of Gibraltar after 1945 may be conveniently divided into three phases. Spain played a comparatively minor role until the mid 1950s with the centre of the stage being held by the struggle to achieve wider self-government. The second phase up to 1969 followed a similar path except that the deteriorating relationship with Spain steadily began to interact with the demand for constitutional development. The third phase from 1970 to the present has been almost wholly dominated by the Spanish question: the constitutional issues now were no longer internal, but revolved around the formal relationship with Britain and the intransigence of Spain.

The seeds of political development within Gibraltar itself had been sown during the war. The City Council in the interwar years had hardly been representative of the mass of the people, but largely reflected the commercial and legal interests of the old Exchange Committee. It had been mainly concerned with those municipal matters which would have been the responsibility of a borough council in the United Kingdom. But as we saw in the last chapter, the

Association for the Advancement of Civil Rights in Gibraltar (AACR) had by 1945 become the focus of local power in the colony. Although the Exchange Committee, the Gibraltar branch of the Transport and General Workers' Union and the Chamber of Commerce still had a voice in future developments, most of the running was made by the AACR which was essentially a workers' party. Although the AACR developed its power base in arguments with the British authorities over repatriation, under the guiding hand of its founder Albert Risso and its leading intellectual Joshua Hassan, it rarely missed an opportunity to assert political rights as well.

The Governor, his main aide the Colonial Secretary, and the Colonial Office in London were slow to recognise this shift in the balance of power. What little consultation as was undertaken was with members of the old order who themselves were no longer representative of the mass of the people. Furthermore, all decisions in the immediate after-

Modern Gibraltar from the Rock. The extent of land reclamation and the difficulties posed by the runway protruding into the bay can be well seen in this view.

math of war were subject to the ultimate veto of the three Service Ministries in London, although in practice this had little impact on political developments. Thus early attempts to move back towards the pre-war system of a City Council with a Governor's Executive Council making all the real decisions was not well received by any of the new centres of political power. An attempt was made in late 1944 to establish an Advisory Council (which had first been proposed by Mason-MacFarlane in 1943) of nominated and elected members, but it would have had no executive or legislative authority and was rapidly rejected by the AACR.

The re-establishment of the City Council nevertheless went ahead with 11 candidates contesting the seven seats which would have a majority over the nominated or 'official' members. The AACR swept the board, despite an electoral system which was biased against them, and managed to secure all seven seats displaying in the process a political acumen and organisation which came as a surprise, if not shock, to the Governor and the establishment. Joshua Hassan who gained the largest vote was elected Chairman. In the space of three years the AACR had been transformed from a pressure group into a political party. Even more significantly, the war years, with all their privations for separated families, had bonded the Gibraltarians together as a nation: it was the evacuation which became the touch paper for all the political developments in the post-war years.

The AACR had enjoyed remarkable success in achieving monopoly control of the City Council. But dustbins and drains were far from the main interest of its leading figures, which was to obtain self-government for the Colony with the power to make laws and exercise financial control with the minimum of interference from the Governor and his Executive Council. Thus the demand for a Legislative Council became the main focal point of Gibraltarian politics for the next five years. It was a battle which looked at in retrospect casts little credit on any of the parties involved. It was confrontation at almost every turn which at times became heated and personal. The two Governors involved (Lieutenant Generals Sir Thomas Eastwood until 1947 and Sir Kenneth Anderson), although privately sympathetic towards the Gibraltarian cause, were frequently at loggerheads with the AACR and the other institutions whilst at times also fighting the Colonial Office in London. The Gibraltar institutions also pursued their own vested interests, often in opposition to each other, with the wealthy merchant class dominant in the Exchange Committee and the Chamber of Commerce resolutely opposing any suggestion of tax measures which would hit their own pockets. Even the AACR split into political and trade union wings as some members sought to distance it from its working-class roots as more and more middle-class and professional people were repatriated. There was also discord in London when the Cabinet refused to accept the recommendations of the Colonial Office. Mr Attlee, for no apparently very good reason, thought that there was too much government in Gibraltar and wanted to amalgamate the City and Legislative Councils into one body. Whilst there may have been some theoretical justification for that view (and it eventually came to pass), it nevertheless flew in the face of everything which had been laboriously negotiated over three difficult years and was totally opposed by all the other parties.

In essence the British Government was prepared to concede a degree of representation to Gibraltarians in the running of their affairs provided that real authority remained with the Governor. Thus all the proposals put forward envisaged an 'official' (that is nominated) majority in any legislative body and constrained the matters which they were empowered to discuss. As the debate progressed, the continued delay in repatriating the evacuees provided a fertile ground for dissension and united the people behind the AACR. The main reason for the postponement was the shortage of housing and concern regarding the sanitary and medical facilities. Today the prevarication looks unreasonable – the last evacuees did not return until 1951 – but it must be remembered that in the late 1940s Britain was almost bankrupt and the need for regeneration at home equally pressing.

The Government in London had conceded in principle the need for a Legislative Council as early as November 1945, but it later claimed, somewhat ingenuously, that it had done so under duress. The details took five years to determine, but in general it marked a gradual retreat from the intransigent position which at first cast the Legislative Council as merely the Advisory Council in disguise. A bitter controversy about a Trades Tax unilaterally introduced in January 1950 detracted for a time from the central argument, but on 23rd November 1950 the Legislative Council was finally officially inaugurated by the Duke of Edinburgh. The Government in London had achieved one major success by insisting on the 'unofficial' members of the Council being elected by proportional representation, which in the event destroyed the AACR monopoly, but did not prevent it retaining power for many years. In fact, although gaining three out of five seats on the Council with the right wing Independents winning the other two, the AACR no longer had the overwhelming support it had enjoyed in its earlier years. The main winner was perhaps Joshua Hassan who had played a clever and subtle hand, distancing himself from the extremists without ever needing to climb too far into other influential pockets. As Chairman of the City Council and a member of the Legislature, he was now in a position to play the leading role in future developments.

As the constitutional storm subsided, the next few years were comparatively quiet although the AACR never gave up its struggle for the abolition of proportional representation which was a serious impediment to its monopoly of power. The main cause of dissension became the introduction of income tax which was strongly opposed by the representatives of the wealthy classes although accepted by the AACR in return for some measures of social reform. The AACR had an understandable grievance, for social security measures such as old age pensions and unemployment benefit, which had been fully accepted within the UK, were not available in Gibraltar.

Until 1954 the AACR could reasonably claim to speak for most of the people of Gibraltar, but the formation of the Commonwealth Party introduced the colony to two-party politics. Although it sought to deny claims that it was the party of the right, it was certainly to the right of the AACR. In the event it failed to provide a viable opposi-

tion to that formidable powerbase which Hassan had constructed. A significant, if mainly cosmetic, development was the redesignation of the Chairman of the City Council as the Mayor, and Joshua Hassan, endowed with all the ceremonial trimmings of office, became the first incumbent in 1955.

*　　　*　　　*

The history of constitutional development in Gibraltar after 1945 is inevitably a story of dissent and confrontation, but before describing the next constitutional crisis it is perhaps necessary to put it into perspective. Decolonisation or, as in the case of Gibraltar, the gradual devolution of power and responsibility to the local population is undoubtedly an incredibly difficult and complex task and was not helped by the intransigence of the majority of members of the United Nations, the extremism of some of the emerging nationalists, or reactionary polemics at home. Compared with many of Britain's colonial outposts the transition in Gibraltar was remarkably trouble free – one only has to compare in this period the violence in Cyprus and disturbances in Malta to see that the Gibraltarians were remarkably restrained in their approach to evolution for which Joshua Hassan must take much of the credit. Unlike so many emerging nations there was also an overwhelming wish to remain British and a pride and respect for the Crown which was amply demonstrated by the ecstatic reception given to Queen Elizabeth II on her visit in 1954. The gathering intransigence of Spain at this time no doubt stimulated the loyalty of Gibraltarians to the Crown.

Nevertheless, 1955 saw the first major constitutional crisis strike the Colony: it was totally unexpected and largely unnecessary. It was kindled by a shortfall in revenue due in the main to the border restrictions imposed by Spain, but also by the reluctance of Gibraltarians in the past to accept reasonable taxes. The Financial Secretary decided it was necessary to introduce a ten per cent import duty on selected goods to balance the budget. This was not only contrary to the long standing status, going back to the reign of Queen Anne, of Gibraltar as a free port, but it was sprung upon the Legislative Council with no prior warning. Whilst there may have been good budgetary reasons for the lack of consultation, it was certainly prejudicial to maintaining an equable political climate. The measure was defeated in the Legislative Council and a new and inexperienced governor, Lieutenant General Sir Harold Redman, used his reserve powers to force through the measure. Uproar ensued and eventually the elected members resigned their seats. The issue by now was less concerned with the imposition of the tax than the question of principle involved in the Governor vetoing the Legislative Council. The Colonial Secretary in London intervened to pour oil on the disturbed waters and the crisis passed, but the incident was undoubtedly a spur to the next round of constitutional change which gave the elected members a majority on the Legislative Council and circumscribed the powers of the Governor. In the ensuing elections the AACR retained its powerbase and effectively destroyed the Commonwealth Party.

After the crisis of 1955 the political scene in Gibraltar was again comparatively placid. The AACR continued to press for constitutional reform and the Colonial Office, encouraged by the peaceful and law-abiding environment in Gibraltar compared with the violent nationalism in Malta and Cyprus, moved steadily towards giving the locally-elected representatives more responsibility. Nevertheless, the situation in the latter years of the 1950s was little changed: the Governor and the Executive Council still ruled the colony, and whilst the Legislative Council had a sort of power 'in extremis', as had been shown in 1955, it lacked authority in the day-to-day business of government. The AACR unequivocally wanted to move towards a ministerial system for the elected members, but the solution adopted was to invite these representatives of the people to become 'associated' with selected government departments. Paradoxically this gave them a measure of responsibility, in that they had to answer for their department in the legislature, without any real power in the decision making.

The AACR under the guiding hand of Joshua Hassan had moved so far towards the centre that with the demise of the Commonwealth Party it was the Transport and General Workers' Union which in effect became the opposition although with little electoral success. After the excesses of the 1940s, constitutional development was now assuming a responsible and pragmatic form. The British Government was duly grateful and Joshua Hassan was rewarded with a knighthood in 1963.

The situation so far may be briefly summarised: the people of Gibraltar had moved slowly towards internal self-government against hesitant British authorities which recognised the need for change in the new international environment reflected in the United Nations decolonisation measures, but which were inherently reluctant to move too quickly. Thus in 1963, in the last resort, Gibraltar was still controlled by the Governor with his Executive Council and his array of largely expatriate civil servants. True the elected representatives had increased influence in the decision making through the 'members', but they did not have absolute power. Much of that was to change in the new constitution of 1964.

The years after 1963 were increasingly dominated by the conflict with Spain which in turn influenced further constitutional development. The appearance of Gibraltarian representatives before the UN in 1963 led to a frank reappraisal of the relationship with Britain. Before that episode the AACR had concerned itself almost entirely with devolving power from the British establishment; afterwards the people and their elected representatives began to concentrate far more on the positive aspects of a close relationship with Britain. The official AACR position was for a 'free association', but there was an increasing number who wished to see a much closer integration leading to the formation of a new opposition – the Integration with Britain Party (IWBP).

Despite the heightened tension with Spain, the revised constitution of 1964 owed more to a new Conservative Government in Britain and in particular the Minister for Commonwealth Relations and Colonies, Duncan Sandys. In essence the Government conceded almost all that the AACR had been agitating for since 1955. The number of elected members in the Executive Council was increased from four to five and in future would be known as the Gibraltar Council. But the main changes occurred in the Legislative Council and the civil service. A

Chief Minister and a Council of Ministers were to be appointed from the Legislative Council who would have full responsibility for their own departments. The Chief Secretary would cease to be a member of the Council, which was increased to eleven elected members with only two 'official' members with limited voting rights. The Chief Secretary was retitled the Permanent Secretary – responsible to the Chief Minister for the efficient running of the civil service. The Legislative Council was now in several respects a miniature equivalent of Westminster with a similar relationship with its civil service. The Governor retained responsibility for defence, foreign relations and internal security with other reserve powers, apparently substantial, but in reality largely unusable except in a serious emergency.

The years after 1964, under pressure from the tension provoked by Spain, saw an increase in support for the pro-integration movement. However, the AACR did not lose its mass backing and Sir Joshua Hassan remained Chief Minister, albeit with a minority government dependent on the support of the Independents. The attitude of Spain had induced a new mood of togetherness among Gibraltarians and on many issues, particularly constitutional matters, members of the Legislative Council were able to unite in coalition. By careful semantics, the AACR and the IWBP were to gloss over the very substantial differences between 'free association' and 'integration' with Britain.

The next constitutional change in 1969 was a logical and progressive development of the 1964 remodelling. However, the preliminary discussions were overshadowed by a widely publicised referendum in 1967 on Gibraltar's future, of which more will be said in relation to the confrontation with Spain (page 169). The new negotiations were not conducted with quite the same harmony as in 1964 due to a somewhat insensitive representative of the British Government, Lord Shephard, and were foreshadowed by a bizarre incident when a series of letters to the *Gibraltar Chronicle* from a small group known as the 'Doves' called for a resolution of the Spanish problem by negotiation. This was seen as, and in essence was, a capitulation to Spain and led to riots in the city which had to be curtailed by the Governor threatening to deploy the military garrison. Troops were deployed in the afternoon of 6th April against the wishes of the Mayor, but the disorder had by then died away. If nothing else it showed the determination of the overwhelming majority of Gibraltarians to remain closely attached to Britain, whatever the economic cost.

It also brought a new bout of co-operation between the two major parties thereby providing a virtually united front in the constitutional talks. As a result the Government again made concessions as it had sooner or later in almost all the constitutional discussions since 1945. The most significant aspect of the new declaration was an unambiguous affirmation that Gibraltar was a part of the Crown's dominions and would remain so unless an Act of Parliament ruled otherwise, and that the Gibraltarians would never be handed over to another state against their freely and democratically expressed wishes. Here in tablets of stone was the security that the Gibraltarian people had come to see as the most pressing question in the relationship between Britain and its erstwhile military fortress. It is of course possible for this provision to be overturned by the will of the British Parliament, but as politicians have subsequently found in the Falkland Islands and in Ulster, it is not a commitment which could be readily evaded.

Other provisions were that the 'Colony', that discredited international nomenclature, would henceforth be the 'City' of Gibraltar although the inhabitants would remain citizens of the United Kingdom and Colonies. The City Council was to be merged with the Legislative Council to form a House of Assembly: although long resisted by the AACR when the municipal body had power, albeit only over mundane matters, it was now anomalous since the Legislative Council had assumed ministerial functions. The division of power under the new constitution was unique in British colonial practice. It was normal to define the powers of the Governor, but in Gibraltar it was the powers of the ministers (known as 'Defined Domestic Matters') which were promulgated, with the Governor responsible for all else. The list has been steadily widened over the years, but still remains the basis of the division of responsibility today.

The Assembly would consist of 15 members elected under a new system for a period of four years. Proportional representation, which had long been anathema to the AACR, was abandoned although the new electoral system was yet to be determined. The Governor retained his responsibilities for external affairs and defence with the Gibraltar Council, on which as we have seen there was already a majority of elected Gibraltarians. The Permanent Secretary, which remained a British expatriate post after the 1965 changes, became Deputy Governor, but although he retains constitutional responsibility for the civil service, the effective control has passed into local hands.

The long evolution of the constitution was almost complete with power and responsibility for internal government now firmly in the hands of the Gibraltarians. If the history of this development is littered with disagreements and compromise, this was inevitable given the attitudes of successive British Governments beset with the vast problems of recovering from the economic and social problems of the war and only slowly coming to terms with the new international environment which saw Imperialism in a totally new and hostile light. The Gibraltarians also had to adjust their expectations in the light of the increased confrontation with Spain and again the process had been traumatic. Despite these difficulties, however, it must be remembered that most of the changes had been conducted in a responsible and sober manner: there had been no terrorism, a little passive but rarely prolonged disobedience, and on the whole genuine commitment on both sides to see progress. It had been slow, invariably too slow for the AACR, but it had been a civilised and peaceful transition. Sir Joshua Hassan and his fellow members of the AACR can take much of the credit for this peaceful evolution as well as the generally considered and careful actions of successive Governors, who it must be remembered were always senior military figures with little experience in the labyrinth of politics.

*   *   *

After 1969 the battle lines changed. The AACR had succeeded in erasing proportional representation, but the complex new electoral system was conditioned by the number of candidates for which the elector was allowed to vote. The practical consequence of this was that any one party was unlikely to achieve at best more than a bare majority, and in fact the AACR had to relinquish the power they had held for so long to a coalition of the IWBP and Independents. This soon fell apart and the AACR, still under Sir Joshua Hassan, resumed power in 1972. However, party politics on the Whitehall pattern was now an established reality in Gibraltar.

The battle lines had also changed in other respects. Under a Labour Government, ministers were now much more inclined to balance the interests of Britain in Europe, which included better relations with Spain since the death of Franco in November 1975, against the concerns of the Gibraltarians. Whilst continuing to assert that the future of Gibraltar was dependent on the democratic wishes of its people, they were no longer prepared to tolerate any constitutional developments which would further antagonise Spain. Britain had gone as far as it was prepared to go. This stance was fundamentally opposed to the policies of the IWBP which campaigned for political, social and economic integration with Britain with representation at Westminster. Hassan was not prepared to go so far although he too wanted closer ties within the bounds of 'free association', but he did not espouse economic parity which he recognised as an unrealistic aim. Roy Hattersley, the minister responsible, was far more outspoken than most of his predecessors: he emphatically ruled out integration or parity and mounted an undisguised attack on the IWBP. Hassan was placed in the embarrassing position of having to support the British Government against his local political opponents – the AACR had moved a long way from its left-wing confrontational stance of the 1940s and 50s and in doing so finally severed its contacts with the powerful Transport and General Workers' Union.

The IWBP, which had displayed few political skills, was destroyed when its leader resigned and the party decided not to contest the next elections in 1976. The AACR meanwhile reigned supreme in the Assembly against a fragmented opposition. The election also marked the emergence of Joe Bossano, who had resigned at an earlier

stage from the IWBP, although he had no support within the Assembly for his Gibraltar Democratic Movement (GDM). Of greater significance was the election of a democratic government in Spain in 1977 which marked a more constructive approach, although it was to be many more years before this resulted in the lifting of restrictions at the border. In the 1980 elections Hassan retained his first place in the poll although only by a narrow 64 votes from Joe Bossano. The IWBP also re-emerged under a new name as the Democratic Party of British Gibraltar (DPBG) and gained six seats.

The nationality issue took a further turn in 1981. In the context of a wider bill which sought to define British nationality, Gibraltar was placed in the second category as 'citizens of British Dependent Territories'. This caused uproar in Gibraltar and all parties once again united to oppose Britain. An amendment to bring Gibraltarians into the first category of full citizenship was defeated

in the Commons but accepted in the Lords. The Government gave way.

The main issue of the early 1980s, apart from the ongoing but exceedingly difficult talks with Spain, was the announcement by Britain that it was to close the naval dockyard. Paradoxically, the partial re-opening of the border with Spain was also posing a potentially disastrous draining away of capital from Gibraltar. These issues dominated the 1984 elections in which the AACR was again returned with a majority, but Joe Bossano's party, now renamed the Gibraltar Socialist Labour Party (GSLP), became the official opposition with seven seats. The integrationist DPBG disappeared again after its brief revival. Politics in Gibraltar was now polarised between a centre right AACR and a new workers' party supported by the unions, the GSLP.

The Brussels Communique of 1984 between Britain and Spain, which led to the full re-opening of the border, will be discussed in more detail later, but it presaged

The closure of the naval dockyard was initially a major blow to the Gibraltar economy, but it is now a successful privatised industry.

the next major split in the domestic politics of Gibraltar. In essence the agreement was welcomed by the AACR but condemned in the strongest possible terms by Joe Bossano and the GSLP. From opinion polls conducted at the time it looked as though the people overwhelmingly supported the GSLP. Bossano played the nationalist card to the hilt and the people responded with all the fervour of a besieged city despite the fact that the border with Spain was now open: the GSLP was now the voice of the people in the way that the AACR had been in the earlier decades after the war. The latter on the other hand was even being identified as little more than the lackey of Imperialist masters. Hassan had been in power for so long that he had inevitably become too closely identified with 'the establishment'.

Following a heated controversy over Spanish use of the airport, the 72-year-old Chief Minister resigned in December 1987. In fact, like so many of his vast experience, he had in his maturity become more prag-

matic and conciliatory – in the 1980s he made the fatal mistake for a politician of seeing two sides to a problem. Perhaps also he had lost the taste for confrontation which had marked his formative years when the AACR was in the forefront of constitutional progress: he now recognised that it was neither sensible nor necessary to die in every ditch. Whatever the cause of his decline, Sir Joshua Hassan had been a great servant of Gibraltar and in his later years a wise counsel for successive British Governments. But in the late 1980s this latter attribute was completely out of tune with the local mood which reacted positively to the strident nationalism of Joe Bossano: he was prepared to dig a ditch and, if necessary, to die in it.

The Brussels Communique came home to roost in the elections of 1988 when the GSLP won a landslide victory. Indeed, had it not been for the electoral rules by which the elector had only eight votes, it is beyond doubt that its majority in the Assembly would have been far greater than the eight to seven advan-

The Queensway Marina. The encouragement of tourism has brought a new source of wealth to Gibraltar – and an improvement in the architecture.

tage it had over the AACR. The wheel had come full circle: Gibraltar was again ruled by a workers' party, but it was no longer the heirs of Albert Risso and Sir Joshua Hassan.

*   *   *

Spain's claim to Gibraltar had been muted for the greater part of a century and a half before 1945. But it would be misleading to assume that either the Spanish Government or people had lost their enthusiasm for recovering this tiny parcel of country forfeited at the Treaty of Utrecht: it was simply that the circumstances had never been propitious for either a military or a diplomatic offensive with any real chance of success. In reality the recovery of Gibraltar was the catalyst which could unite all factions in Spain's still troubled and divided nation, exacerbated by the international opprobrium attaching to Europe's only remaining Fascist dictator. It was thus not surprising that Madrid played this card for all it was worth. On the other hand the British Government, encouraged by the media, attributed the agitation to Franco himself – they too failed to recognise that virtually all the Spanish people could unite on this issue, and were thus the more disappointed when the removal of the dictatorship made little practical difference to the resolution of the confrontation.

General Franco was fairly confident that Gibraltar would fall into his hands like a ripe plum after the end of the war. Although excluded from the United Nations, Franco could well see that the 'bête noire' of this self-righteous emerging organisation was colonialism and that Britain was in the middle of its sights. Furthermore, economically devastated by the war, Britain, either voluntarily or out of necessity, would have to divest itself of an Empire no longer sustainable – and without the Empire what need of a strategic fortress whose role could only be to safeguard this albatross hanging round its neck? On one point the Treaty of Utrecht was quite clear: whenever 'the Crown of Great Britain' no longer needed Gibraltar it had to be offered back to Spain 'before any others'. As we have seen, however, the emergence of the Cold War gave an entirely new slant to Gibraltar's role as the gateway to the Mediterranean: even Franco would have difficulty denying that Britain within NATO still had a military use for the base.

Franco's expectations were dashed almost immediately after 1945 when it became clear that Britain was to make no unseemly dash from Imperial responsibility. Emerging nationhood was to be nurtured by a progressive devolution of power and responsibility to local organisations:it was the only possible course which would reduce the likelihood of internal power struggles, impoverishment and consequent chaos. And whilst the Empire still existed there was a continuing need for a stable network of military bases on the sea routes to the many dependent nations to the south and east. Furthermore, Franco was concerned even in 1945 that Britain was prepared to concede a greater degree of internal self-government to Gibraltar itself thereby, in his eyes, again contravening the Treaty of Utrecht.

The plum did not fall in 1945 and the situation continued to simmer for some years. But the modest constitutional development in 1950 of the introduction of the Legislative Council provoked Franco into a tirade against Britain and Gibraltar gleefully pursued by the Spanish press. Rather like Argentina in the Peron era, when the Maldives became an essential feature of the school curriculum, Franco went out of his way to educate the Spanish people in the iniquities of the Gibraltarians and their British protectors. This was sufficient to stimulate riots in Madrid where students attacked the British Embassy buildings (there had been no ambassador to Madrid since the UN resolution of 1946) and the offices of British European Airways. But this frantic outburst was in many ways counterproductive, for it simply hardened the attitude of the Gibraltarians against Spain, already inherently hostile, and helped to forge the growing national identity within the Colony as well as cementing the loyalty to the Crown. If there was ever a period when the Gibraltarians might have voluntarily acquiesced in union with Spain, which is doubtful anyway, it had certainly passed beyond recall by 1950.

Diplomatic relations between Britain and Spain were restored in 1951 in the wake of a commercial agreement in 1948. This eventually led to direct talks in which Spain developed the theory, which it was later to use in the UN, that the true inhabitants of

Gibraltar were those 'expelled' in 1704 and now living in the Campo, and that the Gibraltarians were really aliens who had come from other countries merely to serve the British garrison. Predictably, negotiations along these lines made no progress. Tension was elevated to a new level when it was announced that the Queen was to visit Gibraltar as part of her Commonwealth tour in 1954. For the first time since 1945 Spain replaced blustering with deeds by imposing restraints on contact with Gibraltar. The consulate was closed, restrictions were placed on Spanish visitors, work permits for new Spanish workers ceased to be approved and a ban was placed on certain goods crossing into Gibraltar from Spain. The measures in themselves were fairly mild, but they were sufficient to make the Gibraltarians, who up to now had been mainly concerned with internal constitutional developments, begin to reconsider their relationship with both Britain and Spain. A new era had opened which was slowly to become the overriding feature of Gibraltar politics.

There was a fourth player in the developing wrangle over Gibraltar – the United Nations. Having served her penance of international purgatory Spain was invited to join the UN in 1955. At first she kept a low profile and it was not until 1963 that Gibraltar was discussed in New York. However, the UN had been very active in the decolonisation process since its inception and the General Assembly had set up the Committee of 24 to supervise the means. In line with that Committee's requirements Britain had submitted a list of dependent territories which included Gibraltar. This was perhaps a mistake, although nobody seemed to realise it at the time, as under the Treaty of Utrecht Gibraltar could not be decolonised unless Spain waived its claim – it had to belong either directly to Britain or offered to Spain. Nevertheless, Britain assured the UN that it was, in effect, handing over power to locally elected representatives who wished to retain a link with Britain. Spain, however, ingeniously turned this statement on its head by asserting that decolonisation meant returning the Rock to Spain – if Britain no longer had the requirement for the fortress, as conceded under the 1713 Treaty, it had to be restored to its earlier status. Sir Joshua

Hassan and the opposition leader Peter Isola, presenting a united case to the UN, eloquently supported the British view.

The Committee of 24 was hamstrung in its consideration of Gibraltar by the ambiguities in the UN Charter and the General Assembly Resolutions which were never intended to apply to the specific intricacies of this kind of dispute. There were three relevant paragraphs. Resolution 1541(XV) of the General Assembly stated that a non-self-governing territory can be assumed to have reached a full measure of self-government by emergence as a sovereign independent state, by free association with an independent state or by integration with an independent state. Gibraltar was sure that the territory fell within the second category although Britain was perhaps more ambivalent on this point. So far, so good. Paragraph 2 of UNGA Resolution 1514 (XV) on decolonisation was almost as helpful by stating that: 'All people have a right to self-determination; by virtue of that right they freely determine their political status and freely pursue their economic, social and cultural development.' Having for the time being apparently subsumed their differences with Britain on constitutional development, this too could be taken to apply to Gibraltar. Para 6 of the same Resolution, however, could be interpreted rather differently. It stated that: 'Any attempt at the partial or total disruption of the national unity and territorial integrity of a country is incompatible with the purposes and principles of the Charter of the United Nations.' Spain used this clause to reassert her territorial integrity, allied to the fact that Britain had reneged on the Treaty which had conceded Gibraltar under duress in the first instance. Invoking the eighteenth century in an organisation as modern as the UN did not appear inappropriate to the overwhelmingly conservative Spanish Government. It was in any case a somewhat spurious claim as the clause was intended to preserve the integrity of a small country threatened by a larger predatory neighbour: once again Spain had managed to turn the provision on its head.

Looking at these three clauses, it is difficult to see how any impartial judicious observer could support the Spanish case against the true principles of decolonisation espoused by the UN. It is a measure, therefore, of the opportunism and self seeking of some of the member states that they could support the Spanish case irrespective of the logic and their own guiding resolutions. Despite the progress being made in decolonisation by Britain in the 1960s, she was still the anti-colonialist's bogey; even the United States was prepared to go no further than abstaining on the issue. It is a sad reflection that the organisation set up in part to prevent the re-emergence of threats to international order like Fascism could so outrageously support, despite the absurdities of its case, a regime which had its genesis in Fascism and which was to a considerable extent still ruled by the same tenets. It is equally a measure of the weakness of the UN that it did no more than invite Britain and Spain to return to the negotiating table to resolve the issue.

Mercifully the UN now receded from the scene. Although the issue remained on the agenda, neither the General Assembly nor the Committee of 24 was able to implement any resolution which was unacceptable to Britain and to the expressed wish of the people of Gibraltar. Spain too realised that it had gone as far as it could profitably go in seeking international support for the return of Gibraltar and turned from political agitation in the UN to economic coercion. Although the border was not closed immediately, the Spanish authorities imposed a melange of restrictions which discouraged tourists, forced Gibraltarians living in Spain to move into Gibraltar, and restricted the passage of goods across the border. The Government did not, however, prevent the 9000 or so Spanish workers from crossing daily into Gibraltar which would have had local repercussions in what was still a very poor and underdeveloped part of Spain.

Britain initially refused to negotiate under duress, but in deference to the UN resumed discussions with Spain in May 1966. Spain was now playing another card, for this was a period when the Cold War was at its height and Gibraltar, although not formally a NATO base, was a linchpin in the Alliance's defensive strategy. Spain hoped to provoke pressure from Britain's NATO partners by banning the overflight of NATO military aircraft en route to or from Gibraltar. It had lit-

tle effect, for NATO and particularly the USA which had major bases in Spain did not rise to the bait, and in the long run Spain needed a NATO presence both for economic and security reasons. The negotiations in London made little progress, for although Spain apparently made concessions in a paper of May 1966, they were only palliatives surrounding the essential requirement for sovereignty to pass to Spain. In July Madrid turned the screw by banning the overflight of Spain by all RAF aircraft, not only those proceeding to Gibraltar, and demanded that Britain should move all military forces from the neutral zone. As the latter contained the airfield it was of course ignored. Further restrictive measures were imposed at the border in 1967, but of greater consequence were restrictions applied in the airspace surrounding the airport. The Spanish Prohibited Airspace (SPA) extended east-west immediately to the north of the runway and in a north-south line midway across the bay. Whilst this did not impede aircraft landing from the east, it meant that aircraft approaching from the west had to make a tight circuit of the Rock to line up with the runway. Whilst no major problem in good weather, low cloud or strong winds could make the approach hazardous for civil as well as military aircraft. A Spanish warship was regularly moored within the bay on the edge of the SPA to add a military threat to any aircraft which might violate Spanish airspace. Despite the safety implications, an appeal to the International Civil Aviation Organisation (ICAO) was of no avail.

The patience of the British Labour Government, as well as the people of Gibraltar, who were now feeling the effects of the Spanish economic blockade, began to wear thin. On 14th June 1967 Mrs Judith Hart, Minister for Commonwealth Affairs, announced that a referendum would be held in Gibraltar on its future status. Whilst perhaps the need for a vote was an apparent admission of weakness, the result left no doubt as to the wishes of the people. The question was very simple: did the people wish to pass under Spanish sovereignty in line with the latest Spanish proposal, or did they wish voluntarily to retain their link with Britain with democratic local institutions?. It was a propaganda *coup d'état*: nearly 96% of the electors voted – far more than a local election had ever generated – with 44 votes for union with Spain and 12,138 for retaining the link with Britain. The United Nations refused to send observers which is again a sad reflection on their impartiality, but the election procedure was verified by a Commonwealth team.

On the 6th of May 1968 the Spanish Government closed the frontier to all but the Spanish workers and a few persons with special passes. Tourists could now only get into Gibraltar by air or on the ferry from Algeciras. The Government was not deflected and in 1969, as we have already seen, self-government in all internal affairs was granted to the Gibraltar Legislative Assembly. In retaliation the Spanish Government closed the frontier completely, depriving the remaining 5000 Spanish workers of their jobs, closed down the Algeciras ferry, and in October severed all telephone and telegraph links. Gibraltar was completely isolated from the outside world except by air or sea – the sixteenth and longest siege of the Rock had commenced.

The closure of the border did not have quite the dramatic impact that Spain would have wished. It had been a long time coming with the progressive implementation of restrictions providing a breathing space for Britain and the Gibraltarians to adjust to the new circumstances. The number of Spanish workers had been progressively reduced from a peak of 12,000 to under 5000 and their loss was partially redressed by the recruitment of a labour force in Morocco. This brought its own problems, the most immediate of which was how to accommodate the immigrant workers. Large numbers still live today in very crowded conditions in hostels such as the old barracks in Casemates Square. Their conditions of employment – alien workers without their families – has caused resentment and protest. The formation of the Moroccan Workers' Association along with unemployment for Moroccans has led to pickets with banners and slogans setting up their stall every day since January 1993 outside the guardroom opposite the Convent. In many respects their situation is similar to the workers who came from Genoa, Portugal and later Malta to serve the garrison in the years after 1713 – it remains to be seen whether they will ever be absorbed into the Gibraltarian community in the same way as their forbears from other parts of Europe.

The British Government provided additional finance to help the economy and the increased garrison brought more spending power. Of equal significance, money was no longer flowing out to Spain in the pockets of workers. But many of these benefits were cancelled out by an increase in inflation and a prolonged period of social and industrial unrest. The closure of the border also saw significant developments in the Campo. Any sense of national hubris or self justification in the Spanish action was hardly reflected in La Linea which had suffered the loss of jobs in Gibraltar and had little industrial infrastructure of its own. The closure of the border led to the building of the monstrously ugly petro-chemical refinery, which pollutes the shoreline at Carteia, and other lighter industries in the vicinity, as well as the construction of numerous blocks of new flats in La Linea itself. But once the initial opportunities, mainly in the construction industry, began to wane, the severing of relations probably resulted in at least as much economic hardship in the Campo as in Gibraltar.

Perversely, the closure of the border heralded a change in both Spanish and British policy. For Spain, the long years of confrontation had clearly not produced the expected result: in binding the Gibraltarians ever closer to Britain and cementing their national identity, it made any rapprochement between Gibraltar and Spain almost unthinkable. But the differences in approach probably owe more to the individual inclinations of the new Foreign Minister, Lopez Bravo, and his British counterpart, the calm and urbane Sir Alec Douglas Home, than to any fundamental shift in policy. A self-confessed anglophile, Lopez Bravo curtailed the anti-British propaganda and ceased the annual ritual of raising the Gibraltar issue in the UN. Equally perverse was the reaction in Gibraltar to the apparently more conciliatory attitude in Spain; such was the fear that the British Government would succumb to the blandishments of Madrid that any suggestion of relaxations on the border was greeted with distrust and a sense of betrayal. They need not have worried; the advent in 1973 of a new Government and new Foreign Minister, Lopez Rodo, soon put the relationship back onto a more traditional and confrontational footing.

British policy too was changing, but in a more subtle and less demonstrative way. 1970 marked the re-opening of British discussions on joining the Common Market in which European attitudes, even though Spain was not yet a member, appeared more relevant than the future of what some politicians and senior civil servants, their eyes fixated on Brussels, saw as a small and increasingly costly appendage like Gibraltar. Politicians from time to time still publicly reasserted their undying determination to ensure that the rights of the Gibraltarians were safeguarded, but there was a clear feeling abroad that this prolonged confrontation with Spain was damaging to Britain's wider interests in Europe as well as across the Atlantic – north and south.

The death of General Franco in 1975 and the transition to democratic rule has been heralded as a false dawn in Anglo/Spanish relations over Gibraltar. In the immediate context it undoubtedly was; democracy in Spain was too fragile a plant to withstand any precipitate change in policy on a subject so deeply ingrained within the Spanish psyche as Gibraltar. But in the longer term Spain's policy was changing significantly and in directions which were unthinkable under the Franco regime. The new Government wanted to improve Spain's links with the rest of Europe and eventually to join the EEC. This opened up many other possibilities: for some Europeans and for the USA, joining NATO was seen as an essential precondition of membership of the wider Western European community. For Britain it gave new impetus to settling the Gibraltar question, for it was inconceivable to London that Spain could be admitted to a European union whilst at the same time keeping its borders closed to a fellow member.

Although there was little overt progress for a number of years, work was intensified behind the scenes to achieve a solution to the problem. The breakthrough came at Lisbon in April 1980. In the Lisbon Statement the fundamental positions of the two parties were pedantically restated: Spain reasserted her claim to sovereignty and Britain's pledge to respect the wishes of the Gibraltar people was reaffirmed. But Spain agreed to lift all restrictions in return for a British undertaking to negotiate on any matter either side wished to raise. This was a clear and unambiguous signal that sovereignty was at least on the table. The agreement was greeted with dismay in Gibraltar and distaste in Madrid as well where it was thought that the Foreign Minister, Marcelino Oreja, who had indeed exceeded the powers given to him by his Government, had conceded too much.

It was to take another five years before the subsequent difficulties were ironed out in the Brussels Communique. Significantly, whatever it might say in public, the Spanish Government was now working steadily towards implementation of the Lisbon Statement: its problem was taking with it the people, the media, the military, and dyed-in-the-wool Francoists. Spain was still inherently a very conservative country. An abortive military coup in February 1981 put a brake on progress and the Falklands conflict the following year, in which the sympathy of the Spanish people was inclined understandably towards their compatriots in Argentina, almost brought the process to a halt. But the attempted military coup had merely heightened the desire of the new Spanish administration to embrace their tender democracy within the security of the EEC and NATO, and for this they needed British support, for not all the socialist and liberal governments in the EEC were yet convinced that Spain had shed the excesses of its recent past. Britain had always espoused the widening of the EEC and certainly wanted Spain within NATO – it nevertheless saw the opportunity for a little gentle diplomatic blackmail. The price Spain had to pay for admission to the EEC was the opening of the frontier with Gibraltar. It took nearly three years of patient negotiation, but on the 5th of February 1985 the border was at last reopened. The sixteenth siege had lasted over sixteen years, but not a shot had been fired and nobody had been killed. The UN, that much heralded arbiter of world peace in 1945, can claim no credit whatsoever for the resolution of the confrontation. In the event it was the EEC, albeit indirectly, which provided the plank for the agreement.

After the re-opening of the border, relations between Spain and Britain entered an era of uneasy equilibrium. At last embraced within the security of the European Community, Spain had many other preoccupations and was unwilling openly to rock the boat in Brussels by acrimonious discussions on Gibraltar. Britain too had wider interests: with a decreasing military commitment, and with the fall of the Soviet Union presaging a significant change in the strategic importance of the Rock, the Government was inclined to keep the dispute in as low a key as possible. Discussions with Spain followed a predictable and monotonous pattern and were sometimes discontinued when the inevitable impasse was reached. From time to time the British Government reiterated the guarantee, albeit not unqualified, to self determination for the Gibraltarians. But to the local inhabitants, still led by the irrepressible Joe Bossano, these protestations of loyalty began to sound increasingly hollow.

The temperature in the last half of the 1980s was by no means muted in Gibraltar itself. Convinced that the British Government was slowly disengaging itself from Gibraltar, the local politicians argued with increasing passion how best, and by a small minority even whether, the link should be maintained. There was considerable support for the integrationist faction, but little desire to see the levers of government in any way reappropriated by a parliament in London. This paradoxical policy weakened the position of the integrationists and another group began to look for independence within the EC rather than under the cloak of a British dependency. There was predictably little support for the proposition that Gibraltar should become a UN-mandated territory. Those advocating 'free association', the fundamental plank of Sir Joshua Hassan's discredited AACR, were hamstrung by the image of a moderate centrist policy which rarely inspires the masses in times when radicals or extremists are in full flow. The end result has been that relations with the British Government have steadily deteriorated over the last ten years with little discernable improvement in those with Spain despite the easing of restrictions.

Although the border was ostensibly open, there were still delays at peak periods with the Spanish customs laboriously inspecting each car which passed through into Spain. This was done as much to deter Spanish people slipping across the border to buy petrol and duty free goods to the detriment of the local economy as to exert pressure on Britain. It must also be recognised that Spain had, and still has, many internal pressures – large scale unemployment and a vulnerable currency, alleged corruption in the highest places, not only among politicians but in some of the major institutions of state, and severe drought which caused considerable hardship in the south until relieved by heavy rain at the beginning of 1996. It was believed that at such times any government would take refuge in high-profile distractions whatever the importance or immediacy of the debate – and the years have shown that all of Spain can safely release its rancour on Gibraltar.

In 1993 occurred one of the periodic stalemates in formal talks with Spain, and when it was planned to renew these towards the end of 1994, the restrictions at the border were once again tightened. It was at first thought that this was merely the conventional turning of the screw before the talks restarted, but it soon became apparent that the Spanish had more substantial allegations which became an embarrassment to the British Government. It was alleged that the Rock had become a centre for drug smuggling and money laundering, particularly of drug-related money. Tobacco smuggling had of course a long pedigree and was carried on or condoned as much by the Spanish as by the Gibraltarians. Few would claim that a handful of people in Gibraltar with their fast expensive launches and equally flashy cars were engaged in an entirely legitimate import/export business. But drugs are another and more serious business and one inevitably shrouded in greater secrecy. It is difficult to believe that Gibraltar itself was on any transit route for drugs from north Africa to Spain; the restrictions at the border virtually eliminate the passage of such commodities by land. There is no logical reason why boats from north Africa, whosoever owns or crews them, should come via Gibraltar and there is no serious drugs prob-

lem and little drug-related crime within the city itself. Nevertheless, the tacitly acknowledged tobacco smuggling does open the door to accusations that the much more lucrative drugs trade was also a growing problem.

The money laundering charge was even more difficult to refute. For quite legitimate reasons the Gibraltar Government promoted the establishment of the city as an off-shore financial centre; after all it has long been a feature of British tax havens such as the Channel Islands and the Isle of Man, and the economy urgently needed to move in new directions after the drastic reduction in military personnel which had been the staple of the economy for nearly three hundred years. Spacious new office blocks were constructed on reclaimed land called Europort and encouragement given to financial institutions to establish a base in Gibraltar. Unfortunately the world-wide recession intervened and there has been little take up of the incentives offered by the larger financial institutions. Spain alleged, however, it seems with some justification, that the regulations governing such establishments were not in accordance with sound practice and the lat

est EC directives, and that as a result the city was attracting some undesirable custom.

It seems the British Government had some sympathy with this view and, it was reported, issued what amounted to an ultimatum to Joe Bossano to tighten up the financial regulations. It also appeared that the Gibraltar Government was somewhat slow to comply, and warned that any attempt by Britain to use its reserve powers could rebound on the Government. All this has driven a wedge between the British Government and Gibraltar as well as souring relations with Spain, already severely strained over the latter's aggressive fisheries policy. As a result of this latest confrontation, innocent Gibraltarians, tourists and Spanish nationals who still come over in numbers to shop in the city had to endure delays at the border which were rarely less than two hours and sometimes much longer. After a swoop by the Gibraltar Police on boats allegedly involved in smuggling, the tension at the border was relaxed and at the end of 1995 it looked as though another crisis may have passed its peak. It is of course too soon to pass judgement on these latest

Europort – the new financial centre on reclaimed land. The refinery outside La Linea can be seen in the background.

developments, for we are now in the realms of journalism rather than history.

*   *   *

It will be very evident to the reader by now that the dispute with Spain over Gibraltar is both long lasting and deep rooted. There were periods in the eighteenth century when Britain was allied with Spain, usually against France, when the dispute was temporarily held in abeyance. But as soon as hostilities resumed, as invariably happened, the fate of Gibraltar moved back to the forefront of politics and war. There was an interregnum in the dispute in the nineteenth and the first half of this century due to the rapprochement in the wars of Napoleon and more directly because of Spain's chronic weakness and internal disruption. But the hostility has returned with renewed vigour in the last forty years. What is the nature of this dispute and can it be resolved? Does Spain have a justifiable case for reassuming control of Gibraltar from the Crown?

It can hardly be argued that the acquisition of Gibraltar would materially improve Spain's economic wealth or strategic security. Whilst smuggling and the proximity of duty free goods for the local Spanish population make the headlines and fuel the dispute, their extinction would have no more than a local effect and make no impression on Spain's overall economic performance. With Algeciras across the bay and Cadiz round the corner, Spain does not require either another commercial port or naval facility in the area. Nor does it need the airfield; a modern airport lies just up the road in Malaga. Apart from ship repairing and tourism, which itself is largely fed from the Costa del Sol, Gibraltar has no economic resources to attract the Spanish aggression. Strategically, as we have already seen, it is difficult to envisage a scenario when the possession of Gibraltar would materially enhance Spain's security.

The recovery of Gibraltar is therefore solely a matter of the heart. It is an emotional attachment which goes back at least to the reign of Queen Isabella in the fifteenth century and perhaps before. It is a tie which is deep in the Spanish psyche: the possession of Gibraltar by the British is an affront to Spanish pride and honour. Let us for a moment consider a hypothetical analogy.

Assume that in 1704, in one of the many wars between Britain and France, the French had captured Lands End and that nine years later Britain had been forced to cede an unspecified part of Cornwall to France by an ambiguous treaty that had been entered into under duress. Exercise the imagination a little more and assume that Lands End had some strategic importance which had caused the area to be retained by France until today, but which had now largely disappeared. Would not the people of the United Kingdom claim, with some force, that it was time the French went home? Such is the Spanish feeling on Gibraltar: as fellow members of the EC and NATO, it seems perfectly logical to them to have the same emotional attachment to a piece of land which is incontrovertibly a part of the Iberian peninsula. This analogy, of course, ignores the rights and feelings of the people of Gibraltar, and to this aspect we must return later.

An international claim to territory, however, requires more than geographical proximity and emotional attachment and Spain has based its claim in essence on the Treaty of Utrecht of 1713. It is therefore necessary at this stage to examine this agreement again and to try to assess its current relevance. The clauses of the Treaty as they affect Gibraltar are at Appendix 2. We have already noted that there were a number of ambiguities arising out of the circumstances in which the Treaty was negotiated. There can be little doubt that some of Britain's actions over the years, and whatever the provocation, have in some areas strained any reasonable interpretation of the provisions of the Treaty. There are some aspects, such as the provisions regarding Jews and Moors, where Britain has clearly broken the Treaty, no matter how justifiable in both moral and material terms. The requirement that Britain needs a fortress on the Rock for strategic reasons now looks hardly credible given the international situation and the almost total withdrawal of British forces. Most pertinent of all, Britain has apparently gone some way to 'alienate... the propriety of the said town of Gibraltar' to the people of the city.

Looking at the Treaty in isolation, therefore, it seems that Spain has a strong case. Nevertheless, there is a convincing argument that it is ridiculous to go back to an agreement signed nearly three hundred years ago to determine the future of a people in the entirely different circumstances of today. But what of the Act of Union with Scotland which was signed at almost the same time (1707) – few would claim, whatever their political aspirations today, that this treaty is not still the fundamental plank of the integration of the United Kingdom. Hong Kong will be returned to China in 1997 as a result of a treaty signed a hundred years ago. What sort of period of limitation should one place on a treaty which itself has no determining limits? It is self evident that much has changed in Gibraltar in three hundred years, but Scotland and Hong Kong have hardly existed in a time warp either. Simply to dismiss the Treaty of Utrecht as irrelevant or time-expired is never likely to satisfy Spain or to provide a platform for a new agreement, if such is ever possible.

It is thus the responsibility of Britain, and the people of Gibraltar, to show that circumstances have changed to such an extent that to alter the status quo by reference to the Treaty alone would be an unequivocal and irrefutable breach of moral justice. That the circumstances have changed beyond any remotely imaginable when the Treaty was signed is beyond dispute. The most significant is the growth throughout much of the world of democratic freedom and with it corresponding rights and responsibilities. It could never have been imagined when the British authorities brought in foreign labour in the eighteenth century to provide the workforce that supported the fortress that the descendants of those very same people would today control the major part of their own destiny in government, legislation, finance and all the other manifestations of a modern state. It would have surprised those eighteenth-century Imperialists even more that such a change could have been accomplished without revolution or violence, even with the cooperation, if sometimes hesitant and grudging, of their masters. Paradoxically, it might not perhaps have surprised them that the descendants of those same menial servants should express undying loyalty to the Crown and passionately wish to maintain an association, even integration, with Britain – for such was the ethos (and arrogance) of British Imperialism. In these terms to regulate the

dispute by reference to the Treaty does look ridiculous.

The other twentieth-century concept that is now at the centre of the dispute is the right to self determination enshrined in various Resolutions of the United Nations. Britain has used this concept to justify its policies in the Falkland Islands, in Northern Ireland, in the Gulf States (albeit a little more equivocally) and in many other disputes which have appeared before the forum of the UN in the last fifty years. The concept is the fundamental plank of its statements in respect of Gibraltar and is allied to the undoubted fact that circumstances have changed irrevocably since Bolingbroke negotiated the Treaty of 1713. Whatever support it may command in the United Nations, it is 'ridiculous' for Spain to claim that she can still simply take over Gibraltar on the basis of a three hundred year old treaty let alone an emotional attachment to an appendage of the peninsula.

So what prospect does the future hold for Gibraltar? Perhaps I should take the advice of my fellow historians and end the book here on the premise that it is not that practitioner's role to speculate about the future. But then in practice most other historians fail to abide by their own dictum.

Most British Governments would doubtless wish that the problem would just go away. In the interests of stability and unity within Europe and the resolution of wider and more immediate issues, a solution to the dispute which would quietly remove the Gibraltarians from its baggage would be welcome. But, of course, so would a similar simple resolution of the Northern Ireland problem, or the Falkland Islands. Even if a British Government of whatever persuasion was of a mind to jettison the Gibraltarians, it is difficult to envisage the circumstances in which the opposition, or their own back benchers, or the general public, let alone a mischievous media would let them get away with it. Britain has little alternative to continuing to support the Gibraltarians and the concept of self determination.

Nor are the Gibraltarians likely to resolve the issue for them. It is inconceivable in present circumstances that they would ever vote for integration with Spain. It is also improbable that this small territory could ever sustain itself as an independent state even if there was a majority in favour of it within Gibraltar. Given the veto system within the EC it is also unlikely that Gibraltar could enter the EC as an independent country, attractive solution though that might seem in some quarters. The possibility has been mooted that Gibraltar could be given special status and guarantees as a 'Territory of Europe (EU)'. There are also co-sovereignty ideas, with many variations, but all would be likely to founder on points of principle and detail. Integration with Britain has a more plausible pedigree – after all the situation would then be almost exactly identical to the Spanish enclaves of Ceuta and Melilla in north Africa and remove at a stroke a major plank in the Spanish case. However, such a move has been ruled out by Britain as recently as 1994 when Douglas Hurd reconfirmed Roy Hattersley's decision of 1976. It is likely to continue to be resisted by any British Government – it would raise the temperature within Spain, the EC and the United Nations to an unacceptable level.

Could a solution emerge from within Spain? It would require a change in the Spanish outlook – official and unofficial – of seismic proportions for Spain formally to renounce any claim to Gibraltar. To seek a military solution to the problem is happily unthinkable in today's European environment and it appears equally unlikely that Madrid's policy of political and economic aggression is likely to subvert the Gibraltarian will for self determination. But it would, nevertheless, need a significant change of heart for Spain simply to let the matter subside. It is a convenient device for distracting the people as well as retaliating against Britain in any other real or theoretical dispute within the EC. As an aside, it is perhaps worth mentioning how much more difficult it might be for Britain to keep the lid on the dispute if she were no longer a member of the EC. It is, for example, unlikely that Spain could again totally close the border whilst the two countries are fellow members of the Community. Spain is a net recipient of European funds and is too vulnerable to EC sanctions to risk antagonising the other member nations with such an overt dispute with Britain even though the latter is hardly the toast of Brussels. But if Britain were no longer a member of the EC – who knows?

It appears that we have here an impasse of insurmountable proportions. The only foreseeable light at the end of the tunnel must arise from a fundamental shift in Spanish policy. Spain has antagonised and frightened Gibraltarians for decades by its aggressive and provocative policies both within the international forum and in bilateral discussions with Britain. But if Spain tried to woo rather than to harass Gibraltar both in actions and in spirit; if Spain should cooperate in border crossings – or even abolish the immigration barrier altogether in accordance with the Schengen Agreement; if Spain sought to cooperate economically with Gibraltar within the EC; if Spain desisted from provocative and inflammatory statements in public forums. Is it possible, over generations, by gradual osmosis that the hostility on both sides would disappear? The Gibraltarians too would have to play their part in the process – there would need to be a determination to eliminate smuggling, either of tobacco or drugs, and the Assembly and the media would need to play their part in not raising the stakes by provocative polemics or too fervent a waving of the Union Jack. The optimist will clutch at such straws with enthusiasm and hope, the cynic will probably laugh, but it seems to be the only possible solution to this continuing saga.

APPENDICES

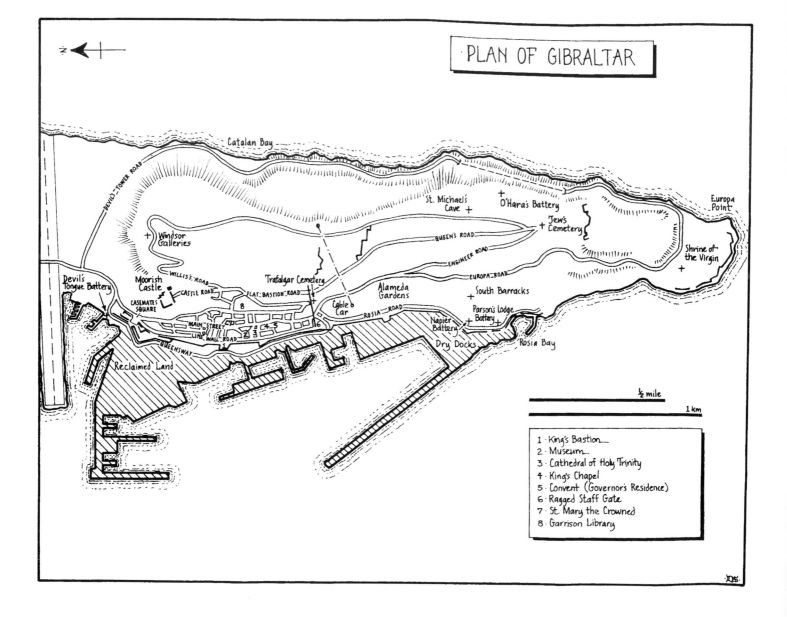

PLAN OF GIBRALTAR

Catalan Bay

Europa Point

St. Michael's Cave

O'Hara's Battery

Jew's Cemetery

Shrine of the Virgin

QUEEN'S ROAD

ENGINEER ROAD

EUROPA ROAD

Windsor Galleries

DEVIL'S TOWER ROAD

WILLIS'S ROAD

Trafalgar Cemetery

Alameda Gardens

South Barracks

Moorish Castle

Devil's Tongue Battery

CASTLE ROAD

FLAT BASTION ROAD

CASEMATES SQUARE

Cable Car

Parson's Lodge Battery

ROSIA ROAD

8

MAIN STREET

LINE WALL ROAD

7 3 4 5 6

2 1

Napier Battery

Dry Docks

Rosia Bay

QUEENSWAY

Reclaimed Land

½ mile

1 km

1 · King's Bastion
2 · Museum
3 · Cathedral of Holy Trinity
4 · King's Chapel
5 · Convent (Governor's Residence)
6 · Ragged Staff Gate
7 · St. Mary the Crowned
8 · Garrison Library

1 A TOUR OF GIBRALTAR

For the visitor to Gibraltar who has no more than a hazy idea of its history, there is no better place to begin than the Gibraltar Museum. Situated just off Main Street in Bomb House Lane, the Museum leads the visitor progressively through the development of Gibraltar from the earliest prehistoric times to its role as a naval base in the Second World War. It charts the military and the social development of the city and the fortress as well as its geological formation and the richness of its flora and fauna. As a bonus, the Museum is actually housed in a building constructed over a Moorish bath house which has been faithfully restored (see page 43).

Fortified by some knowledge of its historical background, the visitor could perhaps best start his tour of Gibraltar by ascending to the Upper Rock. This may be accomplished by taxi or cable car, but the latter is a little more flexible in time. It is not possible to reach the northern summit which is still a military enclave, but the view from the terrace of the restaurant at the top of the cable car is sufficiently rewarding in all directions. The strengths and weaknesses of Gibraltar as a fortress and its geographical relationship to Spain and north Africa may be readily grasped from here. Across the Strait the southern Pillar of Hercules may be easily seen on a clear day with the constant passage of ships a reminder of just how much of the world's trade still passes through this narrow strip of water. The difficulty of finding space for the multifarious buildings of the city is immediately apparent, and the extent of the harbour and dockyard is well seen

The cable car to the Upper Rock.

St Michael's Cave from a print of 1830. (Gibraltar Heritage Trust)

from this vantage point. There will usually be upwards of 20 ships anchored sedately in the bay, some awaiting their turn at the wharves of Gibraltar and Algeciras, or a berth in the dry docks at the southern end of the harbour. The massive water catchment slabs on the east side of the rock, now largely superseded by distillation plants, are a potent reminder of one of the potential weaknesses of the fortress under siege.

The visitor should turn immediately right off the cable car to see the historical artefacts of the Upper Rock. The famous Barbary Apes will always be found milling around the top of Philip II's defensive wall of the 16th-century which runs right up to the summit of the saddle, but a little farther on a short detour should be made to the left to a little Moorish sentry post looking out to sea (page 35). Continuing down the hill, those sound of wind and limb can take the fork to the left to ascend to O'Hara's Battery with its engine house and massive 9.2-inch guns on the southern summit of the Rock. Just below the fork is St Michael's Cave, one of

the most spectacular natural grottoes in Europe, once used by the garrison as a duelling chamber and later as a bombproof store and hospital. It now serves a more peaceful function as an auditorium for concerts and drama. The visitor may now either walk back to the top of the cable car for well earned refreshment and return to the city, or continue downhill to the intermediate station which can sometimes involve a long wait when the cable car fills up at the top.

*   *   *

An historical tour of the Lower Rock and the city is perhaps best divided into three itineraries: the upper old town, the lower city, and the outlying sites. For the upper town and starting from somewhere on Main Street, the visitor should aim for the Moorish Castle. Whichever route is selected, one climbs steadily up streets and steps with evocative names reflecting their past military usage. Some of the buildings date back to Georgian or Victorian days and there are several picturesque vistas which could be carefully preserved and improved where possible by the removal of unsightly wires or other modern accretions. It would be possible without very expensive modifications to designate an interesting scenic route up to the castle which would display to advantage many of the older and more modest buildings of Gibraltar which are currently little known. However, for the present, the visitor will have to take pot luck until he breaks out into the open with the broad bulk of the castle keep staunchly dominating the northern approach to the city. Outwardly the castle impresses only by its solidity and unfortunately the lower part is used as a prison, thereby restricting its presentation. Nevertheless, the interior is partly restored and well worth a visit with its recreation of Moorish artefacts and displays (page 40).

Just beyond the castle are the Upper (or Windsor) Galleries nearly 700 feet above sea level which were commenced towards the end of the Great Siege (page 98). The length of the galleries, approximately 600 feet, may be walked terminating in the Notch, a previously inaccessible natural pillar at the northeast corner of the Rock. The main feature in the Galleries is St George's Hall with seven gun embrasures. There are several cannon and full size re-enactions of batteries of the time of the Great Siege. Although somewhat spurious, in the sense that the tunnels were not actually ready for use at that time, they convincingly bring to life the noise and turmoil of eighteenth-century warfare. Next time you visit the airport, remember to look up at the Rock to see the line of embrasures crossing the north face. Various batteries can still be seen above the castle and on the way down Willis' Magazine houses a good exhibition of Gibraltar under siege.

As you descend from the castle, you can see very well preserved remnants of the zig-zag Moorish wall dating from the 11th-century as well as the typically domed remains of the Moorish gate house, now part of the prison (page 42). Unfortunately much of the visual impact of the castle and its walls is lost by the multitude of ugly post-war blocks of flats which encroach right up to the old foundations and have overtaken them in some areas; it is a telling reminder of the shortage of space for building before the land reclamation was started in earnest. Keep going downhill and you should end up near

Casemates Square which is a good place to start a tour of the lower city.

*   *   *

Casemates Square, now a thriving mass of shops and throbbing traffic, is basically the site of the old Moorish water port, and Grand Casemates Gate was erected on the site of the old Watergate. Outside the Watergate, a new line of fortifications was constructed in the 18th and 19th-centuries in ashlar – the name of each stretch of wall, its bastions and dates of construction are usually prominently displayed. Through Chatham's Wicket Gate and across a drawbridge led originally to the Old Mole. Now one must cross the busy roundabout to the site of the gun embrasures constructed by Prince George of Hesse Darmstadt in 1704 and known as the Devil's Tongue because it was a scourge of Spanish shipping (page 72). Recapturing the appearance of medieval and early modern Gibraltar in this area is now particularly difficult with the massive reclamation of land and modern commerce. Nevertheless, if one stands in Safeway's carpark and looks back towards the city, one can gain a very good idea of the view from one of the Spanish floating batteries of 1782.

Back into Casemates Square, take a detour through a tunnel close to the old barracks now used by Moroccan workers to have a look at the North Defences. These date from Spanish times, but were heavily

The barracks in Casemates Square now occupied by Moroccan workers.

The Guard Post opposite the Convent.

reconstructed by subsequent defenders from the Prince of Hesse onwards through to the Second World War. To your left, as you pass through the old Land Port Gate, now an 18th-century classical structure, is the slope known as the glacis which was the first obstacle which an attacking force had to surmount before assaulting the walls. The North Defences, approached via Crutchett's Ramp, can be explored, but it is essential to have an experienced guide and a strong torch, or you could be lost in the myriad tunnels for a long time. Many of the accretions and artefacts of military history still lie wasting among the debris – another worthwhile target in due course for the Gibraltar Heritage Trust.

In Casemates Square note the modern reconstruction of Lieutenant Koehler's gun carriage, designed in the Great Siege to enable cannon to be depressed sufficiently to fire down from the great heights of the Rock (page 96). Into Main Street, your attention will inevitably be distracted for a while by the range of duty free goods on display, but just occasionally raise your eyes above the shop front level to note the wrought iron balconies and window shutters which give an Italian character to the older buildings above. The first building of note is the Roman Catholic Cathedral of St Mary the Crowned. Largely 19th-century Baroque, it stands on the site of the chief mosque and some parts of earlier structures can be seen.

Just beyond to the left in Governor's Parade opposite Whites Hotel is arguably the best building in Gibraltar, the Garrison Library, in a sedate Georgian style and opened in 1804. It was originally a military club, but now houses an impressive library of reference books – it is an asset of which perhaps more could be made for the visitor to Gibraltar. Unrestrainedly Gothic is the King's Chapel, its entrance hidden away next to the Convent. Originally the chapel of the Franciscan Friars who established themselves in Gibraltar at the end of the 15th-century, it subsequently became the main Anglican church of the garrison. Note particularly the monument to General Boyd on the end wall and, a reminder of Spanish times, the memorial of 1674 to Maria Cueva, wife of the General of Artillery of Cordova. (page 52). The Convent itself, now the residence of the Governor, was partly rebuilt in red brick Gothic in the 19th-century although the beautiful 16th-century cloister can still just be glimpsed through the main entrance.

Just before the South Port Gate on the left

hand side, a Renaissance doorway from a church in the old town has been somewhat incongruously reset in the wall. The Gate itself is cut in the walls built by Charles V of Spain in 1552 and has the weathered arms of Gibraltar and Spain set above the arch which originally led onto a drawbridge (page 55). The second opening was cut in 1883 and bears the arms of Great Britain, Gibraltar and the Governor Sir John Adye. A further opening was subsequently cut to accommodate the burgeoning traffic. Beyond the gate is the Trafalgar Cemetery which houses military graves of around the turn of the 18th-century, but very few of sailors who actually succumbed at Trafalgar. The cemetery, beautifully restored by the Gibraltar Heritage Trust, is a haven of peace after the turmoil of Main Street. After a brief rest, just look round the corner above the cemetery at the massive Spanish bastion of 1552, now known as Flat Bastion, and Prince Edward's Gate opened in the Spanish wall in 1790.

Down to the right we reach Ragged Staff Gates, named after the arms of Charles V (the ragged staff), but of course rebuilt by the British in the 19th-century. However, just to its north is a stretch of Spanish walling in the South Bastion. Continuing to the north, the line of walls, now mainly of 19th-century origin, may be traced more or less back to Casemates Square. The sea, of course, originally lapped the base of these walls until recent times, and all you see on your left is on reclaimed land. Beyond Wellington Front you can take a diversion inland to see the Anglican Cathedral of the Holy Trinity, consecrated only in 1838, despite its Moorish outward appearance – an interesting architectural diversion. Back in Line Wall Road, another style of architecture is displayed in the 'Flemish' synagogue with its elaborate arabesque gable. Beyond is one of the most interesting and complex of the fortifications, the King's Bastion, which played a major role in the Great Siege. Unfortunately, it was overtaken in modern times by the city's electricity works and is in a ruinous state. But the shell, which is largely intact, has some unique features, and would make a most worthy target in the long term for restoration. There is, of course, no entry for the visitor at present, but you can see the typical Victorian barracks fronting Line Wall Road.

Farther along is the City Hall, built by a rich merchant and friend of Nelson, Aaron Cardozo, in the 19th-century and now being restored. On its seaward side is the imposing First World War memorial. Finally before re-entering Casemates Square you will pass

Ragged Staff Gates in the Line Wall.

A 19th-century cannon at the 5th Rosia Battery.

the grandiose American War Memorial erected in 1933 in the Line Wall to commemorate the US Navy presence in Gibraltar in the First World War.

*   *   *

Our third tour starts at the South Port Gate and encompasses the very interesting outlying sites of Gibraltar. Buses and taxis are available, but the more energetic might prefer to take the attractive walk along Rosia Road as far as Parson's Lodge Battery. The walk gives good views of the naval dockyard including the headquarters with its tower built in 1904 (page 129). Most of the old naval workshops are now given over to commercial use as are the three dry docks at the southern end. The New Mole has completely disappeared, but stretches of the sea wall remain with such evocative names as Jumper's Bastion (page 67). Also on Rosia Road is the air vent (reconstructed in Spanish times) of the Moorish aqueduct.

Napier Battery houses one of the most interesting relics of the 19th-century fortifications, the 100-ton gun, immaculately restored, although unfortunately now painted black when the original colouring was grey to blend in with the limestone rock (page 125). The gun site looks down on Rosia Bay, famous as the refuge after

Trafalgar for the severely battered HMS *Victory* bearing Nelson's body before it was eventually transported back to England. Beyond is one of the most successful restorations of Gibraltar's heritage, Parson's Lodge Battery, opened to the public in 1995 and not to be missed. Sitting astride its rocky headland, it is visually the most impressive of Gibraltar's fortifications and was still in operational use until after the Second World War (page 124). Below the Battery is the Naval Victualling Yard, opened in 1812 and containing eleven massive arcaded store rooms (page 123). It is to be hoped that some future use can be found for this internally imposing building and there are embryo plans to adapt at least a part of it as a maritime museum and craft centre. The area around Rosia Bay is one of the most attractive and interesting parts of Gibraltar and could become a major tourist attraction if the necessary resources could be found.

The southernmost tip of Gibraltar is Europa Point, looking across to Ceuta. It is a windswept and somewhat barren area at present, but it should be visited to see the Shrine of the Virgin – originally a mosque in the Moorish period – and particularly the mosaic pavement which formed the cloistered courtyard of an order of nuns (page

36). The Shrine can be found in the midst of the Service housing estate just to the north-west of Europa Point itself. Just south of the new mosque is an underground water cistern known as the Nun's Well and ascribed to the Moors. The return towards the city can be made through a tunnel in the Rock, but take a diversion to look at the impressive South Barracks, now converted into a school, with their Palladian detached pavilions which were completed about 1730. Before reaching the South Port Gate turn into the Alameda Gardens nestling just below the Rock Hotel. Laid out at the beginning of the 19th-century and now the site of the Gibraltar Botanic Gardens, they contain a host of exotic plants and trees as well as statues of General Eliott and the Duke of Wellington, and a number of interesting brass cannon (page 21).

If time permits, a brief visit can be made round to Catalan Bay on the east side of the Rock. It is mainly of interest for the splendid close-up view of the north face of the Rock and from here many of the military accretions and embrasures can be clearly seen. Opposite the cemetery is the still clearly visible site of the Spanish mine (page 81). To the left is the site of the demolished Devil's Tower, one of the original military outposts which played such a prominent role in the sieges of Gibraltar.

There are several other interesting buildings and historical sites which space precludes mentioning, but one of the joys of Gibraltar is that it is small enough for the visitor to encompass most of the city in just a few days and to come upon lesser known sites during the course of one's travels. One of the most useful attributes of Gibraltar is that informative plaques or signs are commonplace and greatly add to the enjoyment and knowledge of the visitor.

APPENDIX 2

EXTRACTS FROM ARTICLE X OF THE TREATY OF UTRECHT

THE CATHOLIC KING does hereby, for Himself, His heirs and successors, yield to the Crown of Great Britain the full and intire propriety of the Town and Castle of Gibraltar, together with the port, fortifications, and forts thereunto belonging; and He gives up the said propriety, to be held and enjoyed absolutely with all manner of right for ever, without any exception or impediment whatsoever. But that abuses and frauds may be avoided by importing any kind of goods, the Catholic King wills, and takes it to be understood, that the above-named propriety be yielded to Great Britain without any territorial jurisdiction, and without any open communication by land with the country round about. Yet whereas the communication by sea with the coast of Spain may not at all times be safe or open, and thereby it may happen that the garrison, and other inhabitants of Gibraltar may be brought to great straits; and as it is the intention of the Catholic King, only that fraudulent importation of goods should, as is above said, be hindered by an inland communication, it is therefore provided that in such cases it may be lawful to purchase, for ready money, in the neighbouring territories of Spain, provisions and other things necessary for the use of the garrison, the inhabitants and the ships which lie in the harbour...

... And her Britannic Majesty, at the request of the Catholic King, does consent and agree, that no leave shall be given under any pretence whatsoever, either to Jews or to Moors, to reside or have their dwellings in the said town of Gibraltar;...

... Her Majesty the Queen of Britain does further promise, that the free exercise of their religion shall be indulged to the Roman Catholic inhabitants of the aforesaid town. And in case it shall hereafter seem meet to the Crown of Great Britain to grant, sell, or by any means to alienate therefrom the propriety of the said town of Gibraltar, it is hereby agreed and concluded, that the preference of having the same shall always be given to the Crown of Spain before any others.

SELECT BIBLIOGRAPHY

ALCANTARA J. *Medieval Gibraltar* Medsun 1979

ANCELL S. *A Circumstantial Journal of the Long and Tedious Blockade and Siege of Gibraltar* Liverpool 1784

AYALA LOPEZ DE. *The History of Gibraltar 1782* London (translated) 1845

BARNETT C. *Engage the Enemy More Closely* Hodder and Stoughton 1991

BARRUCAND M. *Moorish Architecture in Andalusia* Taschen 1992

BRADFORD E. *Gibraltar: The History of a Fortress* Batsford 1971

CARR R. *Spain 1808-1975* Oxford University Press 1982

CARR R. *The Spanish Tragedy* Weidenfeld 1986

CORBETT SIR JULIAN. *England and the Mediterranean 1603-1713* Longman 1904

DENNIS P. *Gibraltar and its People* David and Charles 1990

DRINKWATER COLONEL J. *A History of the Late Siege of Gibraltar* London 1785

ELLICOTT D. *From Rooke to Nelson* Gibraltar 1965

– *Bastion Against Aggression* Gibraltar Society 1968

ELLIOTT J. *Imperial Spain 1469–1716* St Martin's Press 1964

FINLAYSON T. *The Fortress Came First* Gibraltar Books 1991

FLETCHER R. *Moorish Spain* Weidenfeld and Nicolson 1992

GARCIA J. *Gibraltar The Making of a People* Medsun 1994

HILLS G. *Rock of Contention* Robert Hale 1974

HUGHES Q. AND MIGOS A. *Strong as the Rock of Gibraltar* 1995

HUGILL J.A.C. *No Peace Without Spain* Kensal Press 1991

JACKSON SIR WILLIAM G. F. *The Rock of the Gibraltarians* Gibraltar Books 1987

KAMEN H. *Spain 1469–1714* Longman 1983

KENYON E. *Gibraltar under Moor, Spaniard and Briton* Methuen 1911

LAMELAS DIEGO. *The Sale of Gibraltar in 1474* Gibraltar Books 1992

MACINTYRE D. *The Battle for the Mediterranean* Batsford 1964

PALAO G. *Gibraltar: Tales of Our Past* Gibraltar 1981

PENNINGTON D.H. *Seventeenth Century Europe* Longman 1972

RAMSEY W. *After the Battle Number 21* Plaistow Press 1978

RUSSELL J. *Gibraltar Besieged 1779-1783* Heinemann 1965

Spanish Red Book on Gibraltar Madrid 1966 and 1968

THOMAS H. *The Spanish Civil War* Penguin 1965

INDEX